THE PARTHENON ODYSSEY

AN ANGLO-GREEK ROAD TRIP ACROSS A CONTINENT

PETER BARBER

THE PARTHENON ODYSSEY - AN ANGLO-GREEK ROAD TRIP ACROSS A CONTINENT

First published in 2026

Paperback ISBN: 978-1-916574-75-5

Hardback ISBN: 978-1-916574-74-8

Cover Design and Formatting by Kathleen Harryman
https://www.kathleenharryman.co.uk

BOOKS BY PETER BARBER:

THE PARTHENON SERIES:
A Parthenon on our Roof
A Parthenon in Pefki
The Parthenon Paradox

THE MUSINGS SERIES:
Musings from a Greek Village
Musings from a Pandemic

ZORBA'S TVERNA SERIES:
Zorba's Parthenon - A Taverna by the Sea
Zorba's Taverna - The Trouble with Goats & Mayors
Zorba's Embrace - Love, Lie and Lemon Groves

CONTENTS

DEDICATION

I have pleasure in dedicating this book to **Suzi and Simon Stembridge.**

When I sat down to write my first book, I had absolutely no idea what I was doing. I had the familiar, slightly delusional feeling that many of us have, that there was a book somewhere inside me, but no idea how to let it out without embarrassing myself or scaring it back into hiding.

Naturally, I aimed impossibly high.

Suzi's books felt like discoveries. Through her writing, Greece was never just scenery. It breathed, argued, cooked, worried, celebrated, and carried on regardless. Her memoirs were warm, honest, and quietly confident; the sort of books that make everyday life feel important without ever shouting about it. I read them slowly, then all over again much too quickly, and admired her from a safe distance like a sensible person.

She was one of my favourite writers long before I ever thought I might try writing myself. So when I finally sat there with a blank page and a wildly optimistic belief in my own potential, I did something completely out of character. I sent Suzi a message asking if she had any advice for an aspiring writer.

I fully expected silence.

She replied immediately.

What followed over the next few months was an extraordinary act of generosity. Suzi gave her time, her patience, and her kindness with no hesitation at all. She answered questions I didn't yet know were stupid, reassured me when I was convinced I was wasting everyone's time, and never once made me feel awkward for not knowing what I was doing. Which, at that point, was most of the time.

The first book was published. Somehow, it did well. So I kept writing.

Along the way, Suzi and her husband and editor, Simon, became a steady source of encouragement and belief. Quiet, supportive, and unfailingly kind. Their confidence mattered far more than they probably realised, and I will never be able to thank them enough for it.

Simon sadly passed away last year. But through Suzi, and through the wonderful books they created together, his voice, humour, and spirit are still very much present. He is not forgotten – not by readers, and certainly not by me.

So Suzi, and Simon, this book is for you.

With my heartfelt thanks, and more gratitude than I can properly put into words.

THE PARTHENON ODYSSEY

AN ANGLO-GREEK ROAD TRIP ACROSS A CONTINENT

INTRODUCTION

They say Poseidon holds grudges. If you anger him, he doesn't just send a storm, he sends your neighbour too.

Odysseus knew that well. Ten years wandering, poor man, just trying to get home. Every time he thought the sea had calmed, another disaster appeared: a whirlpool, a Cyclops, or a woman who sang beautifully but came with conditions, probably involving immortality so he could keep suffering.

He was shipwrecked, cursed, turned into a pig (well, his men were), blown off course, tied to masts, and lectured by goddesses. All he wanted was a quiet evening in Ithaca with a glass of wine and his wife, but the gods had other ideas, mostly involving storms and character development.

I used to think those were just myths. Then I moved to Greece.

Our version of Poseidon doesn't stir waves; he stirs people.

If you upset him, he doesn't throw you into the sea; he sends Nemesis in her wellington boots, declaring that your river has angered the gods.

We've certainly had our own odyssey. Like Odysseus, we've spent years trying to reach what should have been a simple destination: home. Every time we thought we were nearly there, something else rose from the depths. A flood, a collapsing wall, a rumour, a cat, or some creature that adopted us without permission and then graciously allowed us to stay.

Alex blames me, naturally.

"You've offended someone," she says. "Either Poseidon or Zeus; probably both."

And she might be right.

I can't dig a ditch or plant a lemon tree without divine consequences. Poseidon gave Odysseus whirlpools; he gave me a nemesis.

Sometimes, when the wind howls down the valley and the roof tiles rattle like bones, I can almost hear him laughing. The old gods haven't gone anywhere; they've just bought mobile phones and joined local Facebook groups.

The difference is, Odysseus had a crew.

I have Alex.

And somehow, I suspect the gods find that far more entertaining.

CHAPTER ONE

The Gods Have a Long Memory

Greece has a long memory.

You can live here for years, plant olive trees, pay your taxes, feed the cats, and still discover that you are not quite finished with your past. Nothing dramatic. Just small reminders, delivered casually, that certain things have not been forgotten.

It all started, as most of our worst ideas do, with enthusiasm and good intentions.

Years ago, in a burst of patriotic admiration (and questionable judgement), Alex and I decided to build a Parthenon on the roof of our house in Athens. A small one. Tasteful. A tribute, we thought, to Greece's ancient glory, and to Alex's family, who had lived in the same house for generations.

The authorities did not share our enthusiasm.

Apparently, even in Greece, erecting temples without permission is frowned upon.

There were questions. There were fines. There was, inevitably, an arrest.

Alex stood beside me at the police station, arms crossed, explaining to the bewildered officer that since the British had stolen the original Parthenon marbles, we were simply restoring balance.

That, as it turned out, was not a legal defence.

But we survived. The temple stayed, the fines were eventually paid, and the neighbours. who had long accepted Alex as a force of nature, shook their heads and went back to hanging out their washing. We thought we'd earned our peace.

We were wrong.

When we moved north to the island of Evia, to a sleepy coastal village called Pefki, we imagined tranquillity: sea breezes, olive groves, long lunches, and locals who knew the art of minding their own business. And for a while, that's exactly what we got.

Then came the flood.

Not a polite drizzle or a little "oops, the rain forgot to stop".

No, this was a storm sent by someone ancient, angry, and thorough.

People would talk about that night for years. It would grow into legend, embroidered by memory and myth until it became a saga told in winter kitchens and kafenios across the valley.

They'd call it *The Great Flood of Pefki.*

The old men would slap the tables for emphasis: "Ah, that rain, it didn't fall, it attacked!"

And someone, without fail, would add: "It started near Alex and Peter's house. Of course."

It was a one-hundred-year storm. A brown, furious torrent roaring down from the mountains, carrying branches, bins, and the better part of the village's dignity straight to the sea. Car alarms wailed like frightened goats, plastic chairs floated past the church, and Dimitri's fishing boat, normally parked safely on land, was last seen drifting heroically down the main road like a confused ark, followed by George's car, sideways and upside-down.

Our garden, once full of laughter, olive trees, and Alex's stubborn flowers, became a riverbed. The geraniums floated past like small red witnesses. The chairs vanished, carried off to some unknown sea, along with our illusion of peace.

Maria, naturally, told her own version. In hers, she was waist-deep in water, saving kittens with one hand while phoning the mayor with the other.

Theodora claimed she'd predicted it in a dream.

The priest insisted the bells had rung by themselves, a divine warning to the faithful to move their animals uphill.

Somewhere in all the noise, truth became optional. By the fifth retelling, people swore they saw fish swimming through the square. By the tenth, a dolphin.

But beneath the exaggeration, one fact stood firm: the flood had left its mark. On walls, on roads, and on the hearts of everyone who'd lived through it.

When dawn came, the air smelled of mud and salt and disbelief. People stood in the streets blinking into the pale light, taking in the wreckage: gardens stripped bare, walls reduced to rubble, silence where there had been song.

And then came her.

Nemesis. That's not her real name, of course, but it fits. Nemesis was our neighbour: formidable, watchful, and permanently convinced the universe was plotting against her. She had built her house in what geologists later confirmed was a riverbed, then blocked the watercourse "for convenience". When nature objected, she blamed us.

In Greece, the law doesn't so much *arrive* as it saunters in, orders a coffee, and asks who started it. The assumption is charmingly simple: if someone accuses you of something, you must have done it. Guilt is the house wine. Innocence is à la carte, and you bring your own cutlery.

When the flood came and our garden briefly joined the Aegean, we discovered a new branch of Greek justice: hydraulic responsibility. We weren't just suspected of contributing to the chaos; we were officially promoted to *architects of the flood.*

The village verdict arrived long before any paperwork, as it always does, delivered from the kafenio bench with espresso certainty: "They blocked the river."

Apparently, the water had taken a personal shortcut through our garden because, as one neighbour explained, "It knows you have foreign drains."

"How," I asked no one in particular, "does one prove they didn't block a river?"

"Bring witnesses," someone suggested helpfully. "Fish, maybe."

We had never actually touched the river, not a shovel, not a stone, but in the village, denial is often taken as confirmation. And besides, "Peter and Alex blocked the river" made a far better story than the truth ever could.

So we did the only sensible thing: we hired professionals. A lawyer to translate "*Are you serious*?" into legal Greek, and a land surveyor to interrogate the landscape itself. Soon our home became a small conference centre: lawyers at the table, police in the doorway, and a procession of men in reflective jackets shaking their heads gravely at everything: the wall, the sky, my shoes. If head-shaking were admissible evidence, we'd have been sentenced to life.

We were accused, arrested, then accused and arrested again, like an encore you didn't clap for. Statements were taken. Measurements were made. Tape measures hissed across mud like cautious snakes. A clipboard appeared for every opinion.

One official produced a diagram of uncertain purpose. Another tapped at the ground with a pen, nodded, and wrote "yes" beside something that did not appear to be a question.

Our surveyor – a patient man with the air of someone who has explained gravity to people before – mapped the slope, the channels, the historic riverbed running exactly where Nemesis had built her "convenient improvement". He produced a report so detailed it could have directed migrating birds. The conclusion was simple: water flows downhill; it doesn't take instructions from foreigners with drainpipes.

Meanwhile, our lawyer assembled a mountain of documents: permits, photographs, satellite images, meteorological data, and a letter from the Ministry confirming that, regrettably, I am not in charge of precipitation. We carried folders like shields. Every page had a stamp, and every stamp had a cousin. Greece loves a stamp. If the Parthenon had had this many, it would still be under warranty.

Eventually, slowly, beautifully, the tide turned. The police stopped frowning; the reflective jackets shook their heads less and began to nod in short, careful motions. The report said what the mud had always known: the river was the river, the wall was the problem, and we were simply the people who owned the unfortunate geography where nature came to prove a point.

Did that end the gossip? Of course not. In Greece, the court of law can forgive you; the court of opinion awaits the sequel. But on paper, stamped, signed, and sealed, we were innocent. Or as our lawyer translated it, with a small smile: "Officially, you did not make the weather." Which, in our corner of Evia, is the highest acquittal a person can hope for.

We thought it was over.

It wasn't.

In Greece, gossip travels faster than electricity, and never along the same wires. We were still being accused of diverting the mountain stream, unbalancing the ecosystem, and possibly offending Poseidon himself.

Maria, our faithful messenger of doom, kept us updated.

"Everyone says it's your fault," she'd report cheerfully.

"But the report proved—"

"Peter, this is Greece," she'd interrupt. "Reports don't change opinions."

And she was right.

Truth here isn't about evidence; it's about repetition.

Say something loudly enough in a kafeneio, and it becomes history.

In Pefki logic, if rain falls near you, you summoned it. If a cat gives birth in your garden, you're responsible for its vet bills. And if water flows downhill, well, you should have built the hill somewhere else.

When a Greek village finally makes peace, you'd think it might last. Plates are smashed, wine poured, shoulders clasped, and surely after all that, everyone hugs, sings "Opa Opa," and harmony reigns.

Not quite.

Peace in Pefki is more like filo pastry: delicately layered, easily torn, and held together by honey and hope.

We found ourselves in an interesting position. Our consultant had proved, beyond any doubt, that we were in no way responsible for the village flooding. In fact, the guilty party turned out to be the very person who had accused us, and, incidentally, had managed to get us arrested twice.

It was revealed, with some theatrical irony, that she had built not only a wall across the river, but a house *in* it as well. Technically, we had every legal right to demand its removal.

But instead of summoning bulldozers or invoking Poseidon himself, we did the unthinkable: we forgave Nemesis. We arrived at her door with flowers and a cake.

It caused such confusion that the entire village fell silent. Gossip stopped for almost two days – an event so rare it should have been recorded for posterity. In Pefki terms, that's roughly a decade of peace.

By the third day, though, theories sprouted like oregano after rain. Some said Alex had bewitched her. Others claimed I'd been bribed with baklava.

But something odd happened: grudges began to soften.

Spiros and Eleni, who hadn't spoken since the goat incident of 1978, shared a glass of tsipouro.

Dimitri the baker stopped overcharging Nikos the blacksmith.

Even the cats stopped fighting over sardine heads, briefly.

For one bright moment, we'd stumbled into an age of peace – the kind held together by grilled octopus and reluctant forgiveness.

Alex took full credit.

"It was my idea," she said, stirring her coffee with the air of a diplomat.

"Yes," I said, "but I bought the cake."

Truth be told, we were exhausted, not just by the flood, but by what it revealed.

When the water came, it wasn't just mud that swept through our home and garden. It was everything we'd believed about belonging, washed clean in an instant. And when it was over, the silence was worse than the storm.

Neighbours whispered behind shutters.

Some avoided our eyes.

Others came, awkwardly, with buckets and sympathy, unsure which was needed more.

We'd come to Greece chasing simplicity, dreaming of sunlight and community, of long tables under fig trees and laughter over wine. Instead, we found ourselves drowning in suspicion, bureaucracy, and the strange politics of paradise, where everyone smiles as they sharpen their knives.

It wasn't just a flood. It was a reckoning.

And though the village had moved on, more or less, something inside us hadn't.

The house had dried, the walls had been repainted, the garden repaired and replanted. But peace, once cracked, never sets quite the same again.

Some nights, when the rain starts to fall and thunder rolls over the mountains, I still see it all: the water rising, the lights flickering, the cats leaping for higher ground.

Alex pretends she doesn't think about it.

But I've caught her watching the sky too, as if daring it to try again.

CHAPTER TWO

THE DECISION TO BREATHE

Alex was staring into her cup, stirring the same spoonful of sugar long after it had dissolved. Ten minutes of that calm, concentrated stirring, which, in Alex terms, means a weather system is forming somewhere behind her eyes. I've seen it before: the long, quiet inhale before a major life decision, or a "good idea" that usually gets me into trouble.

Finally, she spoke, "We are both exhausted," she said.

I looked up from my phone.

She gestured vaguely at the walls, the ceiling, the window streaked with rain. "All of this. The gossip, the endless sympathy visits, the damp walls. Every time we fix one thing, something else leaks, and half the village comes to sympathise."

The spoon touched porcelain with a soft, decisive clink.

"We need perspective."

"Perspective?" I repeated, which is English for: yes, but could it also be a sandwich?

"Yes," she said, already impatient I hadn't caught up. "We get away. Clear our heads. Just go."

She said it with no drama, no flourish. Just that calm certainty that leaves no useful place for argument.

"We travel," she added. "Remind ourselves there are other villages with other idiots. Then we come back and sort this out properly."

And just like that, the spell broke. The village, the rain, the rumours – all of it could wait. It was time to go.

We had spent a year repairing what the storm had taken: a new garden where the old one drowned, new furniture where the swollen, salt-streaked pieces had given up, fresh plaster over the scars you can still see if you know where to look. On the surface, everything seemed mended. Beneath it, the cracks still hummed.

Every day had become an act of patching, replanting plants, replacing stones, soothing tempers. We learned the choreography of recovery: one of us to call the electrician, one to calm the neighbour, one to stand in the yard with a hose and pretend it was under control. We were good at it. Too good.

There's a blindness that follows too much mending. You start believing progress is fixing what's broken instead of asking whether it was worth saving in the first place. We were curators of our own life museum, careful not to touch anything too firmly in case it fell apart again.

Maybe that's what travel is for. Not escape, but perspective: stepping outside the frame so you can finally see the picture.

We handed Maria the sacred duty of feeding the strays. She accepted with the solemnity of a nun taking vows and the efficiency of a minister forming a committee. "I'll keep them fatter than when you left," she promised, which is both a reassurance and a threat in Pefki.

Then came the packing. Calling it "packing" is kind. It was more of a panic migration. We had no idea where we were going or for how long, so, sensibly, we packed everything.

Alex began with essentials: clothes, jackets, a hairdryer, a backup hairdryer. Shoes were categorised by purpose: walking, dining, unexpected dancing, and "in case the dining turns into dancing which it usually does in Greece". She added her notebook, three pens, and a small oregano plant she refuses to leave behind because "plants need holidays too".

I contributed my usual: several shirts, one pair of shorts I'd regret, a book I wouldn't finish, a toolkit ("You can't fix people," Alex reminded me), two packets of biscuits, and a bottle of tsipouro – medicinal, spiritual, and occasionally to light the BBQ.

The cats watched from the wall with the smugness of creatures who know you're leaving and don't care. Maria arrived for the briefing and shook her head at the car.

"You take too much," she said.

"We're going to the mountains," Alex replied.

"For how long?"

"We'll see."

Maria sighed in the universal language of Greek women who've already predicted the outcome.

By the time we were ready, the Citroën looked like a travelling bazaar: bags to the roof, a plant buckled in like a nervous aunt, and a faint rattle from the toolkit that might also have been destiny.

I started the engine, looked at Alex, and asked the question that tastes of freedom: "Where to?"

She smiled, the smile that often precedes adventure and frequently ends in story. "Away to the ferry to the mainland, and then we will see."

We rolled out of the gate, the village seeing us off in its casual way. A nod from the baker. A lifted chin from the priest. A suspicious glance from behind Nemesis's curtains – just enough to confirm she was still keeping watch.

The road dipped towards the sea, opening out as it always does just beyond the last houses. Something eased as we drove. The sense of being hemmed in, of having nowhere else to go, loosened its grip. Ahead of us, the horizon no longer pressed back. It opened, quietly, as if it had been there all along, waiting for us to notice.

We set off without a plan and without the faintest idea of where the road might carry us. Even the potholes on the way to the port felt like liberation. Behind us: floods, feuds, court papers, muddy boots, whispered accusations. Ahead: a line where sky met water and everything past it belonged to possibility.

As we climbed the last bend before the harbour, I glanced back at the hills, those green scars giving way to brown sticks that had once been trees before the great fire. You could still trace where the flood had torn through, carving the earth as if Poseidon had taken a swipe in bad temper.

But for the first time since it happened, I didn't see wreckage. I saw the outline of what we'd survived, singed, battered, rearranged perhaps, but stubbornly there. Greece doesn't rebuild; it endures.

Alex reached across and squeezed my hand, a quiet reminder that, somehow, we did too.

"See?" she said softly. "We're still here."

She meant more than the house or the olive tree that refused to drown. She meant us – the part worn thin by sleepless nights and official forms, now tugging itself back together.

Sometimes surviving isn't enough. You have to move, even if it's only far enough to breathe differently.

Poseidon wasn't going to let us go easily. We were still in his territory – the Aegean, his personal playground – and he'd clearly noticed.

The day had teeth. The wind came howling down the quay, snatching at scarves, flipping skirts, and chasing hats across the pavement like escaped crabs. Seagulls flew backwards. Old fishermen clung to their cigarettes for ballast. Thunderclouds were stacking up on the horizon like uninvited relatives at a baptism, each one arriving with a gift of rain and bad attitude. The sky darkened, the sea growled, and the ferry, our noble chariot, bobbed at the dock with all the enthusiasm of a cow at a rodeo.

Poseidon had clearly decided to make an occasion of it. Somewhere deep beneath the waves, you could almost hear him laughing, swirling his trident like a bartender stirring a cocktail called *Regret à la Englishman*. All that was missing was a polite note saying, *Bon voyage, mortals. Let's see what you're made of.*

The ferry would take us to the mainland. After that, we didn't know and didn't need to. Away was enough. We had no idea where we were going, and for once, we didn't care.

The ferry groaned into life, a sound between a bull with a hangover and a priest clearing his throat before the gospel. Below deck, lorries clanked, chains grated, and the crew shouted at each other with the kind of language that, in any other place, would start a feud and here simply meant things were going well.

Passengers hunched against the wind as the boat shouldered itself from the dock. I braced at the rail with the seriousness of a man who wants to appear nautical. Alex did her best Aegean impression: chin up, hair flying, eyes bright, storm as tonic, not threat.

"This is nothing," she shouted. "You should see Santorini in February."

I decided not to reply. My focus was on not turning green in front of strangers.

The coastline thinned to a smudge. Beneath us, the sea, ancient and loud, washed the village noise from our ears.

Ferries are floating theatres. Every deck carries a cast: a chain-smoking trucker balancing frappe, cigarette and phone calls; the honeymooners photographing lifeboats like art; an old woman in black, clutching komboloi and throwing withering looks at anyone who smiles, as if their happiness were a personal insult.

Within ten minutes, Alex had a new friend. She always does. A woman with a clinking shopping bag and a voice that could toast a village.

"This is Eleni," Alex announced, beaming as if she'd been elected mayor of the upper deck. "Her cousin has the best grilled octopus in Greece. We must go."

I nodded as calmly as a man engaged in quiet negotiations with his stomach. The ferry rolled; my insides reconsidered their loyalties. Octopus, usually a joy, became a theory. Eleni studied me.

"He looks pale," she observed.

"He always looks pale," Alex said, flicking a hand. "English skin. He can get sunburn from the fridge light."

Eleni rummaged in her bag and produced a small bottle of something that looked like emergency fuel. "Tsipouro," she declared. "Medicine."

There are rules in Greece. One of them is: if a stranger offers you tsipouro, you accept it and ask the saint of your choice to meet you halfway. I took a gulp. My seasickness evaporated instantly, replaced by a fireball that roared from throat to toes and convinced me the engines had moved inside my chest. Alex laughed, Eleni cackled, and the ferry lurched again for emphasis.

"See?" Alex said, satisfied. "Stronger already."

At last the ship docked into port, heaving itself against the quay with all the grace of a well-fed uncle collapsing into a chair after Sunday lunch. Chains clattered, orders were barked, and drivers sprinted to their cabs with cigarettes still lit, steering with one hand and crossing themselves with the other.

We rolled down the ramp and onto solid ground, greeted by the holy trinity of every Greek harbour: diesel, salt, and frying oil. Somewhere nearby, a café was already serving calamari for breakfast. A priest crossed the road on a moped. Cats prowled between the tyres like they owned the place, and, in fairness, they probably did.

We pulled over just beyond the chaos, the engine ticking, the air still humming with the noise of ropes and horns and shouting. Evia was somewhere across the water behind us – distant, smudged, still drying out from our last disaster – but we were here, standing on new ground with no plan, no timetable, and no one demanding to see our paperwork. We looked at each other and grinned, that quiet, guilty smile of people who've just mislaid a burden they never meant to carry.

I exhaled, feeling the tension leave my shoulders. "There's no list."

Alex closed her eyes for a moment, as if checking the

thought for accuracy, then smiled. "Exactly," she said. "Just a road, and whatever's waiting at the end of it."

She opened her eyes and glanced towards the inland road, where the mountains rose steadily out of sight. "How about Delphi?" she said. "A couple of hours. We can stay in Arachova. Fresh air. Quiet. No Nemesis."

She said it lightly, but the decision was already made. The way it always was with her. Not announced, not debated, simply placed on the table and left there to be accepted.

The word itself felt like a breath: Delphi. The old centre of questions. People used to climb that mountain to listen for the earth's answer; lately we'd been answering everyone else's questions but our own.

"Delphi," I said. "Yes."

We drove without speaking for a while, the road unwinding into hills, olive leaves flashing silver in the light. I could feel the village slipping from my shoulders like a wet coat. Alex's hand found mine again.

Perhaps this is what healing looks like, I thought: not triumph, just movement. The gentle kind that says: keep going; the path will explain itself.

We joined the road that curled towards the mountains. Somewhere beyond the bends, the stones of Delphi were waiting with their patient silence. If we were lucky, the wind might carry an answer. If not, there would be pine air, a firm mattress, and a morning without gossip.

For now, that was enough.

CHAPTER THREE

A JOURNEY TO THE UNKNOWN

It was spring in Greece, that restless, awakening season when the land stretches after winter and remembers it's beautiful, almost smugly so. As we wound our way from the port and began the slow climb into the mountains, the world shifted around us with the confidence of a country that knows exactly how to make an entrance.

Behind us, the sea still fumed beneath bruised clouds, muttering its disapproval at our escape. The waves slapped the harbour wall with the sulky rhythm of someone who had been left out of important plans. But ahead, the hills were already shrugging off the last of their snow, revealing flashes of green so bright they looked newly invented, as if spring had taken up painting again after a long sabbatical.

We felt something stirring too.

Not excitement exactly; something deeper, quieter, almost ancient. A sense that we were crossing a threshold. That whatever waited beyond the next bend would be different from what we left behind.

We didn't say it out loud, but we both felt it: we were beginning our own Greek odyssey. The word hung in the air between us, unspoken but unmistakable. We weren't running away; we were being carried forward. Not escaping; embarking.

Poor Odysseus. He thought he was popping over to Troy for a quick battle. A long weekend, a bit of heroic posing, maybe back by Tuesday.

We, too thought this would be a short trip – some clothes, some biscuits, an oregano plant, the usual essentials. But somewhere between the sea and the mountains, we realised that no one ever truly chooses an odyssey. It chooses you.

And like Odysseus on that first cheerful voyage out of Ithaca, we had no idea how long our journey would become, what storms would rise, what strange encounters awaited, or how profoundly it would change us. All we knew was that home lay behind us, uncertainty lay ahead, and the road between them felt oddly, unmistakably sacred.

The mountains rose, wide and open, ready to swallow us whole and then show us who we were beneath the mud and bureaucracy. Spring clung to the slopes in bright patches, as if the earth itself were beginning again, and inviting us to do the same.

For the first time in a long while, the horizon didn't feel like something closing in.

It felt like permission.

An invitation.

A beginning.

Each bend of the road carried us further from the salt and roar of the coast and closer to the scent of wild thyme, pine, and wet earth slipping through the cracked vents of our faithful Citroën. Poppies flared along the roadside like sparks, almond trees trembled with white blossom, and even the goats looked giddy with renewal. The ferry now felt like a fading dream, left somewhere far below with the waves and the noise, as Greece reassembled itself in colour and light.

The road wound back and forth in dizzying loops, curling around the mountain like a ribbon. Each hairpin bend revealed another postcard view, turquoise bays glittering far below, villages clinging to cliffs that had no business supporting them, goats balanced on impossible slopes as though auditioning for a circus.

Alex didn't drive. She *danced* with the road, swaying into corners, laughing at potholes, waving at oncoming buses as if they were part of the choreography. One hand on the wheel, the other gesturing freely, sometimes waving to passing cars, sometimes explaining a philosophical point about Greek roads and destiny. She took every curve with the confidence of a rally driver and the serenity of a priestess. I sat beside her, silent, one hand gripping the door handle with the solemnity of a man rehearsing his final words. I thought that if Hermes himself appeared in the rear-view mirror, she'd overtake him on a bend and tell him to get a proper job.

She was in her element, wind in her hair, eyes alive, the kind of smile that only appears when she's part of the landscape rather than just passing through it. The little Citroën hummed like a contented bee, following her lead without complaint.

I glanced at the speedometer and then at the drop to the sea below. There was no guardrail between us and eternity. Alex noticed my expression and laughed.

"Relax," she said, tightening her grip on the wheel with a flourish. "I know this road. I was born with these bends."

I considered pointing out that she was born two hundred kilometres away, but decided that silence was the wiser choice. The view was too beautiful to spoil with fear.

The higher we climbed, the more the world unfolded – terraces of olives, white churches perched on spurs of rock, the sea shimmering like mercury far below.

Alex peered out towards the horizon. "Look," she said, "you can see forever from here."

I looked, and for once, she wasn't exaggerating. The mountains rolled away in soft blue layers, the islands floating in the haze like sleeping gods.

She smiled, eyes on the road, and said quietly, "This is freedom."

I nodded, still clutching the door handle. "Yes," I said, "and possibly the afterlife if you miss the next bend."

She laughed, that deep, infectious laugh that belongs entirely to her, and the car carried us higher, winding through the clouds.

I loved Alex with a passion – the inconvenient, illogical kind that refuses to read warning labels. She had given me Greece: not the one in the guidebooks with polite waiters and tidy sunsets, but the real one, loud, chaotic, magnificent. The Greece of shouted greetings, double-parked philosophy, and storms that arrived with personality. She didn't just live here; she *belonged* to it.

And despite my nerves, my white-knuckled grip on the door handle and silent conversations with every available saint, I had to admit it: she was right. There was something exhilarating about surrendering to her way of driving, trusting the road, the car, and the woman who genuinely believed she could out-steer the gods.

For a few glorious moments, fear gave way to wonder. The sea shimmered below us, the sky stretched above in reckless blue, and the woman beside me, this force of nature who could argue with a priest, charm a fisherman, and terrify a mayor, smiled into the wind.

And in that instant, it all merged into something larger than both of us: sea, sky, and love, spinning together on a mountain road somewhere between chaos and eternity.

And as we rounded the final curve, I realised I wasn't rehearsing my last words any more. I was just watching her, driving us through the heavens as if she belonged there.

We pulled into a mountainside petrol station, one of those multipurpose Greek establishments that doubles as a cafe, a hardware shop, and, if you ask nicely, a post office. An old man emerged from behind a rack of olive-oil tins, cigarette glued to his lower lip, and began pumping petrol. Each drag of smoke hovered dangerously close to the nozzle, and I found myself calculating the odds of spontaneous combustion.

Inside, the café section was a small miracle of survival: two plastic tables, a stack of chairs that looked older than democracy, and a faded poster of Mykonos that had clearly seen sunnier days. From a radio in the corner came the steady crackle of laïka music – the kind that sounds like heartbreak wrapped in cigarette smoke.

We ordered coffees. The owner nodded once, disappeared behind a curtain, and we heard the hiss of something being coaxed into existence. A few minutes later, he reappeared with two cups.

Greek coffee isn't really a drink, it's an experience. It arrives looking innocent enough, until you realise it's half coffee, half mud, and strong enough to make your ancestors sit up. You don't sip it. You approach it with respect.

Alex lifted hers carefully, blew on it, and took a small taste. "Perfect," she said, smiling.

I tried mine. It tasted like roasted philosophy, bitter, ancient, and guaranteed to keep me awake until next week.

The owner watched us closely, as though judging our worth by how far down the cup we managed before hitting the sludge. I stopped just short of the line where the spoon stands up by itself. Alex, naturally, finished hers completely, then turned her cup upside down for fortune reading.

The owner's wife appeared from behind the curtain and picked up Alex's cup. She studied the dark pattern left by the coffee grounds with practised seriousness, turning it slightly in the light. Then she nodded, as if confirming something she had already suspected.

"You are travelling," she said.

Alex grinned. "We are."

The woman looked again, her finger tracing a line inside the cup. "And you will go on a very long trip."

I smiled politely. We only had plans to go to Arachova and Delphi. We might be back by the next day. Whatever this woman was seeing in the coffee, it clearly extended beyond our modest itinerary.

"The coffee never lies," Alex said, with the calm confidence of someone who had already decided to believe it.

I wasn't sure whether she meant the woman, the ritual itself, or simply her own instinct. Either way, the comment lingered. I finished my coffee slowly, aware that something had been said which could not be easily unsaid, even if neither of us was quite sure what it meant yet.

Outside, we stepped onto the terrace, where a few plastic chairs clung bravely to the edge of the mountain. The view opened out below us. Far beneath, the sea shimmered in the morning light, as if reminding us that, whatever mood it was in, it could still offer beauty on its own terms. Whitewashed villages dotted the slopes, scattered lightly across the landscape.

The cold nipped at our noses, but after being refreshed by the coffee, we pretended to be hardened mountain folk rather than two coastal refugees in thin jackets. Alex threw her head back into the wind, hair flying everywhere, and declared, "This is good for us. Fresh air. Perspective. No neighbours watching from gardens." I nodded, though my eyes were still on the horizon. I half expected Nemesis to appear up there, glaring down at us from some impossible height.

We climbed back into the car and pressed on. The road tightened as it climbed, the temperature falling with each bend. Soon the air smelled of woodsmoke, and the mountains closed around us like old storytellers leaning in for the next chapter.

So, we were on our way to Delphi and Arachova, though we didn't yet know what kind of welcome the gods, or the locals, had in store.

CHAPTER FOUR

ARRIVAL IN ARACHOVA

By late afternoon, the road finally spat us out of the mountain passes and into Arachova, a town that looked as if someone had stolen a corner of Switzerland, sprinkled it with Greek flags, added a few Orthodox churches for seasoning, and then balanced the whole thing on a cliff just to keep everyone alert.

Red-tiled roofs clung to the slopes like limpet shells, while the streets twisted and turned between stone houses as though they'd been mapped by a cartographer who'd spent the night on raki and decided straight lines were a sign of moral weakness.

Every corner looked ready to slide gracefully into the valley below, but somehow it all held together; a miracle of architecture, faith, and stubbornness. In Greece, even gravity thinks twice before arguing.

Alex slowed the car to a crawl, partly because of the cobbles, partly because she was already craning her neck to inspect the shops. Fur coats in the windows, ski equipment piled up like exhibits, tavernas offering everything from souvlaki to "pizza with mythic taste". To me, it looked like a Greek St. Moritz without the snow. To Alex, it looked like Glyfada with better handbags.

We parked beside a row of 4x4s, all polished to within an inch of their lives, and I felt our muddy Citroën shrink with embarrassment. As we unloaded our bags, a group of Athenians strutted past in designer sunglasses, their dogs dressed warmer than we were. Alex gave them a nod of superiority; she was from Glyfada, after all. I tried to hide my anorak.

The guesthouse sat just above the main square – a stone building with wooden shutters and a balcony that promised "views of Parnassus". Our host, a tiny woman with a voice that could cut marble, greeted us like old friends, and within five minutes she had placed a tray of coffee in front of us, complete with spoon sweets and advice on which taverna *not* to eat at ("their moussaka is a crime against humanity").

From the balcony, the view stretched out across the valley, an entire world painted in evening light. The mountains fell away in folds of silver and green, and there, far in the distance, we could see Delphi itself, a scatter of ruins glowing gold in the last of the sun. The air was so clear it felt ancient, as if every breath carried the ghosts of philosophers and pilgrims who'd once stood on these same slopes asking impossible questions.

For centuries, kings, generals, and hopeful dreamers had climbed to Delphi to seek the truth, to ask the Oracle whether to wage war, make peace, or marry badly. Now it was our turn.

Alex leaned on the balcony rail, eyes fixed on the horizon. "Can you feel it?" she asked softly. "This is where people came for answers."

I nodded. "Yes. And probably left with even more questions."

If Delphi was all lofty wisdom and ancient whispers, then Arachova by night was its rowdy cousin: loud, smoky, and proudly uninterested in enlightenment. Philosophy, as far as anyone here was concerned, could stay further down the mountain where it belonged.

This was no place for oracles. This was a place for menus, open fires, and the kind of grilled meat that made you forget you'd ever asked life's big questions. The only prophecy worth hearing came from the waiter, and it usually began with: "You should try the lamb."

The village lit up like a Christmas card as the sun slipped behind the mountains. Fairy lights strung across balconies twinkled above cobbled streets, the smell of grilled meat and woodsmoke drifting through the air. Designer-clad Athenians paraded arm in arm, their fur coats brushing against the shoulders of their pedigree dogs, who were dressed in cashmere jumpers that probably cost more than my car.

Alex walked among them as if she had just been elected their queen. She moved easily through the crowd, confident, animated, her voice lilting in rapid-fire Greek as she greeted waiters and shopkeepers like old friends. The street seemed to open for her, drawn to her warmth and certainty.

I, on the other hand, drifted a few steps behind, wrapped in my practical coat and mild bewilderment, a foreigner in a place that felt almost too vivid to be real. The air was sharper here, the colours brighter, stone walls glowing gold in the lamplight, smoke curling from chimneys, laughter spilling out of doorways. It was as though the whole village had agreed to perform the idea of Greece just for her.

For a moment, I felt like a smudge in someone else's painting, the quiet observer, out of rhythm but slowly learning the steps. Yet with every turn, every burst of music from a taverna, every flash of warmth from strangers' faces, I began to feel something loosen inside me.

There was something magnetic about the place: a calm beneath the wind, a pull that made you feel small and significant all at once. The light dimmed, the valley turned silver, and bells echoed faintly from the church below. For the first time in months, I felt a strange peace beginning to creep over me. Perhaps belonging isn't about being from a place, I thought. Perhaps it's about learning to love it as if you were.

We found a taverna wedged between a boutique selling

eight-hundred-euro ski jackets and a bar blasting rebetika loud enough to make the windows vibrate. It felt improbably placed, as if it had been holding its ground long before either neighbour arrived.

Inside, the fire crackled and every table was taken. Coats hung from chair backs, glasses clinked, and conversations overlapped in that comfortable, unhurried way that suggests nobody is planning to leave soon. The air was thick with everything that matters on a winter evening in Greece. Woodsmoke. Laughter. The rich, reassuring smell of meat on the grill.

Alex was greeted like returning royalty – kisses, exclamations, and enough gossip to power the national grid. Within seconds she knew the waiter's name, his mother's name, and the precise medical history of his grandmother's knee.

Then there was me.

I clearly looked British; the posture, the polite nod, the faint air of apology for existing. In a village where everyone gestured like opera singers, I stood there holding my coat, radiating understatement. The owner gave me a quick once-over, trying to work out what exactly I was doing with one of his own. He settled on curiosity and poured me a glass of wine large enough to prove that, for tonight at least, I belonged.

Menus were presented but largely ignored – here you ate what the kitchen had. Plates began to arrive uninvited: sizzling loukaniko sausages, hunks of feta dripping with oil, mountain greens boiled into submission. Then came the pièce de résistance: a clay pot of goat stew, steaming like Mount Parnassus itself.

"Goat," Alex declared happily, ladling a portion onto my plate.

Around us, Athenians clinked wine glasses, adjusted their designer scarves, and posed mid-mouthful for selfies.

Alex almost never drinks alcohol. She doesn't need it. If a glass of wine appears in front of her, she'll raise it gracefully for a toast, take the smallest possible sip, and then leave it untouched; a symbolic gesture rather than a habit.

Most people take a glass of wine to loosen up, to find courage, to shake off the world. Alex was born three glasses in. She never needed wine to loosen her tongue. It arrived loose. Opinion was factory-fitted.

Courage was not something she topped up from a bottle either. It was permanently on tap. By breakfast she had usually corrected a mistake, challenged a decision, and won an argument that nobody else realised they were having. Alex can turn a quiet taverna into a festival, stone sober, with one clap of her hands and that unmistakable spark in her eyes.

She's pure kinetic energy. Even sitting still, she vibrates faintly, like a radio picking up every frequency in the village at once. Her laughter arrives before the joke, her gestures could power a wind turbine, and her opinions, well, they arrive at volume.

So when we sat down to eat that night in the little mountain taverna, I wasn't expecting anything out of the ordinary. A bit of goat, some salad, a polite argument about whether we should order dessert. Then Alex opened the menu and froze.

"Mavrodaphni," she whispered, eyes wide. "The wine of my youth."

I raised an eyebrow. "You had wine in your youth?"

She ignored me, lost in memory. "It's the wine they gave us at church, for communion. So sweet, so dark. Every Sunday, the priest would dip the spoon, and I would pray for a bigger sip."

Before I could protest, she'd ordered a *bottle*. When it arrived, she cradled it like a relic from her childhood. The first sip was taken reverently, almost ceremonially. Then she smiled.

"Oh, yes," she said. "Exactly the same."

I took a cautious sip myself. It was thick, sticky, and sweet enough to dissolve teeth on contact. The kind of wine that could make your ears ache with one sip. But Alex was in heaven, sipping between bites of goat, her eyes growing brighter with every glass.

Now, when Alex drinks, on the very rare occasions she does, she doesn't just get tipsy. She gets… *extra Alex*. The laughter begins softly at first, like the warm-up act to a storm. Then comes the storytelling. Suddenly, everyone within twenty feet is family, and the waiter becomes her long-lost cousin. She gestures wildly, reenacting half her childhood with goat bones as props, while I sit quietly, knowing resistance is futile.

By the second glass, she was telling the story of her grandmother's donkey who refused to cross the river unless blessed by a priest. By the third, she was explaining to a startled German couple at the next table why English men make excellent husbands but terrible dancers.

At one point, she leaned in, eyes sparkling. "Do you know what I learned from communion wine?" she said. "It teaches you faith."

"How?" I asked, already bracing myself.

"Because after one glass, you believe you can sing."

And sing she did.

The owner turned down the music. Alex turned it back up. A few claps from another table, and that was all the encouragement she needed. Moments later, she was on her feet, spinning between the tables, shawl flying, Mavrodaphni in hand, laughing like a woman who'd just discovered joy in liquid form.

The locals joined in, of course. A line of strangers formed, napkins waving, everyone shouting *opa*! as Alex led an impromptu dance around the taverna. I watched from my chair, equal parts proud husband and nervous spectator.

When the song ended, she returned to the table, cheeks flushed, hair wild, and took one final sip from her glass.

"That," she announced solemnly, "was the best communion I've ever had."

By the time the fire had burned low and the bill was slapped onto the table (calculated by an ancient formula involving wine stains and random guesswork), we were full, dazed, and oddly content.

Alex exhaled contentedly, that slow, satisfied breath of a woman who has made peace with the universe, or at least with wine.

"Tomorrow," she said, stretching like a cat in sunlight,

"we go to the temple of Delphi. Unless we find something else to do."

It sounded so casual, so gloriously unstructured, that it took me a moment to process. *Unless we find something else to do.* In our recent life, that phrase didn't exist. There was always a list, deadlines, repairs, leaks, goats, bureaucracy. If you weren't doing something, it meant something had already gone wrong.

Now, for the first time in months, we had no *plan.*

None.

No itinerary, no fixed time, no obligations waiting like unpaid bills on the kitchen table. We didn't even know what day it was, and for once that wasn't a sign of stress; it was a sign of possibility.

We were unaccountable. To the village. To the neighbours. To the endless rhythm of *"you should…"*

And yet… the sudden absence of responsibility didn't feel like the freedom we imagined.

It felt, oddly, like we'd misplaced something. A vague, guilty sensation, as if adulthood were tapping its foot somewhere just out of sight.

Freedom, it turns out, takes practice.

There's a peculiar anxiety that arrives when there's nothing to fix, nothing to defend, nothing to brace for. After months of storms – literal and otherwise – the stillness felt unnatural, like a trick set by the gods. A small voice deep inside whispered: *You've definitely forgotten something important.*

It was like stepping outside without your keys, except the house you've left behind is your entire life.

Alex, of course, was thriving.

She was born for unstructured days and roads that don't bother to explain themselves. Chaos is her natural climate. She trusts the world to unfold for her, and infuriatingly, it does. She calls it intuition. I call it luck wearing excellent posture.

I, on the other hand, sat there trying to adjust to the absence of structure. There was just a road stretching forward, and the faint, fragile promise that maybe, just maybe, life didn't need a timetable. For months, we'd been holding our breath, waiting for another accusation, another official form, another storm rolling down the mountain with our name on it. Now, as the engine hummed and the mountains opened ahead of us, I began to realise something unexpected:

This,

this not knowing,

this not rushing,

this refusal to plan,

might be the closest thing to peace we'd touched in years.

Not the peace of everything being perfect, but the peace of finally, blessedly, letting go. Of releasing the life we'd been gripping with white knuckles. Of trusting the road, the sky, and perhaps even ourselves again.

We thought we were merely going on a trip. But somewhere between the sea and the mountains, we stepped into something larger: a pause, a breath, a beginning.

Our own small odyssey, not measured in miles, but in the slow rediscovery of who we were when no one was asking anything of us.

The cold settled around us and bells clanged faintly from the church below. Alex sighed with satisfaction, her face glowing in the mountain air. "See? I told you. Perfect. A new beginning."

I nodded, wrapping my jacket tighter. Perfect, indeed, though I couldn't help wondering if even the Oracle could predict what would happen next.

CHAPTER FIVE

THE GREEK CAT CAPER

We walked from the taverna towards the guest house. A place of cold air, clean snow, and the kind of silence that makes you think the world has finally agreed to leave you alone.

But as I've learned over the years, the village never truly lets you go. It follows you.

Not in body, but in sound.

The sound of my phone ringing.

I held it up and showed Alex the screen. Alex glanced,

sighed, and said the one word that can drain hope faster than a leaking bucket.

"Maria."

I braced myself. Nothing good ever begins with a call from Maria.

"Peterrrrrr!" came the cry, high-pitched and panicked enough to make the shepherd's dog look up. "It's chaos!"

"Good evening to you too," I said carefully. "What kind of chaos?"

"The cats!" she wailed. "They've taken over the village! They're everywhere – on your roof, in your garden, on the road, in the basil! They've formed a colony! I told you not to feed them so much *love*!"

I looked at Alex, who was already rubbing her temples. "What happened?" she asked, resigned.

"I did exactly what you told me," Maria continued. "A little dry food, a few sardines, but they called their cousins! There must be fifty of them! One of them, a big black one with one ear, looks like a criminal. He's giving orders from the olive tree!"

"Ah," I said. "That'll be Black Tom."

"You *know* him?" she gasped. "Then you also know he broke into Dimitri's fishing boat last night! Fish everywhere! Dimitri says your cats owe him thirty euros and a red mullet!"

Alex took the phone. "Maria, calm down. Just feed them once a day. They'll settle."

"Settle?" Maria repeated, horrified. "They've formed a un-ion!"

In the background, I could hear Eleni shouting, "Don't antagonize them! They sense fear!"

Maria huffed. "Eleni's feeding them leftover souvlaki. She says she's keeping the peace."

"Tell her to stop," Alex said firmly.

"I did!" Maria snapped. "She told me I was starving the revolution!"

By now, Maria had apparently declared a state of feline emergency.

"The cats are sitting in a perfect circle outside your door," she said. "They're staring at the house like they expect it to answer back. I've even sprinkled holy water on the gate."

"Did it help?" I asked.

"It made them look at me differently," she replied.

There was a crash, a hiss, and the sound of Maria shouting, "Off the tablecloth!" followed by what I think was the sound of a broom hitting fur.

"Maria?" I said cautiously.

Silence. Then, breathless: "I've negotiated a ceasefire. I offered them rice and fish scraps. They blinked, ignored me, and went back to planning. Peter, I think they're mocking me."

"They're cats," I said gently.

"Exactly," she cried. "They're worse than people!"

I pressed the off button on the phone and we continued our walk. Alex put her phone down with a sigh. "We've been gone for a few hours and the village is already unravelling."

We decided to stop in the square for a hot chocolate before bed. The café we found was perfect. Wooden tables lined the cobbled square, each one tucked under a tall heater glowing orange like a small campfire. Every chair was draped with a soft lamb fleece; the sort of touch that made you instantly forgive the mountain cold. The waiter brought our drinks in heavy cups, thick with melted chocolate that could have passed for dessert. Around us, locals chatted quietly, and the clink of spoons and the drone of conversation mingled with the soft hiss of the heaters.

It was bliss: calm, warm, normal. For five whole minutes.

Then the phone rang again.

Alex didn't even look at the screen. "Of course it's Maria," she said, picking it up with the tone of someone expecting bad news.

There was silence at first, then Maria's voice arrived in a rush.

"The cats have now occupied your terrace. One jumped out of your flowerpot and attacked my apron. He's the pirate, their leader. Theodora says he looks like he owns the place. She might be right. Also, my dog refuses to go near your gate."

Alex listened without interrupting, her eyes fixed on the glowing heater in front of us, as if it were offering an alternative future. When Maria finally paused for breath, Alex spoke calmly.

"Maria, it's fine. Just leave them alone for tonight. Feed them once, then go home. We'll deal with it when we're back."

She waited, nodded once, then ended the call and set the phone on the table.

"We should have known this would happen," she said to me. "You fed one pregnant cat and named her."

"She looked hungry," I said.

"She looked strategic," Alex replied.

We sat there, sipping our hot chocolates under the glowing heaters, the smell of cinnamon in the air, and realised that no matter how far we travelled, no matter how many mountains, ferries, or borders we crossed, Pefki would always find us. Usually through Maria.

As we finished our drinks and got up to leave, a message arrived.

"Congratulations. You now own the most popular taverna in Pefki. It's called Taverna Miaou."

Attached was a photo of our terrace: a sea of cats lounging across every surface.

Some lay draped across the chairs like royalty. Others perched proudly on the table, tails curled, eyes half-closed in aristocratic disdain. In the corner, the BBQ served as the bar, stacked with cat-food tins. And in the middle of it all, Black Tom sat at the head of the table, one ear missing, one eye glinting, the undisputed boss of Pefki.

The caption beneath read: "They've started taking turns guarding the food."

That night, I dreamed of them. A full council of cats sitting around our courtyard table, each with a tiny glass of wine. Their tails swished in unison. Their eyes gleamed with purpose. At the head sat Black Tom, smoking a sardine like a cigar.

He looked straight at me and said, "We're in charge now, Barber. Tell Maria to keep the fish coming, and none of that dried stuff."

CHAPTER SIX

NEXT MORNING IN ARACHOVA

We woke refreshed and strangely optimistic, as if sleep had pressed a reset button we didn't know existed. Morning arrived in Arachova with a brightness that felt personally delivered. Sunlight barged through the shutters like a cheerful relative: loud, insistent, and impossible to ignore. Somewhere below, the church bells rang just slightly off-key, as though the cantor had decided perfection was overrated.

Alex, naturally, was radiant. She stood at the window humming, her hair catching the early light, looking like a woman who had not only danced on tables and drunk half a bottle of wine, but had absorbed the alcohol as nourishment. Meanwhile, I remained hunched in bed, blinking at the world like a startled mole.

She turned to me with the kind of smile that can't be argued with.

"Good morning! Isn't it a beautiful day?"

I made a sound that could have been agreement or simply the contented sigh of a man who'd slept well for the first time in weeks.

She poured herself a coffee, inhaled it like incense, and began recounting the previous night as though reviewing a triumphant theatre premiere.

"They *loved* my dancing," she announced, stretching like a cat in sunlight. "The German couple took videos. The waiter said I reminded him of his aunt from Kalamata. Such a sweet boy."

I nodded weakly. "You do realise he was terrified."

"Nonsense," she said, brushing the comment away. "He was inspired. You English" – she waved a hand at me – "you drink to forget. We Greeks drink to remember who we are."

Then Alex's phone dinged.

She handed it to me silently.

"Read it," she said.

Maria's latest message glowed on the screen: "Good morning from Taverna Miaou," Maria had written. "Full house again. Eleni says the cats have started taking reservations. Theodora is bringing a new tablecloth especially for them. Also, one cat is sitting in your chair, looking disappointed. I think he misses you."

I couldn't help smiling. "Well… that's very touching. I always hoped to be missed by *someone*."

Alex laughed, the soft, delighted kind. "At this rate, when we go back, we'll have to queue for our own seats."

"Naturally," I said. "It's a thriving business now. The cats won't hand it over without negotiations."

She nodded with mock seriousness. "Still, it's nice to know we've left our mark on the village."

I sipped my coffee, looked out towards the mountains dusted with morning snow, and said, "Yes… and I suspect our mark has paw prints all over it."

Outside, the town was stirring back to life. The streets glistened from the early morning wash of mountain mist, and the smell of coffee and freshly baked bread drifted up from the bakery below. Somewhere, a radio played soft rebetika, slow and melancholy, as if the village itself were gently coming down from last night's high.

Alex sipped her coffee, eyes still bright with that dangerous mix of joy and ideas. "We should do this more often," she said. "Not the wine; the living. The laughing. The part where you stop thinking and just say yes to life."

I watched her, all fire, grace, and absolute certainty, and felt that familiar mix of admiration and mild concern that usually precedes one of her plans. "Shall we pack up and head for Delphi?" I asked, ever the man hoping for a clear instruction manual.

She laughed, tossed her scarf around her shoulders like a heroine in a black-and-white film, and threw open the window.

Cold mountain air swept in, sharp and alive. "Not yet," she said. "Let's stay another day. I want to see some snow."

And that was that: our next adventure decreed.

So we would head up into the mountains. Not to ski, you understand – neither of us had the coordination for that – but to *see* it, *touch* it, maybe build a snowman, and almost certainly watch Alex lob snowballs at me with the deadly accuracy of a woman avenging centuries of Greek myths.

Now, Arachova proudly calls itself the "skiing village" of Greece. This is technically true in the same way that my early attempts at Greek were "technically" the language. It looks the part: stone houses, alpine scarves, and plenty of cafés selling hot chocolate, but it rarely snows. When it does, the snow usually lands, admires the view, and melts into slush before lunch.

The real snow lives higher up, forty-five minutes' drive above the village, on Mount Parnassos. That's where the serious skiers go, the ones who own fluorescent trousers and use the word "powder" and know what it means.

Neither of us had any interest in skiing. We'd tried it once. We remember being wet, cold, and emotionally damaged after discovering that skis have neither brakes nor steering wheels.

No, Alex just wanted to see snow. Maybe make a snowman. Definitely hit me with a snowball.

So up the mountain we went.

We climbed through low cloud, past pine forests. Slowly, the brown of the earth gave way to white streaks along the roadside.

Then the fields turned white too, until the entire world looked dusted in icing sugar. It began to snow lightly; it was beautiful.

"Stop!"

A policeman stood in the middle of the road, hand raised.

"Where are your *alysides chioniou*?"

I looked at him blankly.

"Your snow chains," he said in English, with the weary authority of a man who's had this conversation all morning.

I had never heard of snow chains until I moved to Greece. In England, when it snowed, we simply panicked politely, followed the car in front, and hoped for the best. There was always a bit of sliding around, but we considered that part of the national charm.

But here, no chains meant no further. The officer pointed us back down the mountain with the air of a disappointed parent.

We drove halfway back down the mountain and found a petrol station selling *alysides chioniou*. We bought a set immediately and returned up the road, proud owners of what the bag promised were snow chains.

Alex stayed in the car with the engine running and the heater on full, offering occasional encouragement through the glass while I knelt in the snow like a man about to attempt something he did not fully understand.

The bag showed a reassuring photograph of a neat, symmetrical wheel wrapped in shiny chains. It looked calm. Cooperative. Almost grateful.

I opened the bag.

What fell out was a tangled mass of metal links, red plastic hooks. It looked less like safety equipment and more like a jewellery display after a small earthquake.

Still, I remained optimistic. "How hard can it be?" I said, partly to Alex through to glass, partly to the mountain.

The answer arrived quickly.

Very.

I wrapped one chain around the rear wheel. It immediately fell off, tangled around the axle, and wedged itself into the only gap that required me to lie in the snow with my head under the car. I freed it. Tried again. It fell off again.

This went on for half an hour. I wrestled. I cursed. The snow fell harder. My fingers turned a heroic shade of blue.

At last, I snapped the final hook into place and stood back to admire my work. It didn't look *right*, exactly, more like the car had been caught in a metal spiderweb, but the chain was at least on the wheel. Mostly.

I had one more wheel to do.

By the time I finished, I was half-frozen and only dimly aware of my own name. I climbed back into the car, trembling but triumphant.

"Ready?" Alex asked.

"Ready," I croaked.

I pressed the accelerator. The car didn't move.

"Strange," I said, pressing harder. The wheels spun uselessly.

Alex peered out the window. "Peter… are the chains on the back wheels?"

"Yes," I said proudly.

She smiled sweetly. "This is a *front-wheel-drive* car."

I sat there for a moment, staring through the windscreen, wondering what exactly Alex had been doing while I was crawling around in the snow performing mechanical origami on the wrong wheels. But I decided not to ask. Experience has taught me that some questions are better left buried, preferably under snow.

Besides, even if I had asked, I already knew how it would end. Alex always wins arguments. Always. She doesn't even raise her voice; she just looks at me the way Zeus probably looked at mortals before turning them into goats.

So I said nothing, got out to fix it, and let the chains rattle their disapproval. With all fingers thawed, tempers restored, and the snow chains now "correctly" fitted to the *front* wheels, we finally reached the end of the road, or, as the sign proudly declared, "The Ski Centre of Mount Parnassos".

Ahead stood a large white building puffing with life. From its roof, cable cars popped out like bubbles, gliding up into the clouds and vanishing somewhere above civilisation. This, apparently, was where Greeks came to "ski", which in practice meant sitting in cafés, drinking hot chocolate thick enough to stand a spoon in, and watching other people fall over.

We bought our tickets and climbed into a cable car. It creaked, swayed, and began its slow ascent into the mist. Beneath us, pine trees poked through the snow like paintbrushes, and the world fell silent except for the gentle hum of the cables. Alex pressed her nose to the glass. "It's beautiful," she whispered.

At the top, the air was sharp and clean enough to sting. The café terrace overlooked a wide, white slope dotted with tiny moving figures – skiers, technically, though most resembled laundry in a gale. We took our place at a table, steaming mugs of hot chocolate in hand, and admired the spectacle.

Every so often, a skier would sweep past us in a perfect blur of grace, knees bent, arms poised, the very picture of alpine mastery. The next one would appear moments later travelling in an entirely different direction to his skis, legs flailing like windmills and jacket flapping like a sail.

Alex watched them with fascination. "It looks fun," she said.

I wasn't so sure. One young man went by backwards, followed by his poles, then his dignity. Another disappeared into a snowbank and re-emerged without a hat, a glove, or any clear memory of why he was there.

We sat on the terrace, sipping our drinks, and watching the chaos unfold like a slow-motion ballet. The air was crisp, the sky impossibly blue, and every few minutes came the satisfying *whoomp* of another skier discovering the true depth of Greek snowdrifts.

There was laughter, applause, and the occasional distant cry for help: the perfect soundtrack for an afternoon in the mountains.

"This," Alex said, stretching her legs towards the sun, "is my kind of skiing."

I nodded in agreement. "Seated, warm, and without any risk of freezing to death."

And there we stayed, perfectly content, two non-skiers on top of the world, applauding the brave souls who made gravity look optional and balance entirely negotiable.

After our second mug of hot chocolate, I decided we needed something stronger.

"Let's have a proper drink," I said, scanning the menu above the bar. "Look, Irish coffee, special offer, two euros!"

I felt the familiar stirrings of hope. Irish coffee is one of life's great achievements: a beverage that combines caffeine, alcohol, and optimism in a single glass. It was, clearly, destiny.

I approached the counter and pointed at the sign. "Two Irish coffees, please, one without whiskey."

One of the things I love most about living in Greece is the logic. Philosophers once taught it in the agora of Athens. Socrates, Aristotle, Plato, all masters of reason, debate, and clear thought. But somewhere between ancient Athens and modern Greece, something happened. The logic... loosened a little. Diluted, perhaps. Maybe it was the heat. Or the ouzo.

Here, logic is not a universal truth, it's a personal accessory. Everyone has their own version, and they wear it proudly.

Over the years, we've had countless moments when Alex and I have exchanged that familiar look, part amusement, part disbelief, the "Did I just hear that?" look. Or the even rarer, "That cannot possibly make sense, but it does to them" look.

Eventually, you learn not to fight it. Greek logic doesn't need to make sense to you. It just needs to make sense to whoever's explaining it. And it always does, beautifully, completely, and with total confidence.

The girl behind the bar frowned. "Sorry. We're out of that."

"Out of… Irish coffee?" I asked, as if she'd just announced they'd run out of snow.

"Yes."

"Do you have coffee?"

"Of course. This is a coffee bar," she said slowly, in the tone of someone addressing an escaped patient.

"Whiskey?"

"Yes."

"Cream?"

"Yes, lots."

I smiled. "Excellent. Then I'll have a coffee, a whiskey, and some cream on top, one without the whiskey"

Her eyes narrowed. "Ah. Irish coffee."

"Exactly."

She nodded thoughtfully, as though I'd just solved a riddle, then began her calculations. "That will be five euros for the whiskey, four for the coffee, and one fifty for the cream. Ten fifty total."

I hesitated. "But the sign says two."

She shrugged. "That's when we *have* it."

It was hard to argue with logic of that magnitude, so I paid.

She handed me the drink with a faint smile – a steaming cup of strong coffee, one with a generous shot of whiskey, and a luxurious blob of cream that floated on top like a proud little iceberg.

It was, I'll admit, delicious. Worth every penny.

And as I stood there sipping it, I thought of Aristotle, somewhere in the Elysian Fields, nodding in approval. After all, the woman was right. It *was* two euros, when they had it.

That's the beauty of Greek logic: it's never wrong. It just depends on the weather, the day of the week, and whether your cousin's brother's neighbour happens to agree.

I brought it to the table.

Alex raised an eyebrow. "Ten fifty?"

"Worth it for the lesson in logic," I said, taking a sip. "It's not Irish coffee. It's Greek economics in a cup."

She laughed. "You'll never learn."

"On the contrary," I said, "I've learned a lot. In Greece, you don't order what's on the menu, you order what's *possible*."

We sat there for a while longer, watching the skiers tumble past. And for a heartbeat, everything was still. The mountains stood in silent brilliance, their slopes washed in white so pure it seemed to breathe. Alex sat across from me, her smile rising with the steam of her cup, her eyes bright with the kind of joy that needs no words. Somewhere below, a muffled thud and a distant laugh marked another skier's graceful defeat; a small reminder that perfection is only ever borrowed.

For that one moment, the world was whole: snow and sky, laughter and love, everything held gently, gloriously in balance.

CHAPTER SEVEN

Down from the Mountain

Further along, the snowmelt had turned to silver streams that danced beside the road. The air grew warmer, richer, scented with pine and wet earth. It was hard not to feel a kind of peace, the quiet, humbling joy of being exactly where you're meant to be.

Down by the coast, the almond trees were already dressed in pink blossom and children were running barefoot along the beaches.

But up here, in the quiet stone villages tucked beneath Mount Parnassos, winter still lingered. The snow hadn't given up. It lay in patches along the road, melting where the sun managed to reach, then freezing again in the shade. Smoke rose from chimneys, curling slowly into the cold, blue air.

What we'd come for, as Alex put it, was "to breathe the clean mountain air and eat something that was walking around yesterday."

She meant lamb, of course. This was lamb country, where it's not so much a meal as a relationship.

The road wound down through pine forests and past fields still silvered with frost. Streams hurried beside us, swollen with meltwater, catching the sunlight and tossing it back like restless ribbons. Every so often an old pickup truck rattled past in the opposite direction, each one driven by a man in a wool cap wearing the same expression – not surprise exactly, but the quiet curiosity of someone who knows every turn of this mountain and is wondering who on earth *we* might be.

By noon, we were hungry. The kind of hunger that belongs in cold weather: deep, steady, and impatient. But the villages we passed through were silent. Cafés stood closed, chairs stacked, shutters bolted. It was as if everyone had agreed to stay inside until the snow finally admitted defeat.

Then we saw it: a wisp of smoke rising from a low building on the edge of a small square. The window glowed faintly, and the smell that drifted out as we opened the door was unmistakable: woodsmoke, wine, and meat.

We had found our place.

Inside, the light was soft and golden. A stove burned quietly in the corner, filling the room with the sound of popping wood. There were only three tables occupied, all by men of a certain age, wearing thick sweaters and speaking in the rhythm of people who've known each other all their lives. A backgammon board lay open between them, the clatter of dice and laughter blending with the radio in the kitchen.

The owner looked up from behind the counter. He was a tall man, broad in the shoulders, with silver hair and the calm confidence of someone who had never served a bad meal. He nodded as we entered, took two glasses from a shelf, and poured wine from a tin jug before saying a word. Then he spread a paper tablecloth across our table with slow precision, smoothing the edges as though setting the scene for something important.

"What would you like to eat?" he asked at last.

Alex smiled. "What do you have?"

He gave the kind of shrug that means there's a story behind the answer.

"No fish," he said. "The river is frozen. But I have lamb chops. From my cousin's farm. Salad, potatoes, beans. All from here."

"That sounds perfect," said Alex.

He nodded once, not in agreement, but in approval, as though she had passed a small test, and disappeared into the kitchen.

The fire gave a soft sigh. The men nearby raised their glasses to us. The smell of burning pine and roasting lamb filled the room, and for a while, we didn't need to speak.

Outside, the snow began again, drifting past the window in slow, thoughtful flakes.

The food arrived. There was no speech, no theatre. Just food. Sensible, confident food. A simple plate placed on the table, the lamb glistening, the potatoes crisp and golden. The salad was bright with oil and herbs; the bread was still warm from the oven.

The first bite was perfect: tender meat, smoky and clean, tasting of the mountain itself.

Alex closed her eyes for a moment. "This," she said quietly, "is what we came for."

The owner returned and watched us eat, not for praise but to make sure we were silent, that kind of silence that means satisfaction. When he saw that we were, he smiled, poured a little more wine, and said simply, "Good."

The old men at the next table were telling stories now, their voices low and musical. Every so often, one of them would laugh, and the sound rolled gently through the room. A dog wandered in, shook the snow from its fur, and settled by the stove. Nobody noticed. It was that kind of place.

When we finished eating, the owner brought two small glasses of clear liquid. "Tsipouro," he said. "For the cold." It was strong, but honest, like the man himself.

When we stepped outside, the snow had stopped again. The village lay quiet beneath a pale sky. Far below, the valley shimmered where the sun had broken through. The air was so clean it almost hummed.

Alex linked her arm through mine. "I love this," she said

softly. "It feels like time stopped for us."

I looked back at the little taverna, its chimney still smoking, and thought she was probably right. Here, among the snow and the silence, life had slowed to its natural rhythm, steady, unhurried, content.

And as we continued our drive back down the mountain, the firelight still warm in our thoughts, I realised that Greece doesn't only sparkle in summer. Sometimes, its greatest beauty is in the stillness, when even the mountains are half asleep, and a simple plate of lamb chops becomes a small act of grace.

As the road dipped lower, the first lights of Arachova flickered on, golden windows against stone walls, and the sound of laughter spilled from tavernas. We rolled through slowly; past people wrapped in scarves and the smell of grilled meat rising like incense.

It was too late to drive to Delphi. We would save that for tomorrow.

CHAPTER EIGHT

TO DELPHI

The next morning, we packed to leave Arachova. We said goodbye to our host, who waved us away from the steps of the guest house after making us promise to come back soon, and headed down to Delphi. Alex gazed across the valley. "You know," she said softly, "the ancients believed the oracle spoke through the wind."

The air was crisp enough to wake even the most reluctant traveller, meaning me. The road curled like a silver ribbon through pines and olive groves, every bend revealing another postcard view of cliffs, valleys, and the faint shimmer of the sea far below. Alex had her sunglasses on, hair tied back, humming along to the radio with the serene authority of someone who believes the gods had plans for us.

"Today," she said with solemnity, "we ask the Pythia."

"The Oracle?" I asked. "The one who breathed the fumes and told kings what to do?"

"Yes," she said, nodding. "She will tell us where to go next."

"Right. Because navigation by volcanic hallucination is always reliable."

She ignored me, of course.

We arrived in Delphi quietly, without ceremony. There was no grand entrance, no clear moment where you could say, here it is. One minute we were driving through the modern town with its cafés, hotels, and souvenir shops, and the next we were standing at the edge of something much older, trying to work out where the present stopped and the past began.

Delphi is not a city in the way you expect a city to be. There are no streets laid out in neat lines, no obvious centre. Instead, the ancient site spills across the side of the mountain, scattered and uneven, as if it had simply been left there one day and nobody quite knew how to tidy it away again.

The main road cuts through the modern town below, traffic passing in both directions, but above it the ruins climb steadily up the slope of Mount Parnassus. Temples, columns, broken marbles, foundations, all spread out across terraces carved into the rock. Some are protected by low fences, politely asking you to keep your distance. Others sit open and exposed, inviting you to wander close enough to touch the stone and feel the cold of it under your fingers.

There is no single viewpoint that explains everything. You walk uphill along the old Sacred Way, and the place reveals itself gradually. A cluster of columns here. A fallen wall there. The remains of a treasury tucked into the hillside, half reclaimed by grass and time. Nothing is laid out helpfully. You have to move, stop, look, and then move again.

At the heart of it all lies the Temple of Apollo, or what remains of it. You are outside it, always outside, standing where it once stood complete and authoritative, trying to imagine the noise, the crowds, the waiting. It is easier to imagine the effort than the certainty. This was where people came for answers, after all, and the mountain still feels as if it is listening rather than speaking.

Higher up, the theatre and stadium sit quietly above everything else, overlooking the valley. From there, the view opens out in a way that makes it hard to believe this place was ever busy or loud. The land drops away sharply, and the air feels thinner, cleaner. You become aware of how deliberately this sanctuary was placed. Not hidden, but not easy either.

At the very top sits the museum: a sleek, modern building of glass and metal. Inside are the things too delicate to leave outside. Faces, carvings, fragments of stories removed from the weather and the wind. Below it, scattered across the mountain, the rest remains where it fell. Exposed. Incomplete. Unfinished.

What struck me most was the lack of order. Delphi does not present itself neatly. It does not explain itself. It asks you to work for it, to connect the pieces in your own head. Perhaps that was always the point.

We had parked near the monument at the entrance to the village – the statue of the Pythia, the priestess who once inhaled divine vapours and told kings their fates. She was perched regally on her tripod, eyes cast skyward in eternal inspiration. A small sign explained, in three languages, that this was where pilgrims once came to ask questions of destiny. Judging by the empty crisp packets and soft drink cans scattered nearby, modern pilgrims now brought snacks.

We joined the procession of coaches sighing out tourists in every language under the sun. Alex strode ahead with the certainty of a priestess returning home. I trudged behind, already short of breath, wondering if the gods had installed so many steps purely to punish the faithful.

We walked slowly, not because there was too much to see, but because it felt wrong to rush. This was not a place you visited so much as one you moved through, aware that every step crossed ground once charged with expectation. Kings and generals came here seeking clarity. We arrived hoping mainly for a good walk and a sense of space.

And yet, standing there on the mountainside, with stone and sky and silence pressing in from all sides, it was impossible not to feel that something lingered. Not answers, exactly. Just the sense that this place had been asking questions for a very long time, and had never been in a hurry to resolve them.

The shrine to the oracle in Delphi was the Temple of Apollo, home of the Pythia. The stones still shimmered in the early morning sun, humming softly with the weight of all the questions ever asked here.

I stood quietly, trying to look suitably reverent. Alex, however, had other ideas.

Without warning, she slipped her arm from mine and ducked neatly under the rope that kept the rest of us obedient mortals at a respectful distance. Before I could whisper "*don't you dare*", she was already halfway up the ancient steps, moving with the confidence of someone who clearly had unfinished business with the gods.

"Alex!" I hissed. "There are signs"

"I can't *feel* anything from over there," she said, waving me off.

She reached the worn stones, her scarf streaming behind her, and planted herself squarely on the Oracle's rock, chin lifted, eyes closed, arms slightly raised as if summoning the spirit of Apollo himself.

For a moment, the whole place seemed to pause. The wind dropped, the tourists stopped whispering, and even the pigeons froze mid-hop.

Then Alex opened one eye and looked down to me, perfectly calm.

A security guard had appeared further along the path and was already making his way towards us, his pace suggesting experience rather than urgency. This was not his first interruption of the day.

Alex raised a hand in his direction; a small, untroubled wave. "Tell him I'm local," she said. "It's fine."

The guard slowed, took in the scene, and hesitated. Alex was still speaking softly to the stone, entirely at ease, as if this were a perfectly normal conversation to be having on a mountainside.

He stopped a few metres away, considered the situation, then did what Greek officials often do when faced with quiet confidence and no immediate danger. He stepped back, folded his arms, and waited.

Whatever Alex was asking of the oracle, it clearly did not require intervention.

Then, with both hands on her hips and her face lifted to the sky, she called out, clear, bold, and entirely unembarrassed: "Apollo! Are you listening? I have questions!"

Tourists turned.

A man dropped his camera.

A guide paused mid-lecture like someone had hit the pause button.

But Alex didn't notice.

When Alex addresses a god, the mortal world becomes background scenery.

The sunlight caught her hair like a flame. She looked exactly like a woman who had earned the right to ask Olympus a few things.

And this time, her questions were very specific.

"Apollo," she began, in that tone villagers associate with imminent truth, "please explain to me why people prefer a good story to the actual truth."

A nearby tourist murmured, "Ah. A philosopher."

Alex continued.

"Why does a river decide, after hundreds of peaceful years, to take a shortcut through our garden? Why does a neighbour build a wall across a watercourse and then blame us when the mountain disagrees?"

A couple of Germans nodded in vigorous international solidarity.

"Why," she pressed on, warming up, "when the evidence shows we did nothing wrong, do people still whisper behind shutters as if gossip were a national sport? Why must we collect documents, signatures, engineers, lawyers, surveyors, *and still* defend ourselves against rumours that travel faster than the weather? And another thing," she added, pointing at Olympus as if serving a legal summons. "Why does a village forget ten years of kindness the moment something dramatic happens? Why is suspicion easier to believe than innocence? Why must peace be earned again and again when we have already paid so much?"

A ripple went through the ruins. It seemed that even the hawk circling overhead slowed down to listen properly.

Alex placed both hands on her hips, the stance of a woman prepared to renegotiate her relationship with divinity.

"And most importantly, Apollo: how do we begin again? After mud, and anger, and noise, and days when the world sits heavy on your chest… how do you rebuild trust? Community? Even yourselves?"

Her voice softened, catching slightly.

"How do you find calm again, when the ground beneath you, literally, gave way?"

No one moved.

No one breathed.

Even the columns seemed to lean closer.

I felt something too.

Not a divine answer, but a stirring: that mix of rawness and resilience that carried us through those long months. The realisation that asking the gods was not madness; it was hope in its bravest form.

Alex stepped down from the rock at last, graceful, certain, radiant, like a woman who had just filed a formal complaint with Olympus and expected a written response.

I slipped my hand into hers.

"Did he answer?"

She smiled, that quiet, powerful smile she reserves for moments when she understands the world more deeply than I do.

"Yes," she said. "He did. Floods wash things away, but they also clear the ground. We have space now. Space to start again."

And with that, she walked on, leaving even the ancient stones looking a little humbled by her courage.

I closed my eyes and listened too. The wind moved softly through the ruins, and for just a heartbeat, I thought I heard it: not words, but laughter, warm and amused, as if the gods had been waiting for her all along.

For the first time in months, my mind fell quiet. The wind moved through the ruins like a memory, soft and certain, carrying with it the faintest hum of something ancient – not words, not voices, but presence. The kind that makes you realise how small your life is and how vast time can be.

I breathed it in, the scent of warm stone, wild thyme, and dust. These weren't just rocks any more; they were bones of a civilisation that still pulsed faintly in the sun. Here, everything had meant something once: every column, every carving, every shadow falling exactly where it was meant to.

And standing there, I understood why people had come. The ancients weren't just seeking prophecy; they were seeking permission to hope.

We climbed higher, the path winding around fallen stone, until the theatre opened before us, tier upon tier curving perfectly towards the sky. The wind whispered through it like an unseen audience.

Alex told me this was where they once performed in honour of Apollo, celebrating beauty, truth, and music. I could almost hear it, the rise and fall of voices carried on the mountain air.

I stepped down onto the stage, feeling the echo beneath my feet, and resisted the powerful urge to test the acoustics.

But I stood in silence, in a place built for song, and let the wind do the speaking.

We finally left this magical place and returned to the car parked next to the statue of the Pythia.

Alex stood before the statue, head tilted, arms folded in reverence. "Well," she said, "ask her."

"Ask her what?"

"What comes next."

I glanced around. The wind sighed through the pines. The statue offered no opinion. A small lizard darted over the Pythia's marble foot, paused, then scuttled off, possibly with a message from the gods, though I doubted it.

I cleared my throat. "Oh wise Oracle," I said solemnly, "we seek guidance. Where should we go next?"

Nothing.

Alex frowned. "You didn't ask properly. You must believe."

I tried again. "Oh, great Pythia, mistress of prophecy, guide our weary souls to our next destination."

At that exact moment, a bus roared past on the main road below, its exhaust echoing up the valley. On its side, in bold letters, were the words *Patra Tours*.

Alex gasped, eyes wide. "Did you see that?"

I nodded slowly. "Yes. The gods have spoken."

She clapped her hands. "Patra! It's a sign."

And that was that. The decision made, the divine consultation concluded – we were officially on a mission from Apollo, via a coach company.

As we drove away, the statue of the Pythia watched us disappear around the bend, probably shaking her marble head. I could almost hear her saying, *"These two again…"*

Still, as omens go, it wasn't bad. And as Alex always says, if destiny doesn't answer quickly enough, she'll answer for it.

CHAPTER NINE

THE JACKAL OF PEFKI

News from home has a way of finding you, no matter how far you go.

We were somewhere in the mountains on our way to Patra when Alex's phone rang. She looked at the screen and sighed.

"Maria."

That one word said everything. In our village, no sentence beginning with "Maria" has ever ended peacefully.

Alex answered, and I could already hear the shouting before she spoke.

"Alex! Peter! It's an emergency!"

I groaned. "What now? The river again?"

"No! Worse!" Maria said, gasping for air. "It's the animal in your garden!"

"The fox?" Alex asked. "The one Peter keeps feeding?"

"Yes! That's the one! Only, it's not a fox!"

There was a long, meaningful silence.

"Not a fox?" Alex said carefully. "Then what is it?"

"Apparently," Maria announced, "it's a jackal!"

I frowned. "A jackal? Are you sure?"

"Yes! The man from Istiaia came this morning. He had papers, a camera, and a little hat. He said it was definitely a jackal. A *golden* jackal, no less!"

Alex looked at me. "You've been feeding a dangerous predator."

Maria continued, unstoppable. "The whole village is talking! The priest came with holy water, but he missed and hit Yiannis's car. The mayor is thrilled, he says we might get a wildlife sign for the entrance to Pefki. 'Welcome to Pefki – *Home of the Jackal*.' It's going to be very good for tourism!"

I could picture it all perfectly: Maria reporting live from the front line, her apron flapping like a flag of distress, surrounded by villagers forming an emergency committee over coffee and cigarettes.

Theodora, hands waving, would insist it was "just a strange dog".

Spiros would swear it had come from Albania.

And Dimitri, without looking up from his beer, would simply say, "If it eats Nemesis, we should build it a statue."

Maria's voice lowered to a whisper. "The man from Istiaia says it might be part of a family."

"A *family*?" I repeated.

"Yes! He's setting up cameras to check. It's like *National Geographic* here! We're famous!"

I sighed. "Famous for what, owning the local predator?"

Maria ignored that. "Anyway, the priest says it might be an omen. He's praying for clarification."

Alex leaned back, half amused, half horrified. "We leave the village for two days, and we've been adopted by a wild animal."

Maria continued, breathless: "The cats have gone! They all ran away last night. The jackal howled, and the priest's dog refused to go out. Theodora says it walks the same path every night. Right along your fence."

"Maybe it just likes the view," I said.

"View?!" she cried. "It's hunting! This morning, it ate one of George's chickens!"

"Not George?" I asked.

"No, the chicken! But George is traumatised. He says the jackal stared straight into his eyes and licked its lips. He hasn't been the same since."

When the call ended, we drove in silence for a while. The road wound down through pine forests, and the smell of wet earth drifted through the window.

Alex looked thoughtful. "You realise what this means?"

"Yes," I said. "Maria has found a new obsession."

She smiled. "No, it means we officially own a jackal."

"Don't say that too loudly," I said. "Next thing we know, the Ministry will want us to register it and pay tax."

She laughed. "Well, you did feed it."

"Yes, but I thought it was a fox! I wasn't trying to start a nature reserve."

According to village logic, if it's on your land, it's yours, and therefore your problem. Doesn't matter what *it* is: a cat, a tree, a rumour, or a wayward goat. The moment it sets foot on your soil, you're the proud owner, caretaker, and, inevitably, the one who'll be blamed when it misbehaves.

The next morning, another message arrived: a photo from Maria. It showed a blurry creature slinking through the olive trees, eyes glowing like lanterns. Underneath, she'd written: "*It's definitely your one. Everyone agrees. Even the priest.*"

Five minutes later, another message:

"*The mayor says you must report to the police when you come back. And bring the jackal.*"

I nearly dropped my coffee. "Bring the jackal? What do they think I'll do, put it on a lead and drive it to the station?"

Alex was already laughing. "You could put it in the back with the suitcases. It might enjoy the ride."

"Wonderful," I said. "We'll arrive with a wild carnivore in the boot. They will love that."

That afternoon, Maria called again.

"It's sleeping in your garden!" she said, as though announcing the Second Coming. "Under your willow tree. I threw it some bread, but it just looked at me."

"Maria, jackals don't eat bread."

She paused. "That explains the look."

Alex took the phone. "Maria, just leave it alone. It's wild. Don't feed it, don't chase it, and for heaven's sake, don't name it."

"Oh no, I wouldn't do that," said Maria. "Theodora already named it."

Alex groaned. "Of course she did. What's it called?"

"Zorba."

"Zorba?" I said.

"Yes," Maria said proudly. "Because it dances at night. Yiannis saw it in his headlights; beautiful animal. Very elegant. And strong."

By the time we reached the coast, Pefki had apparently entered a new chapter of evolution. The cats had gone underground, the priest was sprinkling holy water twice daily, and Nemesis was telling everyone that *our* jackal was responsible for the latest flood.

Alex scrolled through Maria's messages and sighed. "You know, one day we're going to drive home and find that jackal sitting at our table wearing a collar."

"With Maria serving it sardines," I added.

We both laughed, that quiet, tired laugh of people who love their village but know full well that logic doesn't live there.

Somewhere far behind us, the jackal of Pefki probably yawned, stretched, and turned over under our tree, wondering why the humans were making such a fuss.

93

CHAPTER TEN

ON THE ROAD TO PATRA

We stopped at a roadside café clinging to the hillside – the sort of place that sells petrol, coffee, and spare tractor parts if you know how to ask. I pulled in with the grace of a learner driver, clipping the curb, which Alex found hilarious.

On the terrace we sipped tiny cups of Greek coffee, watching the distant sea glimmering in the afternoon light. The breeze carried the smell of pine and woodsmoke, cool enough to nip our noses. Alex settled back, satisfied, as if she had personally arranged the view. I stared at the horizon, wondering how many more hairpins separated us from Patra, and whether my clutch foot would survive them.

Back in the car, I gritted my teeth and carried on. The road unspooled westward, the land flattening as the mountains faded behind us. The signs began pointing towards Patra, and with them Alex's enthusiasm rose still further.

We arrived at the bridge: the Charilaos Trikoupis Rio–Antirrio Bridge, to give it its full, slightly intimidating title. It wasn't a popular bridge. Especially not with the ferrymen, who until its arrival had been living very contentedly, shuttling people across the bay between Rio and Antirrio in the time-honoured Greek tradition: slowly, with coffee breaks.

For centuries, the ferries had been kings of the gulf, creaking majestically from shore to shore, gossiping with the waves, and making a living from those who needed to cross but didn't mind arriving sometime today, or possibly tomorrow, depending on the wind, the mood, and whose cousin was steering.

Then the government, in a rare burst of modern ambition, decided Greece needed a bridge. Not just any bridge, but a *record-breaking* one – a four-pylon, cable-stayed masterpiece stretching 2.8 kilometres across one of the trickiest bits of water in Europe. Deep sea, shifting seabed, and enough earthquakes to keep the engineers permanently awake. Perfect spot, naturally.

Construction began in the 1990s and, like most Greek epics, took about a decade, several miracles, and possibly divine intervention. When it finally opened in 2004, just in time for the Athens Olympics, it was hailed as an engineering wonder:

elegant, enormous, and expensive enough to make Poseidon blink.

The ferrymen, understandably, were unimpressed. Their monopoly had been replaced by a toll booth and a structure so sleek it looked like Zeus had personally commissioned it to show off. They muttered darkly that the bridge was unnatural, that it angered the sea, and that it would never last a proper winter.

Twenty years later, it's still standing, shimmering over the gulf like a silver lyre strung across the waves. The ferries still run, of course – this is Greece. They now carry people who refuse to pay the high toll, or who simply prefer the company of old engines, strong coffee, and conversations that last longer than the crossing.

As for the bridge itself, it's magnificent. You don't drive over it so much as glide, suspended between sea and sky, half-expecting Apollo himself to appear with a parking ticket. It's Greece in a single span: bold, beautiful, slightly improbable, and guaranteed to upset someone making a living the old way.

But we drove over it anyway. It felt like something that had to be done, a small act of modern pilgrimage. The toll, however, was enough to make me consider turning back and opening a ferry business myself. For the price of crossing, we could have had a very decent meal, complete with wine, dessert, and a waiter who called me "my friend" until the bill arrived.

Still, there's a certain satisfaction in doing it once, just to say you have. A proper bridge, I told myself, deserves a proper crossing. Even if it costs roughly the same as a bottle of

Mavrodaphni and a plate of lamb chops.

We've never had traffic lights in North Evia. There's really no point. Even if someone did install them, the locals would treat them as festive decorations, blinking curiosities to admire, not to obey. Red would mean "have a look around", amber would mean "discuss it", and green would mean "go, but only if your cousin's watching". The few zebra crossings that exist are largely decorative too, cheerful road art designed to brighten your day rather than save your life.

So by the time we finally rolled into Patra, the sun melting into the Gulf behind us and the city beginning to glow like a lantern, the sight of *actual* traffic lights felt almost exotic. Cars stopped when they were supposed to. People crossed the road without divine intervention. It was civilisation – confusing, but impressive.

My knuckles slowly unclenched from the steering wheel, though the imprint of them may still be visible in the leather today; a small souvenir from the mountain roads of Evia, and proof that sometimes even miracles have indicators.

"Carnival," Alex said, eyes glinting, as we drove through the town. "Patra is famous for it. You'll see. Masks, costumes, music. Everyone celebrating."

"Celebrating what?"

"Life," she said simply.

Patra has always been a city that knows how to celebrate life, loudly, colourfully, and without restraint. Its carnival, one of the oldest and largest in Europe, began more than a century ago as a simple gathering of neighbours and friends. What started as a small parade of masks and laughter grew, over generations, into a month-long festival that now defines the city's spirit.

The Patra Carnival, or *Patrino Karnavali* if you want to sound as if you know what you're talking about, runs from January through to "Clean Monday", the moment Greece officially waves goodbye to sensible behaviour and remembers Lent is approaching. It builds slowly, gathering noise, colour, and confidence, before erupting in one final, glorious weekend of floats, costumes, street parties, and the sort of cheerful chaos Greece does so well.

The Carnival of Patra is not just a spectacle. It's a bridge between winter and spring, between the last indulgences of earthly pleasure and the quiet reflection of Lent. For weeks, the streets come alive with music and movement. People wear costumes not to hide who they are, but to remember that life itself is a kind of performance; one that should be danced, not endured. It is somehow both exuberant and family-friendly; a national release of steam before restraint is reluctantly reintroduced.

The end of the celebration marks the turning of a page, the moment when the noise softens and the fasting of Lent begins. On that day, families gather on the hills and beaches with picnics of olives, bread, and fresh air. Colourful kites rise into the sky, carrying away the last remnants of excess and marking a fresh start for the soul.

In Patra, the carnival is not merely an excuse for joy;

it's an act of faith in renewal. It reminds everyone that even after the longest season of storms and struggle, there is always music waiting, always light returning, and always one more reason to celebrate being alive.

Patra was no sleepy village. It was alive; a port city with the energy of somewhere that has always been a crossroads: ferries to Italy, students spilling out of cafés, traders shouting as if volume was the currency. And beneath it all, a buzz I couldn't place at first, until I noticed the masks.

Children in clown wigs darted between cars. Shop windows displayed sequinned costumes alongside sacks of lentils. A group of teenagers in capes and plastic swords ran laughing through the square, pursued by a man dressed as a Roman centurion who may or may not have been their father. Everyone appeared to be dressed either as something mythical, something married, or something in urgent need of supervision. Carnival wasn't coming; it had already arrived.

Alex's eyes lit up. "See? I told you. Patra knows how to live."

I parked the Citroën among a row of cars that looked equally bewildered to be there, and we stepped into the chaos. Drums thudded from somewhere nearby, a brass band parped its way down the street, and confetti fluttered from a balcony as though someone had exploded a piñata over the crowd.

Our arrival in Patra just happened to coincide with the biggest carnival day of the year, entirely by accident, which is the sort of accident that Greece specialises in.

We hadn't booked anything. Of course we hadn't.

That would have suggested foresight.

We spent the next hour circling the streets like hopeful vultures, popping our heads into hotels and being met with the same polite smile and gentle shake of the head.

"No rooms."

"Nothing."

"Carnival."

This last word was usually delivered with the tone of someone explaining gravity. Of course there were no rooms. It was Patra Carnival.

Just as we were beginning to discuss sleeping in the car, or possibly joining a float and seeing where it took us, Alex spotted a small, slightly apologetic sign down a side street. It suggested, without much confidence, that there might be a hotel involved.

We ducked in.

"Hotel" turned out to be a generous description for a building that had clearly been constructed before lifts, regulations, or optimism. The stairs were narrow and steep, as if designed to keep out anyone with luggage, weak knees, or expectations.

The owner appeared immediately, summoned by the sound of confused foreigners and luggage being rearranged for the third time. He greeted us with the warmth reserved for people who were already being folded into the story of the place.

He took Alex's hands in both of his, kissed the air near her cheeks, and spoke rapidly, as if continuing a conversation that had only paused briefly a few years earlier. Before we could ask a single question, he pressed a key into her palm, nodded once, and stepped back, satisfied that whatever needed to happen next would now take care of itself.

"You are lucky," he announced, which is never reassuring. "One room. Last room."

Before we could even look at it, he began listing the tavernas where we should eat that evening, speaking quickly and with complete certainty. Each recommendation was delivered with the assurance of a man who had strong opinions and saw no reason to keep them to himself.

He pointed vaguely down the street, then back up the hill, naming places as if they were obvious choices that anyone sensible would already know. We nodded, grateful, aware that this was less a carefully curated guide and more a reflection of his own loyalties, habits, and preferences. In Greece, that usually amounts to the same thing.

The room itself was simple, clean, and perfectly adequate, which felt like winning a small lottery. From our tiny balcony we looked out over the city. The port lights twinkled below us, ferries sliding in and out like restless giants who refused to sleep. Somewhere a horn sounded, music drifted upwards, and the square below was already filling with people in costume.

One wore a horse's head.

Another was dressed as a priest.

A third appeared to be wearing a wedding dress with trainers.

Alex leaned on the rail, eyes bright, already mentally unpacking her carnival personality.

"Tomorrow," she said, with the calm certainty of a woman who had decided something important, "we join them."

I looked down at the chaos below and nodded.

Of course we would.

I sighed. "Do I get to choose my costume?"

She grinned. "Of course. As long as it isn't boring."

Which, knowing my wife, meant I'd be marching through Patra in something involving feathers, sequins, and possibly a goat mask.

For now, though, I was content. The air was warm, the city alive, and the further away from Pefki I travelled, the lighter I felt. We had left the village behind. Ahead was carnival and whatever chaos that would bring, and heaven help me, I suspected Alex was right to come here.

The next morning Patra woke like it had been waiting all year for this day. The streets were already alive before breakfast, drums echoing down the avenues, whistles piercing the air, and the faint smell of souvlaki smoke drifting as if the city itself had decided to put on aftershave.

From our balcony we could see children in masks chasing each other with foam bats, their parents clapping along to a brass band that was at least two notes behind itself. Shops sold wigs in every colour of the rainbow, while a man wheeled a cart piled high with confetti that looked suspiciously like shredded tax forms.

Tucked down a side street, between a phone repair shop and something selling plastic buckets in bulk, we found a costume-hire place. The window display was a fever dream of sequins, feathers, wigs, and synthetic fabrics that had clearly lived several previous lives. A handwritten sign promised *Everything you need for Carnival,* which felt optimistic but encouraging.

Inside, it was chaos in the best possible way. Rails sagged under the weight of costumes from every decade and no decade at all. Masks stared down from hooks. Wigs spilled out of boxes like startled animals. Somewhere in the back, a radio played loudly enough to suggest the staff had given up on conversation entirely.

Alex, naturally, was in her element. Within minutes she had draped herself in a feathered mask and a shawl so aggressively sparkly it could have been used to guide aircraft. She turned, admired herself in a cracked mirror, and nodded with satisfaction.

I was less fortunate.

My options had been narrowed to two. A clown wig that had definitely known better days, or a toga that smelled faintly of mothballs and questionable decisions.

"You're English," Alex said briskly, fastening the toga around my shoulders. "You'll look dignified."

"I'll look like a bedsheet that escaped from the laundry," I muttered.

She stepped back, assessed me critically, then smiled. "Perfect."

Resistance, at this point, was both pointless and unpatriotic.

We plunged into the crowd. Drums pounded, trumpets blared, and thousands of people surged through the streets in a river of colour. Floats trundled past, one shaped like a giant wine bottle, another like a Trojan horse with small children popping their heads out of the windows and shrieking with delight. Confetti rained from balconies, sticking to my hair and toga until I resembled a poorly iced wedding cake.

At one point, a group of revellers dressed as Roman soldiers spotted me. "Caesar!" they cried, hoisting me into their ranks before I had time to protest. Alex clapped and cheered, delighted at my sudden promotion, while I stumbled along in borrowed sandals, trying not to trip over my dignity. Someone thrust a plastic sword into my hand. I waved it weakly, nearly decapitating a passing clown.

The noise was relentless – whistles, drums, music, laughter – and yet somehow it all blended into a single joyous roar. Old women in black, who normally scowled at anyone daring to smile, were dancing in the square with teenagers dressed as pirates. Taxi drivers abandoned their cars mid-street to join the parades, shrugging as if to say, *the meter's still running, who cares?* Even the stray dogs wore ribbons and trotted proudly at the front of the procession.

By the time night fell, the city was glowing. Fires burned in barrels, music pulsed from every side street, and the air was thick with grilled meat and cheap wine. Alex danced with abandon, swept into circles of strangers who instantly became friends. I joined in too, stiffly at first, then with the loosening effect of three glasses of patraiki wine. By the fourth, I was leading a group of men dressed as monks in a conga line down the main square.

At midnight, the fireworks began. Not orderly, health-and-safety-approved fireworks, but the Greek variety: rockets exploding out of beer bottles, Catherine wheels nailed to telegraph poles, Roman candles fired suspiciously close to balconies. The sky lit up in a wild display of colour and chaos, confetti still raining down, drums still pounding.

Alex leaned into me, eyes sparkling beneath her mask. "Now you see why I brought you here," she shouted over the noise.

And I did.

Patra wasn't just carnival; it was life refusing to be quiet. It was joy wrestled out of history, music hammered out of chaos, forgiveness spun into laughter.

For a moment, toga and all, I felt Greek.

The morning after carnival looked like a battlefield. The streets of Patra were carpeted in confetti, plastic swords, and the occasional shoe that had clearly lost its owner mid-sirtaki. The brass bands had finally fallen silent, leaving only the faint groan of hungover trumpets echoing in the distance.

I emerged from the hotel with confetti still stuck in my hair, toga draped over my arm like a defeated flag, and a headache that felt like Apollo himself was rehearsing with a kettle drum inside my skull. Alex, of course, looked immaculate, not a sequin out of place, her eyes bright as though she had been powered overnight by carnival energy alone. We strolled down towards the port in search of coffee.

Soon we were standing on the harbour wall in Patra, the smell of diesel and grilled octopus hanging in the air, watching ferries the size of small apartment blocks groan and rumble as they loaded cars and lorries for faraway ports. Their hulking silhouettes loomed against the sky, names painted proudly across their bows: *Superfast, Blue Star, Anek*. Each one hummed with the promise of somewhere else. The sea stretched wide and glittering.

"You know what would really upset Maria?"

That's how it began.

Alex had that look, the one that starts as a smile and ends with a border crossing. She tilted her head slightly, the way she does when an idea arrives fully formed and entirely uninvited. Her eyes sparkled with mischief, caffeine, and divine inspiration in equal measure.

"Let's go to Italy," she said.

I blinked. "Italy?"

She nodded, perfectly calm, as though suggesting we pop down the road for olives.

"It's right there," she said, pointing at one of the ships. "A few hours. We take the car, get on a ferry, and see where the road takes us."

I stared at her, then at the enormous white ferry spewing smoke and chaos in every direction. Somewhere beyond that horizon lay espresso, operatic road rage, and possibly an international incident.

"Do we have a plan?" I asked.

"Yes," she said. "Go to Italy."

I hesitated. "Do we even have tickets?"

"Not yet," she said, already walking towards the ticket office. "But the gods will provide."

That's Alex: unstoppable once the idea takes root. She moves with the certainty of a general leading a charge, while I trail behind like a man who's accidentally joined the wrong army.

Part of me wanted to protest, to ask for a map, a schedule, maybe a day to think. But the other part, the part still buzzing from drums, fireworks, and too much patraiki wine, thought: *Why not?*

"Fine," I sighed, falling into step beside her. "But only if you promise not to make me wear a toga in Italy."

She grinned without looking back. "We'll see."

And that was that.

One minute we were still deciding which queue to stand in for the ferry tickets, and then I blinked and Alex was at the ticket desk, deep in negotiation, a living masterclass in charm, confidence, and pure theatre.

The clerk – a man who looked like he'd seen every kind of traveller under the sun: tourists, truckers, pilgrims, and people smuggling unregistered goats – was now nodding helplessly, caught in her current. He started printing tickets he didn't remember offering, pressing buttons he clearly didn't understand, while Alex leaned in, smiling as if she'd just blessed his firstborn.

It transpired that we would be heading for Ancona, on Italy's Adriatic coast, which felt like a bold move for two people who, an hour earlier, had been arguing about where to have lunch.

I hovered a few paces back and watched events unfold, equal parts admiration and mild fear. Alex leaned forward and began speaking in that rapid, musical Greek that seems purpose-built to dismantle bureaucracy. It is not aggressive or demanding. It simply assumes cooperation will occur, and usually it does.

I picked up a few familiar words drifting across the counter. *Kourasi* (tired). *Thálassa* (sea). And the master key, *file mou* (my friend). Used together, they can unlock almost anything in Greece, from missing paperwork to ferry cabins bound for Italy.

By the time I reached the desk, the clerk was smiling vaguely, nodding like a man waking from a pleasant daydream.

"Ancona," he said, handing over the tickets. "Cabin. VIP. Free upgrade."

I stared at them, then at Alex.

She gave a small shrug, modest and entirely unconvincing.

"How did you manage that?" I asked.

She slipped the tickets into her bag and smiled. "I told him the truth."

I hesitated. "Which truth?"

"That you snore," she said.

And with that, she turned towards the ferry to Italy, leaving the poor man still staring after her, possibly wondering whether he had just been expertly negotiated with, quietly seduced, or both.

CHAPTER ELEVEN

Passage to Italy

Greek ferries are not boats. They are floating cities with steering wheels, diesel-scented metropolises where you can buy a cappuccino, lose a car, and witness an argument about olive oil without ever leaving port.

The one waiting for us in Patra towered over the dock like a white apartment block on holiday. Trucks queued in neat rows, engines idling, their drivers leaning on the doors, smoking with the calm fatalism of men who knew time had no meaning here.

At customs, a large man in uniform waved us through without even glancing at the car. In the other lane, an unlucky motorist was being interrogated, their belongings spread across the tarmac like a tragic car-boot sale. We were obviously harmless, or Alex's innocent expression (rare and therefore disarming) and the VIP cabin voucher had done the trick.

The Citroën groaned its way up and into the cavernous belly of the ship, where lorries loomed above us like prehistoric beasts. A man in a fluorescent jacket appeared from the shadows, gesturing wildly and shouting instructions that could have meant "park there" or "prepare for impact".

"Park there! No, not there, there! No, you idiot, again!"

It was choreography by chaos. Eventually, I succeeded in wedging the car so close to the steel wall that you couldn't slide a ferry ticket between the paintwork and the hull. Another car was then wedged beside us so tightly we had to fold the wing mirrors.

When it became clear there was no way to open the doors, Alex climbed out through the window like a glamorous burglar. Thus began our voyage: *Fawlty Towers* at sea.

We dragged our bags up a staircase that smelled faintly of fuel, and frying. At the end of a long corridor en route to our designated VIP cabin, a uniformed man appeared suddenly, blocking our way.

"Go away!" he barked.

Alex held up our cabin pass. "We have a room."

He frowned. "Go away. Not ready!" Then he vanished back into a cupboard.

We decided to wait in the restaurant, which, naturally, was closed. Tables were neatly laid, glasses upside down, not a soul in sight. I found an officer and asked when it would open.

He shrugged. "Perhaps soon. Perhaps not." Then he wandered off to find somewhere quieter.

Eventually, the staff appeared, a small army of black-trousered waiters gliding between tables with military precision and the kind of authority that suggested they'd all once worked crowd control at the Colosseum.

We stepped forward, ready to sit at a table near the window, the one with a view of Patra and the distant Rio bridge.

"Not there!" barked the head waiter, materialising at my elbow. He pointed towards a dark corner of the restaurant as though assigning punishment.

"*There*! Sit there!"

He didn't wait for a reply. His finger remained extended, his expression one of eternal disappointment.

I could only assume he'd trained under the same regime as the parking attendant who had shouted at me recently for daring to park exactly where he'd told me to.

Alex smiled sweetly, the smile that precedes either diplomacy or destruction, and led the way to our new seating assignment.

We sat obediently.

The waiter nodded once, satisfied, and vanished.

I found myself wedged against the wall, my chair half-balanced on a raised floorboard. Alex was pressed beside me, her knee against mine, the two of us now experts in confined dining.

"This is nice," I said, through clenched teeth.

"It's an experience," Alex said calmly. "We're collecting those."

The food, when it eventually arrived, was, against all odds, *excellent.* Perfectly cooked, beautifully served, and presented with that Italian combination of grace and barely suppressed aggression. It was food that tasted as though it had been personally offended by the sea and decided to prove a point.

For a few blissful minutes, peace reigned. The ship vibrated softly beneath us, Patra rolled past the portholes, and even the waiter seemed momentarily content, gliding between tables with the stern poise of a man who had seen far worse passengers than us.

Then the family at the next table finished their meal and left. The waiter approached to clear their plates. He stopped. He stared. His nostrils flared.

"*Pigs!*" he bellowed, loud enough to startle a passing steward. "*Animals*! Look at this! Look at this disaster!"

Every diner froze mid-bite. The hum of the engines filled the silence like a prayer.

The waiter gestured wildly at the table: a half-eaten bread roll floating in a puddle of wine, an upturned fork stuck in a napkin, and what appeared to be a spoon welded to the tablecloth.

"Next time they come," he declared, "I throw the food on the floor! They can eat from there. If they want to eat like pigs, I'll treat them like pigs."

It was not a suggestion. It was a prophecy.

Around the room, diners began to tidy their tables in a quiet panic. Napkins were folded. Crumbs were brushed. Wine stains were blotted with the care of forensic scientists.

I, of course, joined in immediately. Forks aligned. Knives parallel. Salt and pepper standing to attention. I even wiped a perfectly clear glass just in case it offended someone's sense of order.

Alex watched me with mild amusement. "Peter," she whispered, "we're not the ones on trial."

"Not *yet*," I muttered, straightening the water bottle label.

When the waiter finally turned his gaze our way, our table looked like a museum display: untouched, symmetrical, reverent. He paused, scanned it slowly, and gave the faintest nod of approval.

"Good," he said gravely. "Civilised people."

We exhaled in unison. Somewhere behind us, another plate dropped. The entire restaurant flinched as though the ship had hit an iceberg.

I don't remember much about dessert, only that we ate it in silence, using the delicate precision of archaeologists excavating pottery.

When he returned to collect the plates, the waiter glanced at our spotless table, gave a small, approving smile, and said, almost fondly, "Not pigs."

And I swear, in that moment, I felt as if we'd earned a

Michelin star, or at least a certificate of basic civilisation. Alex beamed. I nodded modestly, as if cleanliness had been our plan all along.

But as the waiter glided away with the grace of a man raised on espresso and discipline, I found myself thinking about *logic*, and how it changes shape depending on the soil it's planted in.

Italian logic, for example, is fierce, precise, and gloriously unforgiving. It's the kind of logic that can marshal armies, direct traffic with operatic hand gestures, and deliver a plate of spaghetti to table twelve exactly forty-seven seconds after ordering – al dente, naturally. There's rhythm in it, an elegant madness held together by volume and conviction. When something goes wrong in Italy, someone will shout until the universe snaps back into alignment. It's not personal. It's physics.

Greek logic, on the other hand, is… flexible. Elastic. A philosophy all its own, like a set of rules written in pencil, preferably on the back of a napkin that's already been used for tzatziki.

In Italy, a waiter rages because an untidy table violates the natural order.

In Greece, the natural order *is* the violation.

Back home in Pefki, I've been blamed for everything short of the Trojan War. If a tree falls into the road, it's my fault because it's near my house. If a river floods half the village, apparently that's on me too, "because the water passed by your garden". If the neighbour's goat escapes and eats my basil, I should have grown something less tempting. If the jackal that lurks behind our olive trees starts stealing sheep, well, naturally, it's *my* jackal. Ownership here is geographical, not legal.

Cause and effect have been replaced by location and gossip.

That's village logic in its purest form. The closer something happens to you, the guiltier you are, even if you were asleep, abroad, or possibly in another century.

The Italians would write a report, measure the water flow, and fine the mountain.

The Greeks would sip their coffee, nod sagely, and decide that rivers, like people, simply have moods.

And somewhere between those two worlds, between espresso-fuelled order and ouzo-fuelled fatalism, I was learning to stop arguing and start adapting. Because logic, like language, doesn't always translate.

On the ferry, "Not pigs" was a badge of honour. In Pefki, "Your river flooded us again" will probably be next week's headline.

So I paid the bill, nodded politely to the waiter, and followed Alex back to our cabin, both of us a little wiser in different directions.

She smiled. "See? You survived Italian logic."

"Yes," I said. "But I'm not sure I'll ever understand Greek logic."

She grinned, that knowing, dangerous grin. "You don't have to. You just have to live with it."

And that, I thought, might be the most logical thing anyone in either country had ever said.

At last, our cabin was ready: bright, spotless, and blissfully ours. Two windows over the bow, a real bed, even a sofa. A polite note invited us to breakfast in the à la carte restaurant. We felt honoured. Though, given our track record, we privately hoped it wouldn't be served on the floor.

As the ship rumbled out of Patra and into open water, the lights of Greece faded behind us. We lay in bed, listening to the hum of the engines, the gentle sway of the sea, and the occasional Greek shouting match outside. It was oddly soothing.

Alex has never trusted the sea.

She claims it's because her family were seafarers, men who spent their lives wrestling with waves and engines, but I suspect it has more to do with having watched *Titanic* one too many times. To Alex, every ship is just a slightly newer version of that one, and every crew member is a potential iceberg enthusiast.

So when dawn broke somewhere over the Adriatic, I should not have been surprised when she shook me awake with the urgency of a woman evacuating a burning building.

"Peter! Wake up!"

My eyes opened to find a bright orange lifejacket flying through the air and landing squarely on my chest. Alex was already wearing hers, zipped up to the neck and puffed out like a small, determined marshmallow.

"Put it on!" she commanded. "Quickly!"

I squinted at the window. Outside, the sea was calm, a faint drizzle smudging the horizon.

"What's wrong?" I asked sleepily.

"Look!" she said, pointing dramatically. "The clouds are black, and the rain is coming sideways! This is how it starts!"

"How what starts?"

"The documentaries!"

She may have had a point.

This was the reverse of a journey we had taken a few years earlier, when we'd crossed from Ancona to Patra, expecting something mildly inconvenient but vaguely romantic. The Adriatic. A sunset. A plate of pasta eaten while pretending we were seasoned travellers.

What we got instead was an education.

When we arrived at Ancona port to collect our tickets, the woman behind the glass gave us a polite smile that should have been our first warning. "Ah, *yes*," she said, tapping at her computer. "Your ferry… broke down."

She said it so calmly, as if this happened every Friday.

Before I could open my mouth, she added, "But don't worry, we found a replacement."

What she didn't tell us was that the "replacement" wasn't so much *another* ferry as a *retired* one. A vessel that should have been donated to a museum, or possibly to the seabed.

When we saw it, we both stopped dead.

It was large, technically blue if you ignored the streaks of rust bleeding down the sides, and looked as though it had just survived a small war. The name, *Norman Atlantic*, was painted across the bow in letters so faded they looked embarrassed.

Our tickets proudly declared "VIP Cabin", and for a brief moment, I dared to hope that meant something. It did not.

Our so-called "VIP" cabin was a small, airless box with bunk beds, no window, and a faint smell of despair. The "bathroom" was a corner with a toilet that looked haunted and a torn curtain that flapped half-heartedly with each sigh of the ventilation system. A single lightbulb flickered overhead, lending the whole space the ambience of a forgotten interrogation room.

Alex stood in the doorway, arms crossed, eyes narrowing like a cat who'd just been served skimmed milk.

"This is *not* VIP," she said.

We marched to reception, or rather, we staggered there, because the ship already had a distinct lean to one side.

The man behind the desk smiled blandly. He was clearly a professional at dealing with people on the brink.

"We paid for a VIP cabin," Alex said firmly.

"Ah yes," he replied, as though we'd just congratulated him. "There are no VIP cabins on this ship."

"Then why sell them?" she asked.

He shrugged, the universal Greek–Italian gesture for "What can you do, that was the other ferry. It broke down?"

"You could wait for the next ferry," he suggested helpfully.

"When's that?" I asked.

"Thursday."

It was Friday.

We stared at him. He smiled serenely, as if offering us a wonderful week's holiday in Ancona's industrial docklands.

After a brief but vigorous negotiation, in which Alex's tone reached the pitch that causes seagulls to flee, we managed a small discount, though it felt more like hush money.

The *Norman Atlantic* was, in every possible sense, a *character*.

Its corridors creaked, its carpets smelled faintly of diesel and boiled cabbage, and its air-conditioning system was powered entirely by rubber bands. The restaurant was a windowless chamber where plastic chairs were chained to the floor, the coffee machine hissed like an angry cat, and the buffet offered only two choices: pasta, or pasta.

Even in calm seas, the ship swayed and groaned as if haunted by old storms. I half expected to see sailors with eyepatches and lifeboats stamped *Property of the Titanic*.

Still, we made the best of it. Alex, ever optimistic, declared she would "sleep like a baby" in the top bunk. She did. I lay below counting each groan of metal, each cough of the engine, and each crash of the waves, wondering if the ship was trying to tell us something.

By dawn, we staggered down to the car park, and drove off the ramp in Patra like survivors of a minor campaign, eyes stinging, hair salty, hearts full of gratitude to solid ground. "Never again," I muttered. Alex agreed, though she said it with that tone that meant *until next time.* I immediately cancelled the return trip. I swore that we would never sail on that ship again.

For a few days after, the trip became a joke between us. Whenever something went wrong, a power cut, a leaky tap, Alex would raise an eyebrow and say, "At least we're not on the *Norman Atlantic*."

And then, a week later, back in Pefki, fate decided to remind us how small we really are.

We were sitting at the kitchen table, cats arguing over sardines underfoot, when the television cut to breaking news. A headline flashed across the screen: "Ferry Fire in the Adriatic – *Norman Atlantic* Ablaze."

We froze.

There it was, our old rust bucket, engulfed in flames, helicopters circling like insects above it, passengers being lifted from its deck into a grey, smoking sky.

Alex turned slowly towards me, her face pale, eyes wide.

"See?" she said quietly. "Even the gods couldn't stand that ship."

The reporter's voice wavered as she spoke of panic, rescue attempts, and the rising death toll. We sat in silence for a long moment. Outside, the sun was shining, the sea glittered, and in our quiet Greek village, life went on as usual: someone's rooster crowed, a moped buzzed past, the smell of grilled fish drifted up the street.

But on that screen, the sea that had carried us was black with smoke.

"Do you realise," I said quietly, "if we'd waited for the return ferry…"

Alex didn't let me finish. "We'd still be on it," she said. "And *that's* why we don't wait for Thursdays."

Later, we learned the details.

The fire had begun on the vehicle deck; just a small spark, they said, maybe from a lorry or an overloaded socket. It spread fast, feeding on fuel and air, turning that metal labyrinth into a furnace. Power failed. Smoke filled the corridors. Some lifeboats melted before they could be launched. Passengers were trapped in cabins, others clung to railings in freezing wind and spray, waiting for helicopters to pluck them from the flames.

Rescue ships circled for hours, fighting rain and high seas. The last people were lifted off after more than nine hours. Sixteen were confirmed dead, others never found. Even two Albanian sailors lost their lives during the salvage.

The ship we'd joked about had burned for days, smouldering in the Adriatic like a warning to anyone who ever takes the sea for granted.

When they finally towed it into Brindisi, it was little more than a twisted shell. Years later, it was dragged to Turkey and scrapped – a quiet ending for a ship that had carried so much noise, fear, and human hope.

That night, Alex lit a candle. "For the people," she said softly. "And for the ship."

She looked out towards the sea, dark and calm beneath the stars. "We were lucky, Peter. One trip later…"

I nodded. "Yes. The gods must have been busy elsewhere that day."

She smiled faintly. "Or maybe they liked us."

We never laughed about the *Norman Atlantic* again. But we never forgot it either. Every time we step aboard a ferry now, even the gleaming new ones that smell of fresh paint and optimism, there's a moment, just before the engines start, when we both look at each other and remember.

The creaking corridors. The sighing air vents. The metal groaning underfoot.

And that one thought that neither of us says out loud: *We've been here before.*

It turns out that sometimes, what feels like bad luck at the ticket counter is just the gods steering you gently, and urgently, in the opposite direction.

I sat up slowly, rubbing my eyes. "Alex, it's a drizzle. England wouldn't even notice this."

"That's exactly what the passengers on the *Titanic* said!"

I sighed and examined the lifejacket. "Can we at least get breakfast first?"

She hesitated. "Maybe something light. But keep the jacket nearby, just in case the ferry forgets how to float."

As we waited for our food in the restaurant, Alex unfolded

the ship's evacuation plan from the wall. She studied it as if preparing for an exam.

"Look," she said, tracing her finger over the map. "We're on Deck Five. Lifeboats are on Deck Seven. If the siren sounds, we go up, not down. Remember that."

"Got it," I said. "Up is good."

She ignored me, scanning the horizon through the port-hole. "See that? That's a squall."

"It's a seagull, Alex."

"I'm telling you, if the lights flicker, I'm taking control of this ship."

I smiled. "I'm sure the captain would appreciate that."

Outside, the drizzle softened. The sea shimmered pale silver under a shy sun. The only thing remotely dangerous was the coffee: thick, dark, and strong enough to power the engines.

Alex finally relaxed, though she kept the lifejacket beside her chair, the strap looped neatly around her wrist.

We finished breakfast in companionable silence, the ship humming steadily beneath us.

Then Alex leaned back, finally smiling. "All right," she said. "Maybe we'll survive this crossing after all."

I smiled. "You see? No icebergs, no chaos, no drama."

At that exact moment, a waiter dropped a tray of glasses with a deafening crash.

Alex leapt to her feet. "That's it, I'm getting the lifejackets!"

By mid-morning, the rain had stopped, the sea had flattened, and the ship was gliding through calm blue water like a well-fed whale. Most passengers were sunbathing on deck, enjoying the peace.

Alex, however, had not moved on.

"Come on," she said, tugging at my arm. "We need to inspect the lifeboats."

"Why?" I asked, still clutching my coffee. "We're not on the crew."

"I just want to see them," she said, in the same tone people use when saying I just want to look at puppies. "For reassurance."

I sighed. "Can't we be reassured from here?"

"No. Up. Deck Seven."

And that was that.

We emerged onto the upper deck to find a long row of bright orange lifeboats gleaming in the sun. They looked sturdy, solid, entirely uninterested in being inspected.

Alex walked up and down like a general reviewing the troops.

"This one looks all right," she said, tapping the side. "But what's that dent?"

"It's not a dent," I said. "It's a shadow."

She squinted. "Hmm. I'll make a note anyway."

"Excuse me," said a passing steward. "Can I help you?"

"Yes," said Alex. "How many people can one of these hold?"

He blinked. "It depends. Usually around a hundred."

"And how many passengers are on board?"

"About nine hundred."

She folded her arms. "So we'll need at least nine of them. Good. Just checking you have enough."

The steward smiled uncertainly. "We do, madam."

Alex wasn't finished. "And the captain, he's qualified, yes? He's not new?"

"Madam, he's been sailing for thirty years."

"Thirty? It's been longer than that since *Titanic*."

I stepped in. "She's joking. Mostly."

The steward nodded politely and walked off quickly.

Later, while I sat with a book, Alex decided to "chat" with the crew. She found one of the deckhands coiling ropes and began her interrogation.

"So tell me," she said, "what do you do if there's a sudden storm?"

"Storm?" the deckhand said, looking alarmed. "No storm today!"

"Yes, but if," she persisted. "Hypothetically."

He looked around as if checking for lightning. "We tie things down. No problem."

"And if the captain is asleep?"

He frowned. "Captain never sleeps."

Alex nodded approvingly. "Good answer."

By lunchtime, she'd memorised the nearest muster station and personally timed the walk from our cabin, twice. The second time she shaved off six seconds by using the service stairs.

When I pointed out that the ship was cruising peacefully under clear skies, she gave me that look.

"Complacency, Peter," she said, "is how empires fall."

But deep down, I admired her. She wasn't panicking; she was preparing. The same instinct that made her intercept trouble with Greek bureaucracy and Greek village life was now focused on maritime survival.

Still, as we sat later on deck with the sun on our faces and Italy rising faintly on the horizon, I couldn't resist teasing her.

"So," I said, "if the ship does go down, what's the plan?"

She sipped her coffee calmly. "Simple. You fetch the life-jackets. I fetch the snacks."

By mid-afternoon, the sea was calm, the sky blue, and we'd finally begun to relax and take a snooze in our cabin, until there came a knock at the cabin door.

"Get out now! We clean cabin!"

"We're three hours from port!" I protested.

He shrugged. "Yes, but cleaning is now."

We packed our bags, surrendered our peaceful cabin, and joined the rest of the ship's refugees in the lounge – a vast hall filled with sleeping families, truck drivers on camp beds, and the occasional tourist spread over the chairs using their bags as pillows.

When the announcement finally came, "Arriving Ancona", it was as though someone had shouted "Abandon ship!" People leapt up, grabbed their belongings, and charged for the stairwells. We followed the stream down into the lower decks, where the air grew hotter and thicker with every step.

By the time we reached the garage, the temperature was somewhere between "sauna" and "oven". There was no room to walk between cars, so people began climbing over them, clutching bags, pillows, and occasionally small dogs.

Then everyone decided they needed some air conditioning and started their engines. Within seconds, the air filled with fumes and the distinct sensation that we were all about to die of carbon monoxide poisoning before reaching Italy.

Alex fanned herself with a ferry ticket. "This is madness," she said.

I nodded. "Yes, but at least we're nearly there."

CHAPTER TWELVE

NEWS TRAVELS FASTER THAN THE FERRY

We were just about to dock in Italy, thirty-six glorious hours of peace after leaving Greece. Well, peace at least from the noise, the rumours and the endless symphony of village updates that pass for news in Pefki. For a brief, shining moment, we were unreachable. No messages, no missed calls, no one shouting our names from across the olive grove.

Then Alex's phone found a signal.

It didn't just ring, it detonated.

"You're *where*?!" screamed Maria, her voice so loud it startled a passing pigeon. "I've been trying to call for days! The village thinks you're *dead*!"

And just like that, our little interlude was over.

Because while we had spent thirty-six hours on a ship with no reception, the good people of Pefki had spent the same time composing our eulogies.

In their defence, it's not that they wish you gone. They just enjoy the drama of believing it.

I could hear Maria's voice perfectly from the driver's seat, even though Alex had the phone pressed to her ear. The sound was pure, unfiltered Pefki, vowels stretched to the point of acrobatics, disbelief served at full volume.

"Italy," Alex said patiently, as though explaining geography to a cat.

"Italy?" Maria repeated, aghast. "Why would anyone go *there*? Do they even have proper coffee?"

I leaned closer to the phone. "They do, Maria. It's just smaller and costs more."

A pause. Then a horrified gasp. "So you really *left Greece*?"

Alex sighed, the sigh of a woman who had seen this coming since birth. "Just for a few days."

Back home in England, people vanish for years and nobody notices. In Pefki, you miss two phone calls and you're a headline.

There was a pause. Then an explosion. "You were only supposed to be away for a day or two! I thought you were going to

Athens! Athens is close! Italy is *foreign*! You can't just go to Italy like you're popping to the bakery!"

Alex smiled, enjoying herself. "We got on a ferry."

"Of course you did! That's how it starts!" Maria wailed. "First it's the ferry, then you're drinking cappuccino with strangers, and before you know it you've forgotten where you live!"

I tried not to laugh but failed. Alex glared at me, then turned back to the phone. "Maria, calm down. We're just exploring. A little trip."

"A little trip?" Maria's voice went up an octave. "You've crossed an entire sea! The goats think you're dead! Theodora has lit a candle for you in the church! Dimitri said he saw your car at the port and thought the police had taken it!"

Word spreads faster than wildfire in a Greek village, especially when there's no real news to compete with it.

Spiros had reportedly assembled a "search committee", which consisted of him, his cousin, and two beers. They spent the evening at the taverna discussing rescue strategies.

"They must have been kidnapped," Spiros concluded.

"They've probably joined a tour," said Theodora, ever the optimist. "You know how Alex likes culture."

"Yes," Maria shot back, "but Peter doesn't! He likes chairs and coffee! Someone must have lured them!"

Back in the car, Alex was still trying to calm Maria.

"Listen, we're fine. We'll be home soon."

"How soon?"

"I don't know. A few days maybe."

There was a gasp so dramatic I could almost see Maria clutching her chest. "A few days? You're on the *continent*! What if there's a storm? What if you get stuck? What if Peter eats the wrong thing and swells up?"

Alex sighed. "Maria, it's Italy, not the Sahara."

But Maria was unstoppable.

"Well, don't think the village will wait forever. The strays have left your patio. Even the black one has defected to Eleni's garden."

Alex murmured something reassuring into the phone; the kind of neutral sound designed to keep conversations moving without encouraging further detail.

"Well," Maria said finally, regaining her composure, "everyone will be relieved. I told them you were probably just somewhere with no signal."

"And they believed you?" Alex asked.

"Of course not," Maria said. "They think I'm covering for you."

Alex rolled her eyes and ended the call, tossing the phone into the dashboard tray like it might start ringing again out of spite.

Silence returned: soft, blessed, and Italian.

We looked at each other, both thinking the same thing: thirty-six hours without Pefki, and the village had already held a memorial service.

CHAPTER THIRTEEN

LANDFALL IN ITALY

Alex spoke fluent Italian. Of course she did. She's one of those maddening people who can pick up a language by standing near a television set. She once told me, with professorial confidence, that all European languages come from Latin, and that if you can speak Italian and English, you can understand half of Europe.

I, on the other hand, had spent twenty years in Greece and still panicked every time someone asked me if I wanted a receipt.

"Languages are music," Alex liked to say. "You must feel them."

"I do," I'd reply. "Mostly I feel confusion."

At school, we had language lessons like everyone else. Some pupils were taught Italian or German. I was given French – a decision that suggested someone, somewhere, had a great deal more faith in me than I deserved. One or two hours a week were spent in a classroom that smelled faintly of chalk dust, damp coats, and the collective uncertainty of adolescence.

The teacher would sweep in with enthusiasm that felt wildly optimistic, and write something elegant and entirely out of reach on the board. *Je suis, tu es, il est.* She would then turn to face us and wait, hopeful, attentive, as if one of us might suddenly stand up and reply fluently, surprising us all.

I usually responded by lowering my eyes and pretending to copy the words carefully, as though neat handwriting might compensate for a complete lack of understanding. Around me, others nodded with varying degrees of confidence. I nodded too, hoping that agreement might be mistaken for comprehension.

By the end of the lesson, I had learned very little French, but I had developed a quiet respect for optimism. It takes a certain kind of courage to believe that a room full of confused teenagers, myself included, might emerge fluent simply through exposure and goodwill.

But the English, as a nation, are hopeless with languages. It's not that we're lazy exactly, we just assume that if we speak *slowly* and *loudly*, the world will eventually come round to our way of thinking.

By the end of each lesson, the French teacher would be sighing theatrically, muttering about "pronon-ci-a-tion", while we sat there repeating "le weekend" with deep national pride, believing it made us fluent.

To make matters worse, I was dyslexic, though nobody knew it at the time – not even me – so I had enough trouble with my own language, let alone someone else's. My exercise book was a battlefield of red pen and polite despair. My French verb tables looked like modern art. I once tried to say *Je suis fatigué* (I am tired) and ended up announcing *Je suis fromage* (I am cheese).

Even now, decades later, I can remember the look on my teacher's face, that small, tragic moment when she realised her life's work was collapsing before her eyes.

So when I travelled, I did what most Englishmen do: I started every conversation abroad with a hopeful smile, followed by an apologetic shrug and a loud, clear, "Do you speak English?"

If they said yes, I'd beam with relief.

If they said no, I'd repeat the question, only slower and with more hand gestures, as if volume and mime will suddenly make me bilingual.

Alex, of course, finds my linguistic incompetence endlessly amusing.

"You know," she said once, "you could learn. You just need practice."

"I've been practising English for sixty years," I said. "Still not perfect."

In Greece, this confession usually earns me sympathy and encouragement, often delivered at volume. In Italy, it earns me a look of brisk assessment, followed by an espresso, which seems to function as both consolation and solution. In France, it earns me silence. I've come to regard that not as hostility, but as a form of respect – or at least a decision to conserve energy.

After a lifetime of navigating these small linguistic negotiations, I've learned when to speak and when to step back.

So when the Italian waiter began glaring and barking orders around the ferry restaurant, I didn't take it personally. I simply nodded and smiled, the way you do when you recognise the tone, the tempo, and the fact that this is not a conversation but a system. I'd been through worse linguistic encounters than this, and, if I was honest, with far less coffee at the end of them.

After all, once you've told your French teacher you are cheese, there's not much left to fear.

We'd arrived in Ancona: gateway to Italy and, judging by the horns, also its lungs.

Cars surged forward like greyhounds, every driver possessed by the conviction that disembarkation was a competitive sport. We followed in what I hoped was a dignified shuffle, joining a queue that instantly became a traffic jam. A port official in mirrored sunglasses gestured vaguely at everyone. Nobody obeyed.

"Just follow them," Alex said, pointing to a van full of

Italians who were clearly improvising.

"Right," I muttered, "because when lost, one should always follow people who *look* confident."

We escaped the port through a maze of roundabouts and flyovers, our satnav recalculating with the weary tone of a civil servant on his last day. The first stop was obvious.

"Coffee," Alex announced.

She'd spotted a bar at the side of the road – a proper *autogrill*, gleaming with chrome counters and the faint smell of pastries. We parked between two trucks plastered with religious stickers (always a good omen) and stepped inside.

The barista looked up, assessed us instantly, my pale English confusion, Alex's Mediterranean certainty, and smiled. "*Due caffè?*"

Alex returned the smile. "*Forte, per favore.*"

He served two tiny cups of espresso, liquid darkness, smooth and deadly. We stood at the counter like seasoned locals while the morning chaos of Italy unfolded outside: men in suits arguing with passion and affection, women in sunglasses directing traffic with hand gestures worthy of theatre, and the traffic itself joining in like an orchestra of horns and impatience.

The first sip was like being electrocuted by a poet. Alex sighed with satisfaction; I briefly saw the Virgin Mary.

Alex took in the scene, eyes bright, and nodded with satisfaction. She is Greek, so naturally she considers Europe to be a direct descendant of her ancestors.

"This is how things are meant to be," she said. She was radiant. "I feel European again," she said. "The language, the coffee, the chaos; it's like coming home."

"You were never *not* European," I reminded her.

"Yes," she said thoughtfully, nodding towards the car park, "but here… people drive like me."

And she was right. Within ten minutes I'd seen a man reverse at full speed into a roundabout, a nun overtake a police car, and three motorbikes treating the pavement as an optional extra lane.

Somewhere in that beautiful madness, Alex smiled like she'd found her people.

We climbed back into the Citroën, now perfumed with espresso and mild panic. The plan, such as it was, was to drive north, following the coast for a while and stopping wherever life or hunger demanded. The beauty of not planning, of course, is that you're constantly surprised.

Almost immediately, Italy unfolded before us, soft hills rolling towards the sea, vineyards stitched across the slopes like green embroidery, terracotta roofs glowing in the sun. Alex rolled down the window, letting the wind play with her hair.

"It's beautiful," she said. "Like a painting."

The road signs announced cheerfully that we were heading for Bologna.

We drove through tunnels, past hills and endless toll booths, each one manned by a machine that refused to accept my card and insulted me in Italian. Alex translated helpfully:

"It says you are too slow."

"It says your card is stupid."

"It says welcome to Italy."

Finally, we found a stretch of open road. The sea shimmered to our right, the mountains rose to our left, and for the first time in a long while, the world seemed vast and kind.

Alex leaned back, eyes half-closed. "See?" she said. "We needed this. Greece made us strong; Italy will make us happy."

I smiled, though a small part of me wondered what might happen if we reached France.

The storm was behind us. Ahead lay a new road: new stories, new arguments, and probably more waiters shouting. But for now, with the windows open, the road clear, and the faint hum of the Adriatic still in our ears, it felt like we'd finally broken free.

CHAPTER FOURTEEN

Lunch in the Land of Gestures

By the time we reached the outskirts of Rimini, the air had changed. It smelled of the sea, of fish grilled somewhere nearby, and of perfume strong enough to stun a small goat.

Rimini, Alex informed me, was a place of elegance and history, "like Glyfada with better architecture". I wasn't sure what that meant, but it sounded dangerous.

We'd only been driving for an hour or two, following signs that seemed designed to confuse foreigners. Every turn promised a beach, every beach promised parking, and every car park was full. Alex, whose internal compass is powered by instinct and optimism, declared, "We'll stop for lunch. It's destiny."

She spotted it before I did: a roadside trattoria with faded awnings, geraniums in chipped pots, and two Fiat Pandas parked outside. "That one!" she said, clapping her hands. "Look, it's full of locals."

I looked. It was full of *Italians*.

Which, of course, meant she was right.

Inside, the restaurant was everything a hungry traveller could hope for: chaos, warmth, and the smell of garlic doing battle with frying oil. A TV in the corner blared a football match while a small dog patrolled the floor with the confidence of ownership.

The waiter approached – a man in his sixties with slicked-back hair and the air of someone who'd seen everything, twice. He rattled off a list of dishes at the speed of a machine gun.

Alex listened attentively, nodding in time.

When he finished, she said something in perfect Italian that made him smile, laugh, and slap the table affectionately.

"What did you say?" I asked.

"I told him his accent is beautiful," she replied, as if this were the most natural thing in the world.

That's the difference between us. I spend years trying to learn how to order coffee without causing offence; Alex compliments a man's regional inflection and immediately gets better service.

Food arrived as if we'd been adopted. Bread, antipasto, pasta so fresh it still remembered the chicken, and wine that could have stripped varnish. Alex handled it all with effortless charm, translating the menu, chatting with the staff, and switching languages mid-sentence like a linguistic gymnast.

At one point, the waiter brought us something off-menu – a dish of grilled fish, lemon, and what looked suspiciously like a proposal.

"For you, lovely lady," he said, placing it before Alex with reverence. "Special."

She beamed. "*Grazie, caro*!"

I tasted it. It was divine.

"How do you do that?" I asked. "Everywhere we go, people adore you."

She shrugged. "It's easy. I talk. You look polite."

I couldn't argue.

At the next table, an older couple leaned over and struck up conversation. The man raised his glass. "From where you come?"

"Greece," said Alex proudly. "And he's English."

"Ah!" the man laughed. "Sun and rain. Perfect combination!"

He poured me wine before I could protest. "To Europe!" he declared.

We toasted, drank, and briefly became family.

Dessert arrived uninvited: a generous slab of tiramisu dusted with cocoa. The dog under the table gave a long, satisfied sigh, the universal sound of someone who knows life has peaked. On the television, the football match hit fever pitch, a blur of shouting, arms, and national pride in motion.

Then came the roar: "*Gooooal!*"

The whole taverna – waiters and diners alike – exploded into applause; even the dog thumped its tail in approval. Somewhere in that chaotic harmony of sugar, caffeine, and celebration, I realised there are few things Italians do quietly, and some of them involve food.

Alex joined in. She didn't know who had scored, but enthusiasm is its own language.

By the time the bill came, we had hugs, photographs, and promises to return "next summer". The waiter refused to let us leave without espresso "for strength".

Back in the car, the world felt slightly blurred at the edges, the good kind of blurred. Alex leaned back in her seat, sunglasses on, utterly content. "See?" she said. "You must never choose a restaurant. Let the restaurant choose you."

Then, before we even left the car park, Alex's phone rang. This time it was a video call. The village had apparently reached a state of collective emotional collapse. The call wasn't from just one person, but from everyone.

Maria's face filled the screen first, far too close, as though she believed video calls required physical contact.

"*Peter mou! Alex mou!*" she cried. "We thought you'd emigrated! I told them nonsense, you're just on holiday."

The camera swung violently to Theodora, who said, "Darlings, I told them not to worry, but Maria is *still* worried. She told the postman you were taken by smugglers. Please tell her before she starts a petition."

Before we could process that, the video flipped again, now showing old Yiannis, still on his permanent bench by the harbour.

He had apparently given an unofficial press conference.

"They were good people," he told three fishermen and a cat. "Always polite. A shame they've gone. The English one owes me two euros."

Maria returned the phone to speaker mode and held it up so the entire kafenio could shout at us at once. By now, half the village had gathered: men, women, three children, two dogs, and a goat that wandered in whenever the door was left open.

"ARE YOU ALIVE?" came the collective roar.

"Yes!" Alex laughed. "We're fine. We're on our way through Italy."

Maria clutched her chest anyway, because drama, like olive oil, is never used sparingly.

"We were about to ring the embassy."

"The Italian one?" I asked.

"No," she said. "The Greek one. To ask if you had changed nationality without telling us."

The café exploded. Even Maria was laughing now, though she tried to disguise it behind a stern look that convinced absolutely no one.

"Next time," she said, wagging a finger at the camera, "you tell us before you go abroad. We could have packed you something decent to eat."

"Maria," Alex said sweetly, "we're in Italy. They have food."

"Yes, but not *Greek* food! How will you survive without proper olive oil? Don't come back thin! People will talk; you'll ruin our reputation!"

Somewhere behind her, someone shouted, "Bring back cheese!"

Someone else shouted, "Bring back Peter's two euros!"

By now the camera had dropped to someone's lap, giving us a cinematic view of a table cluttered with coffee cups, backgammon pieces, and the hind leg of the goat. A hand appeared, waving dramatically: "WE MISS YOU! COME HOME!"

Then the connection froze on Maria mid-sentence, her mouth open in what looked like either a blessing or a threat.

When the call finally ended, Alex stared at the phone, shaking her head with that soft, disbelieving smile she reserves only for Greeks and cats.

"They mean well," she said.

"I know," I replied. "It's like being adopted by an entire village of mothers. And uncles. And at least one goat."

We sat for a while, deciding where to go next, the evening air buzzing with the soft promise of new places away from the village.

Behind us, not physically, but in that strange emotional way only a Greek village can manage, we felt Pefki.

The gossip.

The laughter.

The love disguised as panic.

"That's what I miss," Alex said quietly. "They care too much, in the best way."

I nodded. "They'll still be talking about this next week."

She snorted. "Next week? Peter, they'll still be talking about it next year."

And she was right.

In Pefki, a trip to Italy isn't just a holiday.

It's an international incident with lifelong consequences.

THE KAFENIO VERSION OF THE CALL

(As reported, misreported, and enthusiastically embroidered by the village of Pefki)

By the next morning, the village had settled into its favourite pastime: collective storytelling, also known as "Maria said, but I heard."

According to them, the video call with us went something like this:

1. THE CALL THAT SHOOK THE VILLAGE

"The moment the phone rang," Maria told anyone within earshot, "I knew it was them. A mother senses these things."

"You're not their mother," Theodora pointed out.

"I am in spirit," Maria snapped.

Theodora nodded gravely, because arguing with

Maria is pointless after 9 a.m.

2. The Tragic Opening Scene

"We all screamed, ARE YOU ALIVE?" Maria explained, placing a dramatic hand on her chest. "Alex cried! Peter fainted! The screen went black!"

None of this happened.

Theodora corrected her: "Peter did not faint. He simply blinked slowly."

But Maria overruled her. "It was a faint. A man-faint. Very rare."

3. The Embassy Intervention

According to Nikos the fisherman: "We were one click away from phoning the embassy. I had the number ready. I know people."

He does not.

4. The Petition That Never Was

Theodora told the bakery queue: "I said not to worry, but Maria already had a petition written. Forty names! Even the goat signed!"

"A hoofprint is not a signature," someone muttered.

"It counts," said Maria.

5. The Smuggler Theory

By lunchtime, Mrs Stamatis had produced a full narrative: "They were taken by smugglers," she whispered dramatically.

"I saw it in a dream. A black van. A fog. Also a carrot, but I don't know what that means."

The carrot became part of the story. *No one questioned it.*

6. The Hacking Incident That Never Occurred

Spiros insisted: "The call froze. That means someone hacked it. Probably the Italians."

"Why would the Italians hack Peter and Alex?" asked Dimitri.

"To steal secrets," Spiros said.

"What secrets?"

He shrugged. "Greek ones."

7. The Official Kafenio Record

By the afternoon, this version had settled as the "official truth":

Alex was laughing, but it was clearly a cry for help disguised as joy.

Peter was "brave but pale", possibly from captivity.

They were "trapped in a place with food but no olive oil".

They needed "a rescue mission immediately", ideally using Dimitri's boat (which has no engine).

By sunset, this is what everyone in Pefki wholeheartedly believed:

- We had not deserted them.

- We were not dead.

- We were not kidnapped by smugglers (the carrot disproved this).

- We were simply "resting abroad so the village could appreciate us properly".

Maria concluded the day's events with her favourite line: "Anyway," she said, "they will be back. Basil does not water itself."

And everyone agreed solemnly, because in Pefki, plants, gossip, and relationships all grow best with lots of attention and very little accuracy.

As we pulled onto the coastal road, the Adriatic lay beside us, wide, blue, and unhurried. The sun was already lowering, the sky settling into that soft amber that makes even long journeys feel manageable.

The road ahead did not promise drama. It offered space. Distance. The kind of movement that allows things to fall back into their proper scale. There would be beauty, certainly, and no shortage of stories in time, but for now it was enough to keep driving, letting the day close behind us without asking anything more.

"Next stop?" I asked.

Alex grinned. "I don't mind, just drive until we see something interesting."

And with that, we drove north, into Italy, into evening, into the next chapter.

CHAPTER FIFTEEN

The Buzz of San Marino

We reached San Marino by accident, which, in our case, is how all good adventures begin.

The road climbed higher and higher, curling through cypress and olive groves until the world simply dropped away beneath us, Italy unfolding in soft gold and green, a living map shimmering in the afternoon haze.

Alex leaned forward in her seat, eyes bright. "It's magnificent," she said. "You can see half of Italy from here."

San Marino appeared in the distance like something painted rather than built, towers rising from cliffs, flags stirring in the wind, the whole country poised between earth and sky. There was a quiet dignity about it, a sense of time standing still, as if it had decided centuries ago that the world could change as much as it liked; San Marino would remain.

It is the oldest republic in the world, and you can feel that weight of history in the air: solid, calm, and entirely unbothered by the noise of modern life. There were no guards, no checkpoints, not even a gate; just a modest sign by the roadside informing us that we had left Italy and entered another country.

We didn't look for a hotel so much as surrender to the idea that one might eventually appear.

We were driving aimlessly by then, the sort of driving that happens when daylight is fading and optimism is doing most of the work. One moment the road threaded its way through olive groves and vineyards, the next it began to climb, curling upwards with quiet determination, as if it had its own ideas about where we should spend the night.

Somehow, without announcing itself, the landscape shifted. The countryside fell away and the road led us into a place that felt older than directions, carved out of rock, history, and stubbornness. The light softened to amber and we arrived not because we had planned to, but because the road had clearly decided we were done.

The hotel appeared as these places often do in Italy, just in time. Modest, pale, and clinging to the hillside beneath the fortress walls, its whitewashed balconies looked out over a valley so wide and calm it felt like a reward for getting lost properly.

The man at reception could have been thirty or three hundred. He handed us a key, a small map, and a smile that suggested nothing we could do would surprise him, including turning up without a booking and with an explanation that made no sense.

"Breakfast is on the terrace," he said calmly. "Best view in San Marino."

He wasn't exaggerating.

The next morning, the view stopped us in our tracks: layers of soft green hills fading into blue, villages scattered like pebbles, the Adriatic glimmering faintly at the edge of the sky. The air smelled of pine, coffee, and, though we didn't know it yet, impending chaos.

Breakfast was perfectly Italian: paper-thin ham, croissants dusted with enough sugar to ensure guilt, and coffee strong enough to wake the ancestors. Each table had a small vase of flowers and, curiously, a tightly rolled newspaper taped into a cylinder.

Alex, mid-pour, tilted her head. "Maybe it's for reading?"

Before I could test that theory, the hotel owner appeared beside us with the expression of a man who'd already accepted his fate. "Wait," he said quietly, placing a hand on my arm. "Just wait."

We waited.

And then they came.

Wasps. Hundreds of them.

They arrived low and fast, skimming the terrace railings like fighter pilots. Within seconds, breakfast had transformed into a scene of organised panic. Croissants were abandoned mid-bite; spoons froze halfway to mouths. The air vibrated.

Alex asked the waiter, "What's happening?"

"Every morning," the owner said calmly. "They love sugar." He pointed to the rolled newspaper. "Use that."

"Use it how?" I asked.

He demonstrated, swinging his own like a swordsman defending honour and espresso. A wasp spun off into the distance.

"Ah," Alex said, impressed. "It's like fencing."

I attempted the same move and immediately hit my coffee cup. It wobbled but held. The wasps remained unimpressed.

Within minutes, the terrace had dissolved into chaos. Tourists ducked behind menus; waiters darted between tables like boxers; the elderly retreated under chairs. A small child screamed. An Italian man shouted "*Basta*!" with all the authority of a general commanding the air force.

I tried defending my toast but only succeeded in spilling the sugar bowl – a tactical error of catastrophic proportions. The wasps redoubled their efforts, delirious with happiness.

"They smell fear!" Alex said calmly, already positioning herself.

I looked down at my hands, sticky and incriminating. "No," I said. "They smell sugar."

Alex had found her rhythm by then. The newspaper was rolled with care, her stance settled, her movements economical and assured. She swept the air with the composure of someone who believed entirely in what she was doing.

"Stay calm," she said. "Fear excites them."

"I'm not frightened," I replied. "I'm coated."

She didn't look at me. Experience had taught her that explanation was unnecessary.

Guests were barricading themselves with napkins, and one brave soul had armed himself with two newspapers and was fending off an entire squadron. The hotel owner moved through the mayhem with the serenity of a monk, collecting plates as if this were all part of the service.

"Don't worry," he said. "They go away at eleven."

"Eleven?" I said. "How do they know?"

He gave a small shrug. "They just do."

That seemed to satisfy him. It did not entirely satisfy me.

We waited it out, glasses nudged carefully towards the centre of the table, movements measured, conversation reduced to the essentials. The wasps continued their patrols with professional focus, clearly unconcerned by reassurance.

As the hour approached, the momentum shifted. Alex, hair slightly dishevelled but otherwise composed, dealt with one final wasp with quiet efficiency and sat back down again.

"There," she said. "They respect confidence."

And, almost on cue, the rest drifted away. No warning, no announcement. One moment they were there, circling with intent. The next, the air had cleared, the table was ours again, and the evening resumed as if nothing had interrupted it.

Italy, I was learning, runs less on clocks than on agreement. When something is finished, everyone seems to know at once, including the wasps.

The wasps had vanished, the air fell still, and the terrace looked like the aftermath of a minor war: half-drunk coffees, broken pastries, stunned survivors staring into the distance.

The owner reappeared, collecting cups with quiet pride. "See?" he said. "They always go at eleven."

Alex nodded, smiling faintly. "You just have to respect nature."

I looked at the wreckage: a torn croissant, a smear of jam, and one smug wasp doing lazy circles above the sugar bowl.

"Does this happen all year?" I asked.

He shrugged. "Only in spring. And autumn. And some-times summer."

"And winter?" Alex asked.

He paused. "Then we eat inside."

He drifted away, calm as ever, leaving behind two shaken guests and a sugar bowl under quarantine.

As we packed to leave, Alex stepped out onto the balcony, the breeze lifting her hair. The view opened out below us in quiet layers of coastline and sea, the water catching the early light and holding it gently. In the distance, the horizon was pale and clear, blue widening into softer tones, the day unfolding slowly, with-out urgency.

From up there, the café seemed improbably small; a brief

interruption in a much larger picture. The table, the wasps, the sugar bowl, all of it already felt contained, reduced to scale by distance and height.

"You know," Alex said, still looking out, "if that's the worst that happens, we're doing all right."

I nodded, rubbing the faint sting on my arm and watching the light change. "Yes," I said. "But tomorrow, we're having breakfast in the car."

She smiled, the sea carrying the sound away, and for a moment everything felt settled again.

San Marino surprised me. Not with size or spectacle, but with how lightly it sat on the world.

We spent the rest of the morning wandering its narrow streets, lanes barely wide enough for two opinions to pass without an argument. Tiny shops spilled out perfume, postcards, and objects of uncertain purpose. One sold crossbows with the same calm seriousness as fridge magnets, as if you might reasonably need either before lunch. Some of the postcards looked as though they'd been printed before photography had fully made up its mind.

From the fortress walls we stopped and looked out. The stone beneath our hands was worn smooth in places, rough in others, patched and repaired over centuries rather than restored to impress. The walls were thick, practical, built for holding ground rather than admiring scenery. Towers rose behind us, solid and unapologetic, their narrow windows designed for watching, not views. This was not a ruin arranged for tourists.

It was a working reminder that someone once expected trouble and prepared for it.

Below us, the Italian plains stretched away in the pale morning light, fields and towns laid out with improbable order, roads threading through them like careful stitching. From up here it all looked unreal, like a map someone had spread out and forgotten to fold away again.

Alex rested her hands on the stone and fell quiet, which is how I knew the place had got to her.

"It's strange," she said softly. "This country is so small, but it feels free."

And she was right. San Marino has spent centuries doing something quietly radical. It has minded its own business. Perched on a mountain, surrounded on all sides, it simply refused to be absorbed. No grand declarations, no dramatic exits, just persistence. A republic that survived by staying exactly where it was and saying no often enough to make it stick.

We stood there for a long moment, the fortress holding firm behind us, Italy glittering below like a catalogue of possibilities. From that height, borders felt theoretical and urgency felt optional.

Freedom, I thought, comes in many forms.

Sometimes it is a mountaintop republic that refuses to disappear.

And sometimes it is something smaller and closer to hand. Getting through breakfast with wasps, keeping your sense of humour, and still feeling generous about the day ahead.

We left San Marino after breakfast the next day, having decided that surrender was unnecessary but preparation was wise. The terrace had been reclaimed, cautiously, with a new system in place, thought of by Alex. Sugar sachets were opened only at the last possible moment. Cups were positioned like decoys. Napkins were folded with purpose. Alex had constructed a loose perimeter of calm authority, and I had been tasked with defence with a roll of newspaper and hope.

The wasps arrived, of course, but this time they were met with strategy rather than surprise. A plate was stationed at a safe distance, generously provisioned and clearly marked as an alternative option with a spoonful of jam. They inspected it, conferred briefly, and accepted the terms. No negotiations were required.

The hotel owner watched from a distance, newspaper raised like a flag of peace.

"He says the wasps are harmless," Alex reported, sipping her coffee.

I glanced at my arm, where yesterday's sting was still faintly visible; a small but enduring souvenir. "That's interesting," I said. "Because yesterday one of them made a very specific point."

Alex smiled. "You startled him."

"I was sitting completely still," I said. "I was drinking coffee."

"Exactly," she replied.

We packed up without incident, the car carrying the familiar scent of sugar, coffee, and misplaced confidence. The owner waved as we pulled away, the terrace restored to calm, the wasps already moving on to their next opportunity.

Italy, I reflected, rewards those who adapt quickly and complain quietly.

The road dropped down through the mountains, sunlight flashing between pine and olive, the air bright with the promise of distance. Behind us, San Marino rose like a dream half-remembered, towers catching the morning light, steady and still.

Alex spread the map across her knees, tracing lines with her finger. "We don't need GPS," she said. "We'll follow the signs. The journey is part of the joy."

And it was. Every turn revealed something new: a chapel tucked into the rock, a farmer leading his donkey through silver fields, the smell of wild herbs drifting through the open windows.

"Look," Alex said, gazing back up towards the mountain. "They're free up there."

She meant San Marino, still perched above the plains, independent and unmoved, a country content to remain exactly where it was while the rest of Italy flowed around it.

"Yes," I said quietly. "And now, so are we."

Once back on the road, Italy gathered itself again and carried us along. Driving there feels less like following rules and more like joining a moving system. Not chaos, exactly, but momentum. Trucks rolled past like patient whales, steady and unbothered. Motorbikes darted between lanes like fish, quick and alert. Cars slid into gaps with the confidence of people who trust the current and expect it to hold.

Alex watched it all with interest. "Everyone has their own rhythm," she said.

"And somehow," I replied, "it all swims in the same direction."

The motorway carried us north through a countryside brushed in gold and green. Vineyards curved across the hills like handwriting; villages rested beneath church towers; and above it all, the light shifted, softening, deepening, urging us onward.

We didn't speak much. The world did it for us.

By midday, the road shimmered in the heat. We stopped at a small trattoria hidden among vineyards and cypress trees. Inside, the air was warm with garlic and bread. The owner greeted us as if we were family; within minutes, Alex had the whole room smiling.

Plates arrived as though summoned: antipasto, pasta fragrant with basil, bread still whispering of the oven. Children played near the counter; a grandmother stirred sauce; somewhere, an old radio hummed a love song from another century.

We lingered long after the plates were cleared, sipping coffee that tasted of sunlight and soil.

When we finally stood to leave, the owner pressed two small biscotti into Alex's hand. "For the journey," he said.

"For the memory," she replied.

The further north we travelled, the gentler the landscape became. The hills softened, rolling rather than rising, fields pale with olives and wheat stretching out on either side of the road. It felt like a country exhaling.

At a petrol stop, Alex came back to the car holding a small jar and smiling. "Truffle paste," she announced, as if this were an entirely sensible thing to buy between fuel pumps. "We must eat properly."

I laughed. "You've already turned the car into a travelling delicatessen."

She held the jar up to the light, considering it. "This," she said, "is for bread. Warm bread. A little oil. That's all you need." She paused, then added, "And maybe a knife."

The idea settled in my mind more firmly than any map. Not the truffles themselves, but the taste of them. Earthy, dense, unmistakable. The sort of flavour that insists on being noticed, even in small amounts.

She smiled, leaning her arms on the door, the wind lifting her hair. "It's all part of the adventure."

And she was right. Not in a grand sense, but in the accumulation of it. Each stop, each flavour, each unfamiliar sign that slowed us just enough to notice where we were. The road was no longer something to get through. It was something that kept adding itself to us.

It stopped being simply a route north and became a thread, quietly stitching together what we had already lived through and what still lay ahead. The floods, the laughter, the rebuilding. The ordinary persistence of continuing.

Somewhere along that long Italian road, with truffle on our minds and sunlight shifting across the dashboard, it occurred to me that freedom was not about leaving things behind.

It was about learning what to carry with you. A taste. A habit. A way of seeing. Home, it turned out, was not a fixed point on a map. It was something you packed carefully and took along, wherever the road happened to lead.

CHAPTER SIXTEEN

It's Raining in Pefki

We had left Pefki behind to clear our minds, to breathe, to remember what life felt like when it wasn't collapsing under rainwater and bureaucracy. Italy had become a sort of therapy – pasta therapy, wine therapy, driving-on-roads-that-actually-made-sense therapy.

We were truly relaxing.

Almost suspiciously relaxing.

But deep down, both of us knew: if anyone could track us across borders, continents, and emotional states… it was Maria.

We were driving north, leaving San Marino behind. Road signs pointed towards Bologna, and Alex, with prophetic certainty, announced: "Spaghetti Bolognese. That's our destiny."

Honestly, it felt like enough of a plan. After a year of torment, floods, accusations, arrests, engineers, and paperwork thicker than baklava, the idea of sitting in Italy with a plate of pasta felt like salvation.

The sky ahead was soft Italian blue. The air gentle. The road smooth.

Greece, beautiful, chaotic, exhausting Greece, was far behind us.

I almost believed we were free.

Then Alex's phone rang.

Peace shattered like a plate at a wedding.

She glanced at the screen and closed her eyes for a moment, the way someone does just before lightning strikes.

"Maria," she said.

I felt my stomach drop.

Maria doesn't call casually.

Maria calls like a fire alarm.

Maria calls when destiny demands it.

Alex answered. "*Kalimera*, Maria. What's wrong now?"

There was silence on the line. A long, dark, heavy silence – the kind found in Greek tragedies just before someone announces the arrival of a messenger drenched in doom.

Then—

"WHERE ARE YOU?!"

She screamed so loudly that a motorcyclist overtaking us nearly swerved into a vineyard.

"I've been calling for HOURS! It's raining again!"

Alex winced, holding the phone a full arm's length away. I could still hear every word from the driver's seat.

"Maria," Alex said carefully, "it's just spring rain."

"SPRING RAIN?" Maria shrieked. "This was NO normal rain! This was a DISASTER! The river came down the mountain like a MONSTER! It took fences, chairs, a chicken house, and Theodora's clothesline!"

At the word *river*, my heart tightened like a fist.

Alex's eyes widened. "Oh God… is our house OK?"

Maria continued shouting, but she didn't answer the question, as though Alex had asked something irrelevant, like the price of lentils.

I pulled the car into a layby and switched on the hazard lights. Alex hit loudspeaker.

Maria kept going, unstoppable: "THE POLICE CAME! WITH BOOTS! THEY WERE CALLING YOUR NAME!"

"OUR name?" I mouthed.

Alex nodded grimly.

I took the phone.

"Maria. IS OUR HOUSE FLOODED AGAIN?"

But Maria was on a parallel conversational plane.

"They wanted to know if you have been redirecting the river again!" she shouted. "I said, 'Not them!' but they didn't believe me. They said your name is on a LIST!"

"What list?" I whispered.

Alex gave me a look that meant "do not ask questions the universe will answer painfully".

Maria continued with unstoppable momentum.

"The water came down next to your land and flooded the whole street. There is a river running all the way to the sea!"

"Nemesis has ideas," Maria said darkly. "About the water. About you."

She lowered her voice, as if the pipes themselves might be listening.

"She says it's not natural."

"Maria," I said loudly, "HAS. OUR. HOUSE. FLOODED?"

"No," she replied, "but every garden below yours has."

"Well then it's not our problem," I said with hopefulness bordering on delusion.

"OF COURSE IT'S YOUR PROBLEM!" she yelled. "It's YOUR river! The police said your name TWICE!"

Alex exhaled sharply, the dangerous, controlled kind of exhale Greek women make when internally selecting between diplomacy and war.

"How bad is it?" she asked.

"Well," Maria said, "Nikos's chickens are swimming, Theodora's cat has moved upstairs, and George says his new patio furniture is in the sea."

In the background I heard barking, shouting, and what sounded very much like a siren, or possibly someone blowing into a hosepipe.

Maria resumed: "I told the police you were abroad, but they said that's not an excuse. They think you changed the landscape AGAIN!"

"Maria," I said, "we are in Italy. The only thing we've changed is the menu."

She sniffed dramatically.

"Well, you'd better come back soon. They are talking about foreign interference in the natural system."

I closed my eyes, letting the absurdity wash over me.

"Tell them," I said, "that I am available for interviews… from Bologna."

Alex ended the call with a sharp tap, then held the phone in both hands the way someone might hold a live grenade: carefully, respectfully, suspiciously.

For a moment, neither of us spoke.

Cars whooshed past on the motorway. The Italian sky shone obliviously, cruelly blue.

Alex finally broke the silence.

"Peter," she said slowly, "tell me that Maria is exaggerating."

I opened my mouth. Nothing came out.

Because we both knew something terrible: Maria only exaggerates emotionally. Her facts are terrifyingly accurate.

Alex stared straight ahead, jaw tight.

"She ignored me twice when I asked about the house."

"Yes," I said. "That was… noticeable."

"She never ignores direct questions."

"She once ignored a fire alarm," I reminded her, "but not questions."

Alex ran a hand through her hair.

"Oh God, Peter. Not again. I can't do another flood. I can't do another year of accusations. I can't do another lawyer. I still have the last one's email notifications muted."

"We don't know anything yet," I said, trying to sound calm and wise, and failing at both.

She turned to me with eyes that said: "Do not attempt optimism. Not today."

"Foreign interference in the natural system?" she repeated slowly. "Do you hear yourself?"

"That wasn't me," I said quickly. "That was Maria."

"Exactly! That's worse!"

She put the phone down on the dashboard like it offended her, then took a long, steady breath; the kind that's supposed to help but usually precedes shouting.

"We leave Pefki for a few days," she said. "And already the police have boots, chickens are swimming, and Nemesis is accusing us of conspiracy with the heavens."

She stared at me.

"Peter," she whispered, "I swear to God, if we get blamed for rain again, I will move permanently to Italy and become a woman who owns a vineyard."

"I support that life choice," I said. "Do I get a small cottage?"

She ignored me.

Instead, she pressed her hands to her temples and muttered, "I knew it. I knew it. We should never have got too relaxed. This is exactly what happens when you let your guard down."

"That's what Poseidon wants," I said solemnly.

"Don't joke," she snapped. "I'm serious. This has 'Nemesis has been talking nonstop' written all over it."

We sat in silence for a moment, listening to our thoughts clatter around inside the car like loose marbles.

Finally, I said what we were both thinking: "This feels like déjà vu."

"No," Alex corrected. "This feels like the *sequel* to déjà vu. The one where everyone knows the plot and still pretends to be shocked."

I nodded, staring at the road ahead, Bologna in the distance, tension in the air like static.

"Should we call the lawyer?" I asked weakly.

Alex shot me a look that could have stopped the flood itself.

"Peter. We are not calling a lawyer while driving to Bologna."

"I wasn't suggesting it immediately," I said. "Just… emotionally preparing."

She sighed, long, deep, heroic.

"We're going to enjoy today," she said firmly. "We are going to eat pasta. We are going to drink wine. And then – *then* – we will find out whether our garden has become a tributary of the Aegean again."

"And if it has?" I asked.

She stared ahead, determination settling on her face like armour.

"Then," she said, "we fight. Again. But first, we eat spaghetti."

I smiled, relieved the fire had returned to her voice. "That's my warrior."

She reached over, squeezed my hand, and said softly: "Not again, Peter. Please God… not again."

I squeezed back. "I know," I whispered. "But whatever happens, we'll face it."

She nodded silently… then added, "And Nemesis is not winning this round. We beat her before; we will beat her again."

We didn't have to wait long.

The phone buzzed again, not a call this time, but a series of notifications:

Maria has sent 12 photos.

Maria has sent 7 videos.

Maria has sent 1 voice note (duration: 4 minutes, 38 seconds).

Alex inhaled sharply.

"Ready?"

"No," I said.

We opened the first photo.

And stared.

Our house, our long-suffering, traumatised, repeatedly accused house, stood there glorious. Dry. Unbothered. Sparkling like it had just had its portrait taken for a real-estate magazine.

The paint gleamed. The tiles shone. Even the basil looked smug.

Alex gasped. "It's perfect!"

A second photo arrived. A close-up of the terrace: dry. The furniture: dry. The flowerpots: dry.

A third photo: the garden – green, calm, untouched, not a pebble out of place.

"My God," I whispered, "it survived."

Alex put a hand over her heart. "It's… immaculate."

We tapped open the first video.

The camera focused lovingly on our walls, panning slowly as though Maria were filming a royal baby.

Then her voice narrated over the top: "Look! Not one stone moved! Not one! Even the lemon tree is smiling!"

Another video followed.

This one lingered on the drainpipes, our infamous, allegedly criminal drainpipes, gleaming like polished silver.

"See?" Maria continued breathlessly. "They are innocent! Innocent and beautiful! I always said so!"

I blinked at the screen. "Did she?"

Alex shrugged. "She's rewriting history. Let's allow it."

We opened the next video.

It started just as reassuringly: our house, proud and dry. But then, slowly… ominously… the camera drifted away from our immaculate walls and began turning towards the road.

Alex and I leaned in at the same time.

The moment the view cleared the corner of our garden, we both sucked in a breath.

The road had become a river.

A wide one.

Fast.

Brown.

Raging.

Water thundered past where there should have been asphalt and cats sunning themselves on pavements. Garden walls further down the slope had disappeared entirely. A plastic table shot by like a distressed surfboard. George's patio chair drifted past at worrying speed. A chicken, floating on what appeared to be a purple bucket lid, looked calmly resigned to its fate.

Behind it all, our house stood proudly, utterly untouched, like an ark that had decided to stay on dry land.

"Oh my God," Alex whispered. "It missed us."

"It respected us," I corrected her reverently. "For once, the flood respected us."

Another video played. this time zooming in on the chaos below. Children yelling. Dogs barking.

Someone shouting, "WHO CAUSED THIS?!"

Someone else shouting, "IT WAS THE ENGLISH MAN!"

And Maria shouting back, "NO IT WASN'T!"

We sat in stunned silence.

Finally, Alex spoke, her voice low. "I feel terrible for the others," she said. She paused, watching the screen. "But also…"

"Yes," I said. "I know."

"… relieved," she finished. "Incredibly relieved."

I nodded. "So am I."

We watched another video.

Below, the river surged with unnerving force, swollen and fast, the kind of water that ignores arguments and follows its own rules. But our house remained there, dry and intact, an improbable pocket of calm while everything around it rushed past.

Alex let out a long breath.

"At least this time," she said quietly, "it isn't us."

"And," I added, cautiously hopeful, "it cannot *possibly* be blamed on us."

We shared a long look. A look filled with love. A look filled with hope. A look filled with the absolute certainty that Pefki would *absolutely* still blame us.

But for now, just for this moment, our relief was pure and unspoiled.

Alex leaned back in her seat and whispered, "Thank God."

I stared at the screen a little longer, watching the last frame of Maria's video: our house standing there like a hero returning from battle.

A strange mixture washed over me: relief, exhaustion, and that quiet dread that comes from knowing the universe is not finished with you yet.

I turned to Alex.

"Shall we go back?"

The question settled between us, heavier than I'd expected.

It was the sort of question that carries consequences even before it's answered.

Alex answered it immediately. She snapped the phone shut and shook her head.

"No," she said. "Absolutely not. You've just seen it: the house is perfect. The garden is perfect. Even the basil is thriving. Why would we go back now?"

She gestured towards the horizon where Bologna waited for us like a warm, carbohydrate-based embrace.

"We finally escaped. We finally exhaled. We finally slept without dreaming of mudslides. Let's keep going. Let's clear our minds properly, not halfway. We'll be in a better state to deal with everything when we return."

I blinked. "But what about—"

"Let them fight among themselves," she said firmly. "Let them accuse us. Let them form committees and theories and WhatsApp groups. We have done nothing – *nothing* – except repair the damage to our home caused by the last flood. We have changed exactly zero rivers."

"That's true," I admitted.

"We haven't touched a stone," Alex continued. "We haven't moved a wall; we haven't shifted a pebble; we haven't even swept the driveway aggressively. So no one can accuse us again."

I nodded, reassured.

Then I immediately shook my head, because this is Greece and people can always accuse you again.

Alex placed a hand on my arm. "Peter, we are innocent."

"Yes."

"We are relaxed."

"Mostly."

"And we are on our way to Bologna for pasta."

That settled it.

She smiled. "So unless Maria sends us footage of our house floating towards Turkey, we are not turning around."

I let out a long breath – the kind that empties your chest and fills your spirit.

"You're right," I said. "We keep going."

"Yes," she said, clicking her seatbelt with the authority of a woman declaring war or ordering dessert. "We go forward. Let Pefki sort itself out for a few days. They'll survive."

"And if they don't?"

She shrugged. "Then at least we'll have eaten well."

She reached across and squeezed my hand.

"Today, we go to Bologna."

I pulled back onto the road.

The mountains opened ahead of us and the sky lifted, just enough to let in a little light. The knot in my chest loosened – it didn't vanish, it just eased.

We were still leaving in a hurry. Still carrying the weight of what we'd driven away from. But now, the road wasn't only an escape.

It was also a direction.

And that felt like something worth holding on to.

CHAPTER SEVENTEEN

IN SEARCH OF SPAGHETTI BOLOGNESE

We were almost in Bologna when the mood in the car finally lifted.

"Okay," I said, stretching my neck as the skyline began to rise ahead of us, "Home of the famous spaghetti bolognese."

Alex didn't miss a beat. She gave me a sideways smile – the kind reserved for moments when she is preparing to educate me lovingly.

"That's what you think," she said. "Prepare to be enlightened. Italians don't call it that. To them, you've just committed a culinary crime."

"Again?" I sighed. "I feel I've only just recovered from the last accusation."

She patted my arm sympathetically. "Relax. Here, the police arrest you for parking, not pasta."

During our last stop we had done what any rational, exhausted travellers do: we booked an Airbnb in the very heart of Bologna. In a moment of pure, reckless optimism, we decided nothing could possibly go wrong.

And so, with the blind trust of people who have clearly learned nothing from experience, we followed the satnav straight into the historical centre, a labyrinth designed in the twelfth century specifically to confuse invading armies, delivery drivers, and modern tourists with rental cars.

The streets narrowed.

Then narrowed again.

Then narrowed further, achieving a width only previously known to shoeboxes.

"Are we sure this is a road?" I asked.

"It says it's a road," Alex replied.

"It looks like a hallway."

We crept forward. Stone walls brushed past the wing mirrors like disapproving librarians. The satnav chirped unhelpfully: "Turn right… now."

"Impossible," I muttered. "That's not a corner. That's a suggestion."

But Alex was unshakeable.

"Trust it," she said. "Italian roads make sense to Italians."

"Yes, but I'm English and traumatised."

We crawled deeper into the maze, under archways, between ancient buildings leaning conspiratorially towards each other, past scooters parked at angles that defied physics. A man on a bicycle overtook us with the pitying expression of someone who knew exactly how lost we were.

At one point, the road became so narrow I had to fold the mirrors in, and even then, Alex held her breath, as though her lung capacity might affect the car's width.

The satnav cheerfully announced: "You have reached your destination!"

We looked around. We were in what appeared to be someone's medieval living room.

"This," Alex said gently, "is not the Airbnb."

"No," I agreed, "but it might be the Airbnb's neighbour's panic room."

She laughed, and the tension evaporated.

"It's all part of the adventure," she said.

A narrow street? A confusing satnav? Mild, Italian spatial terror? We could handle this. We'd survived Pefki.

We pressed on, inch by inch, as Bologna rose, warm and red and ancient, all around us.

Adventure – real, delightful, non-watery adventure – awaited.

And then, suddenly, there it was.

The building stood at the corner of a small, cobbled square, its ochre walls catching the mid-day light, wooden shutters half-open as if in conversation with the street below. Balconies overflowed with geraniums, tumbling in bright red cascades that made the whole facade look quietly proud of itself.

The entrance was an arched doorway with a brass handle worn smooth by time, and inside, the air held a gentle mix of polish, old wood, clean cotton, and history – not museum history, but lived-in history; the sort that has cooked a thousand meals and heard a thousand late-night conversations.

There was no reception, just a key left in a little ceramic bowl and a note in elegant handwriting welcoming us by name. Still, it had presence, as if the walls themselves were observing us, deciding whether we'd behave. This was Bologna, after all.

Our apartment was on the third floor, reached by a lift the size of a confession booth. Two people could fit, provided they breathed in and had already made peace with each other. It groaned its way upwards like it had been installed sometime around the time of the Medici and had regretted it ever since.

The doors parted with a weary creak and we stepped into a proper old Bolognese apartment – the kind that still remembers horses outside and arguments inside.

The ceilings were impossibly high, with faded fresco traces and hairline cracks that looked like they had formed slowly over centuries from gossip, smoke, and too many dramatic hand gestures. The terracotta tiles underfoot were cool and uneven in places, polished by generations of feet, slippers, and the occasional furious stomp. Thick plaster walls held the room in a soft hush, keeping out the city noise as if the building had decided modern life was not welcome upstairs. Sunlight spilled in through tall, shuttered windows, cutting bright rectangles across the floor and warming the bed, which was dressed in crisp white linen like a promise.

Alex stood still for a moment, taking it in, and I did too, because even I could tell this was not just a place to sleep. It was a room with a past.

Alex leaned against the window, eyes soft. "Do you know," she said, "Bologna is called *La Grassa*, the fat one."

I nodded. "A city that celebrates appetite. My kind of place."

Outside, bells rang from a nearby church, mingling with the murmur of voices and the distant clatter of plates from the trattoria below. The smell of garlic and bread drifted up through the open window.

"Come on," she said. "Let's find out why they call it fat."

And with that, we stepped back into the streets, past colonnades that whispered of centuries, past shop windows gleaming with wheels of cheese and hanging prosciutto, following the scent of something wonderful, and the promise of dinner.

I had always imagined Bologna would smell of spaghetti bolognese, simmering tomatoes and garlic – an entire city perfumed by its most famous dish. Instead, it smelled of espresso, rain on warm stone, and the faint sweetness of bakeries. Everywhere we looked, cafés and trattorias offered *tagliatelle al ragù*, tortellini, mortadella, but nowhere, was there *spaghetti bolognese*.

We walked through the narrow streets, following our noses and our hunger. Porticoes arched above us like stone umbrellas, offering shade and echoes of centuries past. Every doorway seemed to lead to another treasure: a bakery filled with golden pastries, a wine shop glowing with bottles like stained glass, a butcher arranging hams the size of violins.

Finally, down a quiet side street, we found it: a small trattoria with a hand-painted sign, a few tables outside, and a smell that could make a saint hungry.

Inside, the walls were hung with framed family photos and faded football scarves. The waiter greeted us with the weary affection Italians reserve for people who clearly don't belong but mean well.

Alex ordered in Italian. "Two *tagliatelle al ragù*," she said confidently, "and whatever wine you recommend."

He smiled approvingly. "No spaghetti?"

She shook her head. "We know better."

He laughed and disappeared into the kitchen.

I'd always assumed, in Bologna, spaghetti bolognese would be everywhere – the national anthem in edible form. In my mind, every restaurant would have people sitting at pavement tables, wearing heroic white bibs, red sauce looping gracefully around their ears, and waiters hovering with buckets of Parmesan like confetti bearers at an Italian wedding.

But no.

Not a single plate of spaghetti bolognese was to be found. Not on the menus, not whispered in the backstreets, not even scribbled on a chalkboard outside a tourist trap. Nothing.

It was as if the whole city had disowned the dish that made it famous.

Alex, said, amused by my confusion. "It's *ragù.*"

"Ragù?" I said. "That's what you buy in a jar when you've given up hope."

She sighed, that patient, long-suffering sigh that has accompanied much of my education in life. "This is the real thing," she said. "What you call spaghetti bolognese is British fantasy food. The Italians would never serve spaghetti with meat sauce."

That hit me harder than I expected – a second culinary betrayal in my lifetime.

When I was about ten, my mother, bless her, was not what you would call an experimental cook. Variety was viewed with suspicion. Foreign food even more so. The nearest I ever got to "spaghetti bolognese" as a child came in the shape of spaghetti hoops: small, tinned circles swimming in a pinkish tomato liquid so thin you could have drunk it with a straw. The sauce was more suggestion than substance.

I honestly thought that was Italian cuisine.

For years, I believed spaghetti grew on trees, already shaped in hoops, and ripened quietly in tomato juice until someone from the factory picked them.

It wasn't until my late teens, when I started learning to cook things other than toast, that I realised I'd been misled. My childhood "spaghetti bolognese" was a culinary hallucination in a tin.

And now, decades later, here I was in Bologna, and it was happening again.

The truth landed like a wooden spoon across the knuckles: spaghetti bolognese doesn't exist in Bologna.

In Bologna, they make ragù, a slow-simmered sauce of beef and pork, onions, celery, carrots, wine, and patience. It's served only with tagliatelle, because spaghetti, apparently, is for amateurs and children.

Alex explained this as though she were reading from sacred scripture.

"So spaghetti bolognese," I said slowly, "is fake news?"

"Exactly," she said. "A British misunderstanding."

I felt strangely bereft, like a man discovering that Santa Claus had never owned a sleigh, or that fish don't actually have fingers.

But then the tagliatelle arrived, golden, soft, coated in a sauce so rich it seemed to hum quietly. It didn't shout, didn't slosh, didn't splash your shirt in triumph. It was measured, serious, the product of centuries of quiet Italian confidence.

I twirled a forkful, tasted it, and understood everything.

This wasn't spaghetti bolognese. It was truth in edible form – the kind that makes you question every meal you've ever eaten and every decision you've ever made in a supermarket.

Alex watched me, arms folded, smug in victory. "Well?"

I sighed. "Alright. Fine. Ragù it is."

She smiled. "See? Italy always wins."

And I had to admit, as I wiped the last trace of sauce from my plate, sometimes losing can be delicious.

We'd eaten magnificently: tagliatelle al ragù that melted into silence, bread that still breathed heat from the oven, and a red wine that convinced me that God had moved to Emilia-Romagna.

I could have died happy right there.

But Alex had other plans.

She sat back, eyes shining, and said in that tone that meant destiny had arrived, "I must learn how to make it."

I froze. "Learn what?"

"The real Bolognese," she said, as if announcing a calling. "I will ask the chef. He will show me."

"Alex," I said carefully, "the chef is Italian. In Italy. They don't teach people how to make it. They probably guard it like a family secret."

She ignored me, stood up, and waved the waiter over.

Within minutes, she was deep in conversation with the chef – a large man with forearms like hams and an expression that said *I have met your kind before.* His name was Lorenzo, and he spoke with the calm authority of a man who had spent his life surrounded by boiling things.

"You want to learn?" he asked.

"Yes," said Alex, smiling. "I am Greek. We invented sauce."

Lorenzo blinked. "You invented… what?"

"The principle," she said.

He looked at me helplessly, as if I might offer translation, intervention, or at least an apology on behalf of all foreign husbands. I did none of the above.

To my surprise, he sighed, nodded, and said, *"Va bene.* You may come to the kitchen. But only to *watch.* No touching."

"Of course," said Alex with angelic sweetness – the kind that always precedes trouble.

She handed me her bag like a queen divesting herself of earthly possessions and disappeared behind the counter with Lorenzo.

The kitchen wasn't hidden away, but part of the dining room itself: half stage, half confession booth. The diners could watch the cooking, and the chefs could watch the eating – a perfect circle of scrutiny.

From my table I could see Alex tying on an apron, already talking with her hands, and Lorenzo looking like a man who regretted all his life choices in one moment.

Lorenzo's kitchen was spotless, precise, and warm. Copper pans gleamed, knives lined up like obedient soldiers, and the air was heavy with the perfume of olive oil and patience.

"Va bene," said Lorenzo, "we begin."

He chopped onions with a rhythm that was almost musical. Carrots, celery, a small mountain of minced meat – pure simplicity.

Alex watched for exactly thirty seconds before frowning. "You forgot the garlic."

Lorenzo paused. "No garlic."

Alex blinked. "You mean not yet?"

"Not ever," he said firmly.

Her hand hovered in mid-air. "But… garlic is life."

He shrugged. "In ragù, it is death."

There was a silence so tense the onions stopped sizzling. Then Alex crossed her arms. "That is nonsense."

Lorenzo's eyebrow twitched. "Madame, this recipe is four hundred years old."

Alex was visibly shaken when she learned that garlic was not part of the recipe. It was as if someone had told her that the sky was optional, or that Greece had decided to stop being sunny.

"In Greece," she said, hand to heart, "everything begins and ends with garlic. Without it, food has no soul."

Lorenzo shrugged in the quiet, weary way of a man who has fought many such wars. "No garlic," he said firmly, as if reciting law.

She made a small sound at the back of her throat, the prelude to a longer argument that never quite arrived. She let it pass. Temporarily.

He added wine. White.

Alex inhaled. "White wine?"

"Yes."

"With meat?"

"It lifts," he said.

"It interferes," she replied.

He laughed softly, still stirring. "You Greeks," he said, "you want the food to announce itself."

"And you Italians," she said lightly, "prefer it to whisper."

I stayed where I was, glass in hand, saying nothing. This was not my conversation.

Lorenzo tasted the sauce, nodded to himself, and lowered the heat. Alex leaned in slightly, still careful not to cross an invisible line. "You stir gently," she observed.

"Yes," he said. "Ragù does not like being rushed."

"That's where we differ," she said. "In Greece, food likes emotion."

He finally looked at her properly and smiled. "It has emotion," he said. "It just doesn't raise its voice."

Around us, the kitchen carried on as normal. Orders were called. Plates went out. Nothing paused for philosophy.

After a while, Lorenzo wiped his hands and stepped back.

"The important thing," he said, not lowering his voice, "is not what you add."

Alex waited.

"It's knowing when to stop touching it."

She considered this, weighing it carefully.

"That's not very dramatic," she said.

He shrugged. "It works."

She smiled then, recognising a man who would not be persuaded and did not need to be. No recipes changed hands. No boundaries crossed. Just two people who took food seriously, acknowledging each other and moving on.

As we left, Alex leaned towards me.

"It still needs garlic," she said.

"I know," I replied. "But at least you didn't try to fix Italy."

She smiled. "Not today."

By the time we left, they were friends, or perhaps sparring partners who had agreed to a ceasefire. Lorenzo handed her a small jar of his sauce and said, "No garlic."

She smiled sweetly. "I will respect your tradition," she said, slipping a bulb of garlic into her bag.

After dinner we drifted out into Bologna, pleasantly overfed and slightly disoriented, as if the city had provided more than was strictly necessary. The streets were alive in that unforced way Italian cities manage so well. Students lounged on church steps, arguing philosophy and weekend plans with equal conviction. Music spilled out from beneath the arcades. The smell of roasting coffee followed us everywhere, persistent and reassuring.

Somewhere between a violinist and a bar that appeared to specialise entirely in standing room, Alex's phone rang. Maria.

She had waited, which in itself was ominous.

I answered, already braced. Maria exhaled heavily, the sound of a woman who had survived an event and intended to provide a full account.

"Yes, yes, it is calming now," she said. "The road river has stopped running. Only a few puddles left. So, fine. For now."

I allowed myself a careful breath of relief.

Then she asked, inevitably, what we had been doing.

"Eating," I said. "In Bologna."

There was a pause. Not alarm. Assessment.

"And Alex?"

I looked at Alex beside me, strolling happily, entirely at ease with herself and the evening. "Earlier," I said, choosing my tense carefully, "she was talking to the chef."

Another pause. Longer this time.

"Talking how?" Maria asked.

"Thoughtfully," I said. "With observations."

The silence that followed was profound.

"You let her near an Italian kitchen," Maria said slowly. "In Italy."

"Well, yes."

Her intake of breath was impressive.

"Peter," she said, with genuine concern, "these people invented pasta. You cannot simply interfere."

Alex took the phone from me.

"Maria," she said calmly, walking on, "it was cultural exchange."

"Cultural betrayal," Maria replied. "They have rules. Sacred rules. What is next? Opening a souvlaki stand in Rome?"

Alex smiled. "It could work."

There was a long, wounded silence.

Then Maria asked, quietly, "Tell me something. Did he add oregano?"

"No," Alex said.

Another pause.

"And garlic?" Maria asked.

"No."

Maria groaned, long and low, like a woman mourning the steady decline of civilisation.

"*Madre mou*," she said. "You people travel too much."

She hung up, clearly convinced that Italy, like Greece, now required monitoring.

We continued on through the city, untroubled. The evening wrapped itself around us, generous and unhurried. Alex slipped the phone back into her bag, entirely unrepentant.

Beside me, she walked with the easy confidence of someone who believes, deeply, that most things are improved by conversation. And perhaps, occasionally, by restraint.

For the moment, Bologna seemed to agree.

Back in the restaurant, I imagined Lorenzo stirring his family's century-old sauce and pausing thoughtfully. *Not bad… needs garlic.*

We still had no plan when we left Bologna.

That, oddly, had become the plan.

Over breakfast, maps spread across the table and coffee going cold between us, we talked without really deciding anything. Not in the decisive way people usually mean when they say they're "planning". More in the gentle, speculative way of people who had discovered that the road itself was doing some of the thinking for them.

"We could go anywhere," Alex said, tracing a finger northwards on the map.

I looked at the line we had already drawn without meaning to. Greece. Italy. Further than we'd ever driven from home before without an actual destination. Far enough that it no longer felt like a detour. It felt like a story that had slipped its leash.

"How far is too far?" I asked.

She smiled. "We'll know when we feel it."

The village felt a long way off now. The river. The arguments. The endless phone calls. Even Maria's voice, which still found us daily, had lost some of its power. We could answer. Or we could silence the phone, sit back, and let the scenery do the talking for a while.

That, I realised, was new.

We were no strangers to distance. We'd driven overland from the UK to Greece before, and back again, ticking off countries with the quiet efficiency of people who know where they're going and when they're meant to arrive.

We were used to movement like that. Flights back and forth. Timetables. Return journeys booked before the outbound one had properly begun. Purposeful travel. Sensible travel.

This was different.

This had no edges.

The distance wasn't measured in borders or motorway

signs, but earned mile by mile, slowly enough that it crept up on us. One morning you're dealing with village drama and swollen rivers, and the next you're drinking coffee in Bologna, suddenly realising you've driven here from Greece.

There was something liberating in that lack of direction. No deadline tugging at the wheel. No obligation waiting at the other end. Just road, choice, and the quiet pleasure of not knowing exactly where we'd sleep next.

And we were loving it.

Alex studied the map again. "Lake Como," she said, tapping the page lightly. "It looks beautiful."

"Doesn't everything look beautiful on a map?" I said.

"Yes," she replied, "but this looks calm."

"From there," she added, almost casually, "we could cross into Switzerland. Just to have a look around."

Just to have a look around.

The phrase hung there, absurd and liberating at the same time. Greece felt very far away now.

The next morning, we packed, paid, and loaded the car without ceremony. Just a shared glance that said, *why not.*

As we drove north towards Como, Bologna slipped quietly behind us, a warm blur of red stone, coffee, and slow-cooked wisdom receding into the distance.

And ahead of us, the road stayed open.

CHAPTER EIGHTEEN

Nemesis Has Questions
(and Pefki Has Feelings)

Nemesis was at it again.

You didn't need an announcement. There was no official signal, no bell rung in the square. You simply felt it, a faint tightening in the village atmosphere, like the moment just before a summer storm when the air goes flat and the cicadas stop shouting.

People began lowering their voices when her name was mentioned. Conversations paused mid-sentence. Someone changed the subject to olives when she walked past. Another suddenly remembered an urgent errand in the opposite direction.

Logic, sensing trouble, quietly packed a small bag and left town.

We were, at that moment, somewhere between Bologna and Lake Como, gliding through mountain tunnels and service stations with improbably good coffee, blissfully unaware that back in Pefki the early stages of organised confusion were already underway.

The flood itself had come and gone, as these things do, leaving behind a trail of mud, rumours, and opinions.

The river had behaved badly, then retreated, apparently satisfied with the chaos it had caused. Our land sat there quietly, unchanged, as if nothing had happened at all.

There had been sightings of the police, of course. A rumour (from Maria) that the police had been seen in our garden. A patrol car slowing as it passed. A pair of uniforms pausing a little too long at the edge of the track. The unmistakable sense of people *sniffing around*, which in Greece is often the prelude to paperwork.

But this time, remarkably, nothing followed.

No knock on the door. No polite enquiries beginning with "just a few questions" – the kind that sound friendly and end with legal fees. No sudden interest in permits, boundaries, or decisions made twenty years earlier by someone else entirely.

Most surprising of all, no one had officially blamed us. Not yet, anyway.

In village terms, this was extraordinary restraint.

For once, disaster had passed without attaching our names to it, and that small mercy was enough.

But our house was not merely dry. It was offensively dry. The walls were clean. The garden upright. The basil flourishing with an arrogance that bordered on provocation.

It looked smug. And smugness, in Pefki, is dangerous.

Nemesis noticed the moment the water receded.

According to eyewitnesses – meaning Maria, the postman, two pensioners, and a man who only appears when drama reaches critical mass – Nemesis emerged from her house, planted her hands firmly on her hips, and began a slow, forensic survey of the scene.

Her garden was a swamp. Her steps had last been seen migrating downhill. Her wall was broken again; now less a structure and more a suggestion. Her cat was furious.

Then she looked up. Our house stood there untroubled, as if it had been staged for a property brochure titled Foreigners *Who Somehow Escape Consequences*.

Something inside Nemesis fractured.

"This is IMPOSSIBLE!" she shouted, loud enough for the olives to lean in.

"How can *their* house be dry? The river came THIS way! Through MY land! MY wall! MY chrysanthemums!"

The audience assembled instinctively, forming the traditional five-metre semi-circle, close enough to hear everything, far enough to avoid involvement.

"It's their foreign drains!" Nemesis cried. "They call the water! They whisper to it from the mountain!"

George the fisherman scratched his chin. "I don't think water works like that."

Nemesis rounded on him. "YOU DON'T KNOW WATER!"

This was deeply unfair. George has known water his entire life. He works on it, argues with it, and occasionally curses it in several dialects.

Silence followed.

Maria stepped forward, voice calm, face already tired.

"Well," she said, "at least their house is safe."

Nemesis stabbed a finger towards the sky.

"This is an INSULT. My wall breaks and their house is dry? They must be doing something. Something… hydrological."

Maria sighed.

"Please don't use words you learned on the news."

But Nemesis was already accelerating.

"If they come back and tell me 'the water flows downhill'," she said, vibrating with anticipation, "I swear I will throw myself INTO the river!"

"It's gone now," Eleni offered.

"THEN I WILL WAIT!"

And with that, the village knew. This was no longer a rant. This was the opening move.

By this point, Pefki slipped seamlessly into its natural defensive posture: organised confusion.

Outsiders call it chaos. They are wrong. This is not panic.

It is choreography.

Everyone could see where this was heading.

Nemesis had tangled with us before. She hadn't won, not in the end, but it had cost us dearly. Thousands of euros in legal fees. Surveyors pacing our land with expensive equipment and solemn expressions. Reports written, rewritten, translated, misfiled, rediscovered, and quietly ignored. At one point, we even hired a drone pilot to trace the course of the river, as if gravity itself required aerial verification.

We had survived.

Barely.

And everyone in Pefki remembered it. They remembered the tension that lingered like damp after the water receded. They remembered how close it came to becoming irreversible.

Most importantly, they remembered that Nemesis does not forget.

So when she began again, measuring, asking, hinting, using words like *clarification*, *process*, and *procedure*, the village did not debate whether to act.

It acted.

An informal meeting took place at the café.

Nobody announced it. Nobody needed to. By mid-morning people had simply drifted in, one by one, drawn by the familiar sense that something required collective consideration. Chairs were pulled closer. Coffee arrived without being ordered. Someone shut the door, more out of habit than intent.

Maria stood near the counter, arms folded.

"We are not starting this again," she said.

There was general agreement.

The flood had been bad, yes, but it had passed. The river had risen, spilled where it shouldn't, and then retreated, leaving behind mud, damaged tempers, and competing explanations. What mattered now was what happened next.

And more specifically, what *didn't* happen next. Nemesis needed to be defused before she could begin to stir up trouble.

The story, as it circulated through the village, began to soften.

Walls that had collapsed were now described as "old walls".

Problems that appeared suddenly were said to have "always been there".

The flood itself became "heavy rain".

"The mountain decides," Dimitri said quietly, which settled the matter more effectively than any argument.

The police had been seen, of course. Driving slowly. Looking around. Asking nothing. In village terms, this was encouraging.

By lunchtime, the tone had shifted from outrage to acceptance. Not because anyone had changed their mind, but because there was no longer any energy in the accusation. Nemesis was still unhappy, but unhappiness on its own carries little weight.

Later that day, Alex called the café.

Maria put her on speaker.

"Hello," Alex said. "Just to say we're fine. We're still travelling."

Maria closed her eyes briefly, the way she does when taking on responsibility. "You are not coming back yet?"

"No," Alex said. "We're heading north."

There was some murmuring.

"How far north?" Theodora asked.

"We haven't decided," Alex replied. "We're taking it day by day."

Spiros shook his head slowly. "That is dangerous."

"Yes," Alex agreed cheerfully. "But enjoyable."

Maria sighed. "As long as you are safe."

"We are," Alex said. "And the house?"

"Standing," Maria said. "Still innocent."

That seemed to satisfy everyone.

When the call ended, the café returned to its normal rhythm. Coffee was finished. Chairs were pushed back. The matter, for now, was closed.

In Pefki, that is often how things are resolved. Not with conclusions, but with fatigue.

And north of Bologna, with the village momentarily quiet behind us, we continued on the road, grateful for the rare luxury of distance.

CHAPTER NINETEEN

ARRIVAL AT LAKE COMO

The road north wound gently through farmland and villages, the fields glinting with morning dew, the sky a soft, endless blue.

We stopped briefly at a petrol station where a man in an apron was roasting chestnuts beside the pumps. Only in Italy, I thought, could you buy both unleaded and lunch from the same counter.

Alex rested a hand on the car and looked out across the plains. "It's strange," she said. "The further north we go, the more it feels like we're climbing into a dream."

The flat fields gave way to hills, and the air grew cooler, cleaner, more deliberate. Villages appeared like brushstrokes: red roofs, tall church towers, washing lines that fluttered like flags of everyday life.

We arrived in Como by late afternoon, sunlight still glimmering over the mountains. The road narrowed, curling like a ribbon through stone archways and sudden tunnels that opened to views so beautiful you almost forgot to steer.

The satnav led us, with its usual confidence, through streets that seemed designed for donkeys rather than cars. Shopkeepers waved helpfully; one man even stopped sweeping to guide us with the air of someone rescuing lost tourists for sport.

Finally, the street opened into a small piazza, and there stood our hotel, a graceful old villa painted the colour of honey, its green shutters half open as though the building itself was stretching after a long nap.

The reception was tiled in marble and smelled of lemon polish and history. The receptionist, a woman with perfect posture and an even more perfect smile, handed us our key as if presenting a rare artefact.

"Your room has a view," she said, lowering her voice. "A very good view."

She wasn't wrong.

When we opened the shutters, the world seemed to spill into the room, the lake shimmering beneath us, the mountains rising like guardians on every side, their slopes scattered with villas and olive trees. The water below caught the last of the sun, turning gold for a heartbeat before fading into blue.

Alex stood by the window, silent. "It looks like it's breathing," she whispered.

The view from the balcony that evening was almost too perfect. The lake stretched before us like a vast mirror of silver and blue, rippling only slightly as if trying not to disturb its own reflection. The mountains stood in quiet majesty around it, their peaks softened by mist. Somewhere below, a church bell chimed, and the sound drifted across the water, gentle and forgiving.

For a long while, neither of us spoke. The air felt different here – clean, weightless, almost kind. But peace, I've learned, is never just about where you are; it's about what you've carried with you to that point.

Alex leaned against the railing, her eyes fixed on the stillness below.

"It's funny," she said quietly. "When I see water now, I don't just see beauty. I see danger. I hear it."

I knew what she meant.

Because for all the serenity of that Italian lake, some part of us was still standing knee-deep in that first flood back in Pefki.

It had begun with a noise we'd never forget: not thunder, not rain, but a deep, relentless roar. Like something ancient and angry had been woken from the mountain. Within minutes, the street had become a river, brown and furious, dragging branches, buckets, and parts of people's lives with it. The smell of mud and water, the crashing of rocks, the shouts of neighbours – it had all fused into one memory we couldn't wash away.

Even after the water receded, it left behind wreckage. The house and garden had been gutted, and covered in silt, furniture swollen and warped like the aftermath of a bad dream. But worse than the mess was the betrayal, the sense that something we loved had turned against us. That the rain and the earth itself had briefly decided we didn't belong.

For weeks afterwards, we'd lived with the scrape of shovels, and the smell of damp stone. We told ourselves we were strong, that it was just a setback, that people survive worse. And we did. But something shifted. You don't go through a flood without learning that everything – safety, comfort – can be taken from you in an hour.

That's what Alex meant when she said she "heard" it. It wasn't just memory. It was the echo of helplessness, the moment when even reason gives up, and all you can do is hold on and hope.

Now, as she stood gazing out over Lake Como, her posture softened. She had that look she gets sometimes, far away and utterly present at the same time.

"I could live here," she said quietly.

I smiled. "You say that everywhere we go."

She didn't answer. She was watching the light shift over the water, how the mountains reflected upside down, how even the ripples seemed deliberate. "No," she said finally. "Not everywhere. Here, it feels like… forgiveness."

And I understood.

Because Lake Como was everything the flood wasn't. Where the water in Pefki had been wild, this was calm. Where that storm had taken, this place gave. It gave silence, and order, and beauty without threat. It gave her back something I hadn't realised she'd lost: trust.

I watched as she reached out and touched the stone railing, tracing her fingers along it, as if grounding herself. Beyond it, the lake lay perfectly still.

"It's so calm," she whispered, looking out across the water. "I keep expecting the lake to move."

"It does," I said. "Just quietly."

She smiled, and the strain had eased from her face. The weariness was gone from her eyes. What remained was relief, steady and unguarded.

We sat together in silence as the light faded. Boats crossed the lake like slow-moving thoughts, leaving soft trails behind them. We caught the smell of bread baking, the laughter of people at dinner.

"This," she said, gesturing at the lake, "is how I imagine peace feels."

I nodded. "It's hard to believe water can do both: destroy and heal."

"Everything can," she said simply. "Even people."

We didn't speak again for a while. The memory of the flood lingered, as it always would, but it didn't feel sharp any more. It felt... distant. Like an old scar you can finally touch without flinching.

Later, as we walked down towards the water's edge, the air cooled and the lights of the village shimmered on the surface of the lake. I watched Alex take it all in, the reflections, the faint lapping of the waves against the stones, and I realised she wasn't just admiring the view. She was measuring it against what had come before, comparing two worlds: one that had broken her heart, and one that, slowly, was stitching it back together.

We hadn't been there when it happened.

That almost made it worse.

We were away from the house when a neighbour sent us the video. Floodwater surging where our kitchen should have been, the camera shaking, the sound distorted by rain and panic. Watching it on a phone screen, far from the village, far from the noise, made it feel unreal and intimate at the same time. Like seeing your own life from the outside.

Alex turned to me suddenly.

"You know," she said, "when the water came into the house that day, even though we weren't there, I thought it would never end. Watching it, I kept thinking, this is what forever feels like. Loud. Endless."

I nodded. "And now?"

She looked back out at the stillness below.

"I listen for it," she said. "Even when it's quiet. Now," she said, looking out across the lake, "I think forever might feel like this too: quiet and full of light."

And she was right.

For all our travels, the borders crossed, the ferries, the

wasps, the floods – it was that moment by the lake that made it all make sense. We hadn't left Greece just to escape the damage; we'd left to remember what it felt like to be unafraid of the world again.

I reached for her hand. She squeezed mine, and I felt that small, impossible shift – the one that turns memory from a wound into a story.

Behind us was chaos.

Before us, peace.

And somewhere between them, floating quietly on the surface of a lake in Italy, was us – still learning how to trust the water again.

We walked down to the waterfront just as the lights were coming on. The air was cool, perfumed with pine and woodsmoke. Along the promenade, couples strolled hand in hand, their laughter echoing softly across the water.

A waiter outside a small trattoria waved us in. "Come," he said, "you look hungry, and a little lost."

He was right on both counts.

We ate outside, the tables lit by small candles flickering in the breeze. The food was simple – grilled lake fish with lemon, a salad so fresh it still tasted of sun, and a carafe of house wine that seemed to refill itself when we weren't looking.

"See?" Alex said, smiling. "No rush. No noise. Just peace."

I raised my glass. "To peace," I said.

She laughed, that pure, musical laugh that always makes strangers turn their heads, and for a moment the entire evening seemed to pause just to listen.

We lingered long after the restaurant had emptied, watching the moon lift itself over the water like a silver coin.

The morning light at Lake Como has its own personality: gentle, elegant, never in a hurry. Sunlight slid between the shutters, laying soft golden stripes across the bed.

From outside came the faint sounds of life beginning: the clink of cups on saucers, the creak of boats on their ropes, the murmur of voices greeting the day.

Alex was already at the window, hair tangled by the breeze, a cup of coffee in her hand. "You need to see this," she said.

I joined her, still half asleep. The lake lay perfectly still, a mirror of sky and mountain, so calm that even the birds seemed to hesitate before flying across it.

"This is why people fall in love with Italy," she said.

I nodded. "It's also why they never leave."

Breakfast was served on a terrace draped with vines; the kind of place where even the toast looks photogenic. The air smelled of warm bread, fresh coffee, and the faint perfume of wisteria.

We ate slowly, as if hurrying might insult the view. Below us, the lake shifted from silver to blue, the sunlight breaking into ripples.

After breakfast, we wandered down to the dock and boarded one of the small ferries that glide across Como like lazy dragonflies. The air was cool and clean – the kind that makes you breathe deeper.

We stood by the railing as the boat pulled away, leaving a trail of silver foam behind. Villages passed like postcards, pastel houses clinging to the hills, laundry flapping in the sun, church bells chiming from towers that looked far too fragile to survive a breeze.

Bellagio appeared like a mirage, cobbled lanes climbing between flower-covered walls, shop windows filled with silk scarves, gelato counters glowing like stained glass.

We wandered without aim. Alex stopped at every balcony to take photos, every cat to offer conversation, and every bakery to sample something "just for research".

Eventually we found a small café perched above the lake. The waiter brought us cappuccinos that smelled like heaven and sugar-dusted pastries that left our fingers sticky and happy.

Alex looked out across the water. "You know," she said, "life could be this simple."

"It already is," I said. "You just have to sit still long enough to notice."

By late afternoon, we were back on the ferry. The lake was calm again; the air tinged with that golden stillness that comes before evening.

Alex rested her head on my shoulder, and for a while we didn't speak. The only sound was the hum of the engine and the soft slap of water against the hull.

I looked out at the reflection of the mountains, the sky turning slowly to amber. It struck me then how far we'd come, not just across Italy, but through everything that had brought us here.

Alex squeezed my hand. "Promise me we'll always keep travelling," she said.

I smiled. "We will. But let's wait until tomorrow."

She laughed quietly, the sound floating out over the water.

And as the ferry slid back towards the dock, I realised that journeys like this never really end. They just change shape, from roads to memories, from mountains to moments.

For now, it was enough to sit there, still, watching the lake shimmer, knowing that tomorrow would bring another road, another story, and another chance to fall in love with the world all over again.

CHAPTER TWENTY

GOOLIES, HOLY WATER, AND THE CAR WASH

We were back in our hotel room at Lake Como, the day finally catching up with us.

Not dramatically. Not with exhaustion so much as agreement. The sort of tiredness that arrives politely, waits until you sit down, and then places a hand on your shoulder to suggest that perhaps now would be a good time to stop moving.

Shoes had been abandoned by the door without ceremony. One lay upright, the other tipped onto its side, as if they had disagreed about who had done more work. The curtains were half drawn, not to shut anything out, but to soften the light that still lingered over the lake. Outside, the water had settled into evening calm; the kind that makes you lower your voice instinctively, even when no one has asked you to.

Alex sat on the edge of the bed, scrolling through photos from the day. Every now and then she stopped, tilted the screen slightly, and smiled. I lay back, arms folded, attempting to convince my legs that walking was no longer required of them and that they could officially stand down.

This was when Alex's phone rang.

Maria.

There was a pause while Maria gathered herself. This is always worth waiting for. Maria does not rush announcements. She assembles them carefully, like furniture that will later need to be rearranged.

"It's not all bad news," she said at last, her voice softening. This was the tone she used when she believed what followed might provoke mixed emotions. "Kostas, you know. The man with the taverna by the river. He's doing very well."

Alex raised an eyebrow. This was muscle memory by now.

"How?" she asked.

Maria released a triumphant sigh, the sound of someone unveiling a solution they were particularly proud of.

"He's turned his taverna into a car wash."

Alex and I looked at each other.

There are moments when Greece explains itself perfectly, without needing additional context or translation.

"A car wash," Maria repeated, warming rapidly to her subject. "The pipe that feeds water from the mountain into his fish tank came loose during the storm. Now it sprays across the car park like a fountain. Cars were already covered in mud, so people started stopping. Kostas put up a sign. Taverna Plimmyra. Eat and Rinse."

Alex laughed. Properly laughed. The kind of laugh that starts somewhere low and has to work its way out.

"He's charging them?" she asked.

"Of course he's charging them," Maria replied, faintly offended by the question. "One euro for a rinse. Two euros for wax. If you order lamb chops, the wash is free. People are queuing down the road. It's chaos."

I could picture it instantly. Kostas in his apron, half cook, half entrepreneur, directing traffic with the confidence of a man who has discovered a new purpose. One hand waving cars into position, the other turning souvlaki on the grill. Children shrieking as they ran through the spray. Men standing around offering advice that no one had requested. Cats sitting on higher ground, watching puddles that smelled faintly of grilled fish with profound disapproval.

"The priest came to bless it," Maria added. "He got soaked. Now everyone says it's holy water."

"And the health inspector?" I asked.

Maria hesitated, just long enough to enjoy what came next.

"He came today," she said. "Twice. Once to get his car

washed, and once for lunch."

Alex and I burst out laughing.

The health inspector was universally disliked. Not in a dramatic or personal way. Just communally. The sort of dislike that settles quietly across a village and never quite shifts. He was one of those men who arrived with a clipboard and the unshakeable belief that rules should apply equally, regardless of geography, weather, or common sense.

His job was to enforce European regulations on village tavernas that still judged cheese by smell and cucumbers by personality. He did not enjoy this. Nor did anyone enjoy him.

In theory, Maria said, the car wash should have been shut down immediately. Washing vehicles beside food preparation was ambitious, even by village standards. There were questions of hygiene. Questions of water pressure. Questions no one really wanted answers to.

In practice, the inspector's car emerged spotless.

Not just clean, but transformed. Mud removed from every crevice. Dust banished from places it had lived in for years. The inside smelled faintly of soap, lemon, and something that might once have been pine. This service, Maria noted pointedly, was provided free of charge.

While the car was being attended to, Kostas insisted the inspector sit down. A plate of lamb chops appeared. Hot, perfectly cooked, seasoned without apology. Bread arrived. Wine followed. It would have been impolite to refuse.

At first, the inspector ate carefully, as if reminding himself of his official role. Then, Maria said, something shifted. He relaxed. He reached for a second chop. By the time he finished, he declared them the best lamb chops he had ever tasted, which was not something he was known to say lightly.

This, Maria explained, softened his views considerably.

By the time he left, the car gleamed, the plate was empty, and several regulations had quietly lost their urgency.

So when Maria said he had come twice that day, we understood perfectly.

Once to inspect.

And once to eat.

"At least everyone's happy," Maria said contentedly. "The road is clean. The taverna is full. And for once, nobody's arguing about the flooding. They're too busy polishing their bumpers."

When the call finally ended, we sat in silence.

Across the lake, the hills rose gently, vineyards stitched into their slopes with patient care. Poppies caught the last of the light. Everything looked orderly. Contained. A landscape that obeyed itself.

Alex reached for my hand.

"You realise," she said quietly, "even when we leave Greece, Greece doesn't leave us." She smiled, already thinking ahead. "So. Switzerland."

"To Switzerland," I said. "Where the clocks work and the rivers know their place."

Later, as we packed, Maria rang again.

This is rarely a neutral development.

"Tourists are getting lost everywhere in North Evia," she announced, with the quiet satisfaction of someone reporting a recurring natural event. "Everywhere."

"That's normal," I said. "People have always got lost."

"No," she corrected me. "This is different. They all have the same thing now. In their cars. Goolies maps."

"Google Maps," Alex said gently.

"Yes, that," Maria replied. "It tells them where to go, where to eat, how to get there. Whatever happened to asking directions?"

It was a fair question.

Asking directions in Greece is not about accuracy. It is about connection. You ask three people and get four answers, but you also get opinions, local history, commentary on the weather, and sometimes a chair and a coffee. Google Maps removes all of that and replaces it with a calm voice that has never met a Greek road in its life.

Alex and I had already learned the hard way that Google Maps does not work particularly well in Greece.

The problem is not the technology. The problem is Greece.

Most Greek roads were not built. They were discovered. The original road engineers were goats and shepherds, who worked on the principle that the quickest way home was the way that got you there before dark, regardless of cliffs, rocks, or common sense. Over time, these paths were adopted by humans, then donkeys, then eventually local councils who added a thin layer of tarmac and called it infrastructure.

Some of these routes became respectable roads, complete with white lines and signs that suggested authority. Others were given gravel and encouragement. The rest were left exactly as they were.

According to Google Maps, there is no distinction. A goat track clinging to the side of a mountain is considered just as valid as a four-lane motorway. Google believes in equality.

This is how we once found ourselves following what Google described as a scenic route to an ancient monastery.

The road narrowed. Then it stopped being a road and became an idea. We bounced along a dirt track no wider than a shopping trolley, rocks scraping underneath, the edge dropping away into a gorge that appeared to lead directly to the centre of the earth.

"Are you sure this is right?" I asked, gripping the steering wheel as if it might file a complaint on my behalf.

"Google says we're nearly there," Alex said cheerfully.

We turned a corner and found a cow standing in the middle of the track, calm and immovable.

I looked at her. She looked at me. She did not move.

I took this as advice.

Later, Maria explained what was now happening at scale.

People wanting to visit the ancient olive tree above Artemisio were following their Goolies straight up the mountain, through George's freshly ploughed field. The potholes were impressive: each one roughly the size of a traditional olive-oil-press basin. Deep enough to swallow a car and most of its optimism.

Cars got stuck.

Deeply stuck.

George adapted.

He stopped ploughing. He waited with his tractor. He charged for rescues. He dragged the cars down the mountain to Kostas's taverna/car wash.

George got paid for the rescue. He got commission from Kostas. Kostas got customers. The tourists got stories. The cars got cleaned.

Everyone was happy.

Except Google.

Somewhere, an algorithm was quietly recalculating, entirely unaware that it had just created a local economy.

Alex listened, nodding thoughtfully.

"So," she said, "the goats design the roads, the tourists follow the phones, and the villagers get rich."

"Yes," Maria said. "This is progress."

I looked at Alex.

"Shall we turn Google Maps off?" I asked.

She considered it carefully. "No," she said. "It's doing very well for George."

And that, I realised, is Greece in miniature.

Chaos, yes. But useful chaos. The kind that feeds people,

rescues strangers, and turns ancient problems into modern solutions, preferably involving tractors.

Somewhere in North Evia, a goat is still choosing the quickest way home.

And somewhere behind it, a tourist is following their Goolies, confident they are on the main road.

CHAPTER TWENTY-ONE

OVER THE ALPS

April had arrived quietly, bringing with it a crisp new light – that pale, promising shimmer that makes even the cold feel hopeful. We left Lake Como early, following the curves of the road northward. The sky was high and clear, the air sharp with the scent of pine and melting snow.

The climb began almost immediately. Each bend revealed another postcard, waterfalls tumbling beside the road, slate-roofed villages clinging to hillsides, and forests dusted in white like sugar on a cake. Higher and higher we went, the air thinning, the valleys deepening, until the world was nothing but blue shadows and bright snow.

Alex was entranced. "It's like driving through silence," she said softly.

It was. Even the car seemed to understand, whispering gently as if afraid to disturb the peace.

Every now and then a train would glide past along the mountainside, silver, precise, almost unreal in its grace. I'd always imagined the Alps to be wild and daunting, but there was something deeply human about them too: tidy woodpiles, smoke curling from chimneys, small churches perched on impossible ledges as if held there by faith alone.

We hadn't really formed a plan for getting home yet.

Switzerland, at that point, was not a destination. It was a curiosity. A place we would dip into, admire politely, then retreat from with stories and photographs. We told ourselves we were only crossing the border to have a look around, perhaps stop for coffee, maybe find somewhere to stay the night, and then sit down properly and work out what came next.

This was how all our plans were being made now. Lightly. With room for escape.

Alex unfolded the map again. "Let's just see," she said. "One day. Maybe two."

"And then?" I asked.

"Then we decide," she replied, which sounded reasonable, until I remembered this was how we'd ended up in Lake Como.

The border itself was wonderfully unceremonious. A nod. A small charge. A sense that things here were expected to function. We drove on, the road smooth, the signs calm, the scenery quietly rearranging our expectations.

Mountains rose without drama. Lakes appeared where you felt they should. Everything looked composed, as if Switzerland had been tidied before we arrived.

We stopped at the first motorway service station, partly for fuel and partly to pretend we were about to make sensible decisions. I went in for a coffee and came back lighter in the wallet having felt like I'd paid for the espresso machine too, but strangely alert, as if I'd just bought clarity rather than caffeine.

"Peter," Alex said gently, seeing my expression, "you mustn't convert the prices into euros."

"I didn't," I said. "I converted them into astonishment."

She laughed, linking her arm through mine. "Think of it as a lesson in minimalism. We only need one coffee."

Alex was already scanning hotel options.

"For tonight," she said. "Somewhere with fondue."

"Of course," I said. "Naturally."

We sat there for a while, Swiss cars slipping past with quiet efficiency, many of them powered by clean electric motors that made little more than a courteous whisper as they went. Maps lay open on our laps, phones in our hands, all of us pretending this counted as planning.

In truth, we were doing what we had done all along.

Watching. Waiting. Letting the road make the first move and trusting ourselves to follow, one decision at a time.

We stood in the car park overlooking the valley, watching the sun strike the snow peaks until they glowed rose-gold. Even surrounded by strangers, there was a feeling of quiet belonging. Perhaps beauty, like love, makes you part of everything.

The road began to drop, winding through tunnels and across bridges so graceful they looked drawn by hand. The snow grew thinner, the valleys greener. Streams burst through the ice, tumbling beside the road in a glittering rush.

And then, suddenly, the landscape opened, and there it was: Lake Lucerne.

A sweep of deep blue water cradled by mountains, each peak still capped with snow that blushed pink in the afternoon light. Villages nestled at the water's edge, their roofs reflected perfectly in the still surface. The air smelled of woodsmoke and cold metal, clean and bright.

Alex pressed her hands to the window. "Look at it," she whispered. "It's like a dream that forgot to end."

I could only nod. The lake seemed both endless and contained, a perfect balance of motion and stillness, like a breath held by the world itself.

We found our small hotel near the old bridge, where the water ran so clear you could count the pebbles beneath it. The receptionist gave us a smile that said, *Welcome to Switzerland – please mortgage your house.*

After settling in, Alex announced her mission. "We're in Switzerland," she declared. "Time for fondue."

And so began our pilgrimage.

For an hour we wandered through Lucerne's cobbled streets, the scent of chocolate drifting from shop windows, church bells echoing against the hills. Every restaurant we passed seemed to serve everything *except* fondue. One offered sushi, another vegan curry, and one memorable place claimed to do "Fusion Alpine Tapas".

Alex refused to give up. "It's impossible that in all of Switzerland no one melts cheese any more."

Away from the noise and the better-lit roads, a narrow side street opened up in front of us. There we found it: a small wooden door beneath a carved bear, with the faint sound of laughter and the unmistakable aroma of bubbling cheese.

Inside, the air was warm and rich with the scent of wine, garlic, and comfort. A smiling waiter brought us a pot of molten gold and a basket of bread.

Alex's face lit up. "This," she said, stirring reverently, "is civilisation."

We dipped, we laughed, we watched the snow begin to fall again outside the window, soft flakes swirling down through the lamplight, settling on the cobbles and the lake beyond.

"Do you know," Alex said, "we've been chasing peace since the day we left Greece. I think we've found it, and it tastes of Gruyère."

I smiled. "Then let's stay until the pot is empty."

We walked back to the hotel through the quiet streets, our breath rising in clouds. The lake lay still beneath the stars, the mountains standing guard beyond. Somewhere, a church bell chimed nine times, echoing across the water.

The world felt steady again. Calm. Kind. Whole.

And I realised that somewhere along the road, without ceremony or decision, the balance had shifted. We weren't running from anything now. We were simply moving towards what came next.

And that was enough.

Then my phone buzzed.

Maria.

Nothing on earth can deflate serenity faster than those five letters.

"You're on speaker, were in the taverna, everyone can hear you."

"Hello, everyone!" Alex chirped. "We're in Switzerland now. Everything is beautiful. Don't worry, we're fine!"

Silence.

Then Maria exploded.

"SWITZERLAND?! Why another country?! Are you opening an embassy?!"

"You said you were coming home!" wailed Theodora.

"No," Alex corrected her, "we said we were heading north."

"North is EDIPSOS!" Spiros shouted. "North is NOT Switzerland!"

Arguments erupted: "Check the map!"

"Where is Switzerland?"

"I think it's above Turkey!"

"No, that's Bulgaria!"

"Maybe they were kidnapped by yodellers!"

Alex laughed gently.

"Don't worry. We're happy. Tell everyone we're safe."

Maria sighed deeply, the sound of a woman who has personally taken responsibility for two fully grown adults' wellbeing. "Well," she said, "at least Switzerland is safe. Nobody steals anything." She paused, then added proudly: "Here, you leave your washing on the line, and by morning it's dancing in someone else's garden. But they bring it back ironed. That's the difference between us and the Swiss."

Theodora crossed herself. "They will come home when the time is right."

Spiros nodded solemnly. "And when they do, we will tell them we never doubted them for a second."

Everyone agreed, despite having doubted us every second.

By evening, the story had evolved: half the village believed we were invited to a royal wedding on the Swiss border. Nemesis still believed our drains controlled the weather.

We heard later that at Mass that Sunday, the priest raised his hands and proclaimed: "They are far, but they are blessed. Wherever they go, they carry a small piece of Pefki with them."

A murmur of agreement filled the church.

And somewhere far away, sitting by a lake beneath the same sun, we clinked our coffee cups together, blissfully unbothered that back home, our absence had become the village's greatest miracle *and* its gravest concern.

Back at the hotel, we sat out on the balcony and watched the lights dance across Lake Lucerne. The air had a polite bite to it – the kind that nips your nose rather than assaults it. Everything below us shimmered quietly, as if Switzerland had decided to show off.

It was beautiful. Impeccably so.

Switzerland felt like the exact opposite of our Greek village. Where Pefki runs on instinct, memory, and raised eyebrows, Switzerland ran on schedules. Here, things happened when they were supposed to. Trains arrived exactly when promised. Roads made sense. Pavements were clean enough to eat from, though nobody did, because that would be strange.

It was all very impressive.

And slightly unsettling.

In Pefki, a normal day begins with the sound of a rooster that cannot tell the time, followed by Maria shouting someone's name from three houses away. A delivery van blocks the road while the driver stops for coffee. Someone argues about politics. Someone else argues about goats. The electricity might flicker. The water might stop. By lunchtime, you have already spoken to six people you hadn't planned to see and learned three things you did not need to know.

Here, by contrast, nothing unexpected happened at all.

We realised, with some surprise, that we were beginning to miss the chaos we had fled from. The noise. The interruptions. The gentle disorder that keeps you alert and slightly amused. Switzerland was calm in a way that made you lower your voice instinctively. It felt respectful. Civilised.

Too civilised.

We'd been away for almost two weeks now and still had no idea where we were going. We had left to clear our minds, and we had certainly managed that. Somewhere along the way, the clearing had turned into wandering, and the wandering had quietly become an adventure.

The sort you don't announce. It just happens while you're busy looking at lakes.

Alex unfolded the map on the small balcony table and studied it carefully.

"What about France?" she said.

I leaned over. "France?"

"Yes. Look. It's not far. We could be in Strasbourg by tomorrow."

I looked at the neat little line she'd traced with her finger, crossing another border as casually as popping out for bread.

"I've heard it's beautiful there," she added.

Below us, Lake Lucerne carried on glinting, perfectly behaved. Somewhere beyond it, another country waited, another language, another version of normal.

We sat there a while longer, letting the idea settle, already knowing that the map would win.

It always did.

CHAPTER TWENTY-TWO

THE JACKAL COMMITTEE

By the time Maria called again, we were already in France.

This, I would later understand, was unhelpful.

Distance gives you perspective, but it does nothing to protect you when a Greek village decides something requires attention, interpretation, and at least one notebook.

"Where are you now?" Maria demanded.

"On our way to France," Alex said, with the mild pride of someone who had crossed several borders without incident.

There was a sharp intake of breath.

"France?" Maria said. "Is that near Italy?"

"It's between Switzerland and somewhere else," Alex replied patiently.

A pause followed. Not panic. Not outrage. Calculation.

"Well," Maria said carefully, "you might want to come home soon. Things here are becoming… focused."

I took the phone.

"Focused how?"

"The police came."

That word landed heavily.

"Not about the flood," I said.

"Yes," Maria replied. "About that too. But now also about your jackal."

I closed my eyes.

"It is not my jackal."

Up until now, the jackal had been a novelty. A distraction. Something to talk about while stirring coffee. But once the police appear, novelty hardens into responsibility.

"What do they want?" Alex asked.

"They want it relocated."

"Where?"

Another pause.

"That," Maria said, "is the problem."

Nobody wanted it relocated to *their* land. The hills were suggested, then rejected once it became clear those hills technically belonged to someone's cousin. Athens, when consulted, proved spectacularly vague. Jackals, it seemed, were not something the system had prepared for.

So responsibility slid downwards, as it always does, until it landed where it always lands.

At the kafenio.

A sub-committee was formed.

Not the main committee – those are reserved for weddings, funerals, and olive oil disputes – but something more specialised. A *situation*.

Dimitri wanted to trap it and sell it to the zoo in Halkida. He knew a man with a van and a net. Nobody asked follow-up questions.

Theodora announced it was the reincarnation of her mother-in-law and forbade anyone from touching it until fifty euros were repaid.

The priest wanted to bless it.

The mayor wanted to fine it.

The schoolteacher suggested it might make an excellent mascot.

After three hours of discussion, voting, recounting, and shouting, the committee reached consensus on exactly one point.

The jackal was male.

This was obvious, apparently, because it ignored everyone and did exactly what it wanted.

Up to this point, Nemesis had been unusually quiet.

She had attended the meeting. She had listened. She had taken notes, not in a notebook, but in her head, which is far worse. She did not interrupt. She did not shout.

And that, in itself, worried Maria.

Nemesis waited until the room began to tire. Until coffee cups were empty and opinions had softened around the edges.

Then she spoke.

"This animal did not arrive by accident."

The room fell quiet.

Maria felt it immediately. "What do you mean?" she asked.

Nemesis folded her arms. "I mean it was summoned."

The word landed badly.

"Summoned how?" someone asked, carefully.

Nemesis gestured uphill, towards our land.

"It sleeps under their tree. It walks their fence. It appeared only after they began changing things."

"What things?" Maria asked.

"The land," Nemesis said. "The drains. The flow. You think animals don't notice?"

A murmur moved through the room. Not agreement. Interest.

"He feeds foxes," Nemesis continued. "Everyone knows this. What happens when you feed wild animals? They return."

"Foxes," Maria snapped. "Not jackals."

Nemesis shrugged. "You call it coincidence. I call it invitation."

Invitation was worse than accusation. Accusations can be argued with. Invitations suggest intention.

From that moment, the temperature shifted.

Nobody openly agreed with Nemesis, not yet, but fewer people laughed. Fewer people corrected her. The idea was allowed to sit there, quietly, like a damp patch on a wall.

By the next morning, the theory had evolved.

Some people said the jackal only appeared when we were away. Others suggested it was "guarding" our land. Nemesis was telling anyone who would listen that animals sense imbalance, and foreigners bring imbalance naturally.

The jackal itself remained uninterested. It wandered when it wished. Slept where it liked. Ignored committees entirely.

Maria called us late that evening. Her voice was lower now.

"She says you called it," she said.

"Called it how?" Alex asked.

"With food. With comfort. With foreign thinking."

I stared at the road ahead.

"And do people believe her?"

"They are listening," Maria said. "That's worse."

By sunset, the jackal, unregistered, untamed, and blissfully indifferent, had achieved what no human ever could. It had united Pefki.

Not in agreement. In argument.

Everyone agreed something must be done. No one agreed on what.

And through it all, the jackal slept peacefully under our willow tree, unaware that its presence had shifted from curiosity to accusation.

"Anything else?" I asked.

"Yes," Maria said. "Spiros has started a rumour that the jackal only appears when you leave the village. Some people think it's your spirit animal."

Alex laughed.

Maria did not.

"So please come home soon," she said. "It's eating more chickens, someone saw it nibbling a tortoise, and we are running out of committees."

I promised to call the mayor and hung up.

Alex was quiet for a moment.

"Maybe," she said, "we should head home."

I nodded. It made sense. It always did, right up until it didn't.

"Yes," I said. "Before the river remembers us."

She smiled faintly. "Before they decide we've caused something else."

We drove on in silence for a while, the road unwinding ahead of us, the landscape opening rather than closing. The further we went, the lighter everything felt.

Alex glanced at the map again. Then at the road.

"Not yet," she said.

I nodded. "Not yet."

And without making a ceremony of it, we kept going.

CHAPTER TWENTY-THREE

SPRING IN STRASBOURG

Morning light lay silver over the mountains, the air still sharp with the memory of snow, as we wound our way north through France.

The valleys below were softening. Green shoots broke through the melting drifts, streams sang beside the road, and every bend smelled faintly of thawing earth and pine.

Alex rested her head against the window, watching the snowfields slide past. "Spring is here," she said quietly.

"Yes," I said, "and it's chasing us north."

The drive from Switzerland to Strasbourg was long, but

it unfolded like a slow meditation. One country slipped gently into the next, language changing on road signs first, then the rhythm of the landscape. The neat Swiss chalets had given way to vineyards and flat fields dotted with red-roofed villages. Church spires replaced peaks, and the sky widened as if to welcome us.

At the border, a cheerful customs officer waved us through with a smile that seemed to say, *Enjoy France – but not too much.*

The moment we crossed into Alsace, the air seemed different, softer, scented faintly with bread and possibility. The villages glowed in pastel shades of cream, peach, and rose.

We stopped at a roadside café for lunch – a small, sunlit place with three tables, six cats, and a menu that looked like it had been written by a poet after several glasses of wine. The chairs were mismatched, the smell of coffee was strong, and the owner wore an apron that had known flour, fire, and possibly combat.

Alex, ever the linguist, took charge.

"*Buongiorno!*" she said cheerfully in Italian. "*Vorrei due panini e due caffè, per favore.*"

The man stared at her, expression blank.

She tried again, slower, as if he were hard of hearing. "*Due. Panini. Due. Caffè.*"

Nothing. Not even a blink.

Alex frowned, switched to English. "Two sandwiches and two coffees, please."

He frowned back, unimpressed.

"Try Greek," I suggested helpfully.

So she did. "*Dyo sandwits kai dyo kafedes!*"

That didn't work either. He shrugged, turned to me, and raised an eyebrow as if to say, *Is she all right*?

I shrugged back. "Sometimes," I meant.

After a brief silence, Alex turned to me with her hands on her hips. "Why is he pretending not to understand?"

"Maybe he's French," I said.

She looked scandalised. "We're in France?"

I nodded. "Just about."

"Ah," she sighed. "That explains everything."

Alex speaks Greek and English fluently, Italian confidently, a bit of Spanish, and the particular village dialect that exists only between the bakery and the café. I've seen her talk her way through airport security in three languages before I've even found my passport. But here, at this tiny French café, her powers met their match.

"Alex," I said, grinning. "I love this. I've watched you communicate in every language known to man. Finally – *finally* – you know what it feels like to be me."

She looked at me over her sunglasses. "I'm not having trouble with a language," she said coolly. "He is."

The café owner scratched his head, then wandered off. Moments later, he returned with two sandwiches and two coffees – exactly what she'd asked for.

Alex gave me a triumphant smile. "See? He understood perfectly."

I looked at the sandwiches. One was filled with something

mysterious and purple, and the other apparently contained lettuce.

We ate in silence for a while.

As we got up to leave, the café owner waved and said, in perfectly clear English, "Have a nice day."

Alex froze.

I smiled sweetly. "He *was* French."

She narrowed her eyes. "You're driving next."

And that was that: the first official truce of the language wars, sealed with caffeine and confusion somewhere in the French countryside.

By late afternoon, the road led us into Strasbourg – a city that looked like a dream built by two countries who couldn't decide which one loved it more. Half the streets smelled of croissants, the other half of sausages, and everyone spoke with the calm assurance of people who know they can order beer *and* crème brûlée without leaving town.

It's a place where French flair flirts shamelessly with German efficiency, where the buildings stand in jumbled alignment but wear window boxes like jewellery, and where you can't tell if the music drifting through the square is an accordion or a small brass band rehearsing for Oktoberfest.

In short, Strasbourg feels like what happens when France and Germany go on a date, drink too much Riesling, and wake up the next morning having built a cathedral together.

The cathedral rose like a sculpture of lace, its spire catching the last of the sun. The streets were lined with half-timbered houses leaning companionably towards one another, their windows overflowing with geraniums that had somehow survived the winter.

The canals glimmered between the old bridges, reflecting the lights of cafés just beginning to fill for the evening. It was the kind of place where time seems to walk at half speed.

We parked near the old quarter and strolled towards the water. The air smelled of woodsmoke and pastry, and a violin played nearby – slow, romantic, a little wistful.

Alex stopped on a bridge and rested her arms on the rail, looking down at the water sliding past below us. "It feels like a fairytale," she said softly.

"It does," I agreed. "Only this time we're not reading it or passing through. We've somehow wandered into the middle of it."

The moment was broken by hunger. Proper hunger. The kind that sharpens your thinking and lowers your standards; the sort that makes you briefly wonder whether paper maps might be edible if folded correctly.

Every restaurant we passed was full. Not "busy" – completely claimed. Tables packed tight, queues curling around corners, waiters moving at speed with the hollow-eyed focus of people who had not sat down since breakfast and no longer believed in time. The air was thick with food we could not reach.

We kept walking. Spirits dipped. Stomachs complained.

Then, just beyond the main square, past the souvenir shops and the last of the fairy lights, we noticed something that immediately felt wrong.

A restaurant with space.

Large plate-glass windows revealed tables that were mostly empty. Waiting. Outside stood a waiter, not rushing anywhere, cigarette in hand, watching the street with the tired calm of a man who had already seen how the evening was going to unfold.

"Are you open?" I asked, hopeful but cautious.

He exhaled a cloud of smoke that might have been a laugh. "Yes," he said in heavily accented English, then waved us inside with a gesture that felt halfway between welcome and a quiet warning.

At that point, hunger overruled curiosity.

Inside was… empty. Completely empty.

Not a single diner. No chatter, no clinking glasses, no background music. Just rows of tables, white cloths, polished cutlery, and the faint echo of our footsteps.

Alex hesitated. "Why is no one here?"

"Maybe," I said, "we're early."

It was early evening.

We sat anyway. Hunger had defeated logic.

Then the smell hit us. Not the warm, comforting scent of cooking, of garlic, herbs, or roasting meat. This was… different. A strange, lingering aroma somewhere between boiled cabbage, wet dog, and something that might once have been fish but had long since retired.

Alex wrinkled her nose. "Peter," she whispered, "something died in here."

"Let's not jump to conclusions," I said bravely. "It could just be the house special."

The waiter appeared silently beside us, as if summoned by despair.

"Menu," he announced, placing two laminated sheets before us. They were sticky.

I glanced down. It was a curious mix of French and German dishes – the kind of culinary diplomacy that probably ended more wars than it started.

Alex frowned. "What's *Boeuf à la Sauerbraten*?"

I scanned the description. "Apparently, it's beef… marinated in vinegar… served with sauerkraut… and—" I paused, "—a hint of danger."

She gave me *the look*. "Order something safe."

"Safe doesn't exist here," I muttered, eyeing the next item: *Poulet mit Kartoffelcreme und Mystery Sauce*.

When the food finally arrived, it looked… unresolved.

Alex's plate held something that may once have been chicken, now lacquered in a glossy brown sauce that caught the light in an unsettling way, like furniture polish. My "house speciality" arrived in a bowl and appeared to be having an identity crisis. It slumped. It sighed. It gave off the quiet confidence of something that knew it would not be eaten.

We stared.

"Maybe it tastes better than it looks," I said, because I am English and this is how we cope.

Alex did not answer.

I took a bite.

The meat collapsed under my fork, not with tenderness, but with surrender. The sauce was sweet, then sour, then salty, then metallic, like licking a coin you'd just found in a puddle. Somewhere in there was a flavour that might once have been ambition.

Alex tried a mouthful.

She froze.

That's never a good sign.

Her expression shifted slowly, thoughtfully, as if her brain were processing whether this was to be eaten, or thrown at the wall. She swallowed, very carefully, then leaned towards me and whispered, "Peter… I think this food is angry."

"It's not that bad," I said automatically, even as my fork began to bend away from the plate for safety.

Alex pushed her dish away, gently but firmly, the way you move something that might explode.

"What," she said quietly, staring at it, "is this?"

"I think," I said, "it began life as a chicken."

She narrowed her eyes. "No. Chicken has dignity."

"Perhaps," I offered, "a chicken that made poor choices."

Her fork hit the table. That was it. Alex stood.

Now, there are moments when being married to a Greek woman is a great comfort. This was not one of them. She marched towards the kitchen with purpose. Not shouting. Not waving her arms. Calm. Deadly calm. The kind that makes grown men suddenly remember childhood promises to their mother to behave.

I slid down in my chair and stared very hard at my plate, hoping to look foreign enough to be forgiven.

From the kitchen came voices.

Alex's first. Controlled. Precise. Greek in its most efficient form.

Then the chef. Defensive. Louder. French accent, possibly German confidence, definitely offended.

Alex replied, faster now. Sharper. The tone of a woman explaining something obvious to someone choosing not to understand it.

Hands appeared in the air. I couldn't see whose, but they were definitely gesturing.

A word floated out that I recognised: "**Απαράδεκτο**." Unacceptable.

There was a pause.

Then Alex again, slower now, each word carefully placed, like cutlery laid out for inspection. She wasn't insulting him. That was the clever part. She was explaining. Explaining what food should be. What chicken should aspire to. What human beings deserved when they sat down hungry.

The chef attempted a comeback.

Alex shut it down.

A chair scraped. Someone sighed. A pan was moved with unnecessary force.

Finally, Alex returned. She sat down, picked up her napkin, and folded it neatly.

"Well," she said calmly, "he is offended."

"Only offended?" I asked. "That feels like a win."

"He says the dish is inspired by French technique and German precision."

"That explains everything," I said. "Including the suffering."

She looked at my plate, then hers.

"I told him," she continued, "that if this is precision, it needs a doctor."

I nodded. "And if it's French, it needs an apology," I added.

The waiter appeared, eyes wide, smile gone.

"There will be no charge," he said quickly. "And perhaps… dessert?"

Alex smiled sweetly. "No, thank you. I need to survive the evening."

As we left, I glanced back at the table. The dishes sat there untouched, quietly reflecting on their life choices.

We stumbled out into the cold night air, gasping like divers resurfacing after too long underwater.

"I feel better," she said.

"So do I," I replied. "Morally restored."

She squeezed my arm.

"This," she said firmly, "is why you married a Greek woman."

I nodded.

"Next time," I said, "we eat somewhere with fewer ideas."

The funny thing was, we weren't hungry any more. Neither of us had actually *eaten*, but the experience itself had filled us in some deeper, more permanent way, like a spiritual fast gone wrong.

Alex took a deep breath. "We nearly died."

"Yes," I said. "But on the bright side, we won't need to eat again until tomorrow."

She nodded thoughtfully. "Next time, we queue."

"Next time," I said, "we will find a restaurant with people in it."

As we walked back towards the lights of the old town, our stomachs still empty but our souls oddly heavy, I found a small comfort in the thought that we'd finally found a restaurant with no queue, and now we knew exactly why.

Back at the restaurant, the waiter lit another cigarette, exhaled slowly, and waited for the next hopeful couple to appear.

It took a while to get the taste of dinner out of our mouths, but it soon became a memory as we walked through the quiet streets, our footsteps echoing softly on the cobblestones. The air was cool, the city hushed. Strasbourg's lights shimmered on the water, turning the canals into ribbons of gold.

We stopped by the cathedral, now shadowed and majestic under the moon. Alex reached for my hand. "Do you feel it?" she whispered.

I did. The calm, the grace, the pulse of a city that had lived through centuries and still found time to glow.

We stood there for a while, the night around us like a held breath. And I thought how travel, at its best, doesn't just show you new places; it shows you the parts of yourself you'd forgotten existed.

Alex smiled. "Tomorrow," she said, "we go west. Maybe to Burgundy. Or maybe we just see where the road takes us."

I smiled back. "Wherever it goes, I'll follow."

When we got back to the hotel, Alex got in the shower, humming cheerfully, while I sat on the edge of the bed, coffee in hand, and decided to consult TripAdvisor.

I was curious, morbidly so. The restaurant still haunted my taste buds like a bad dream, and I wanted to know whether anyone else had survived it.

It didn't take long to find it. The name alone was a warning: Le Coq et la Kartoffel – Traditional Franco–German Cuisine.

I clicked on *Reviews*. They were all one star.

- "An unforgettable experience. Mostly because my tongue still hasn't forgiven me." — *Pauline, Bristol*

- "Went in hungry, came out fluent in regret. The waiter told us the chef 'cooks with emotion'. We think it was anger." — *Hans, Munich*

- "My schnitzel arrived swimming in something that looked like tea and smelled like an argument. My partner ordered the fish. We're no longer together." — *Lucia, Milan*

- "Atmosphere: empty. Music: none. Smell: unforgettable. I think the wallpaper cried." — *Gareth, Cardiff*

- "We were told the sauce was a family recipe. I assume the family was cursed." — *Anonymous (for legal reasons)*

- "If this is fusion, then someone should defuse it." — *Pierre, Lyon*

- The final review stopped me in my tracks: "If vomiting were an Olympic sport, this place would host the finals. We were the only customers that night. The waiter was smoking outside, possibly for emotional support. The food smelled faintly of despair and the inside of a damp cupboard. My husband insisted it wasn't that bad. Bless him. He lies to protect me." — *Alex, Greece*

I stared at the screen. "She's quick," I muttered.

From the bathroom came her voice, echoing through the steam. "Did you find it?"

"Yes," I called back. "And apparently, we're part of the historical record."

She laughed. "Good. Someone had to warn the others."

I scrolled to the bottom of the page. Under "Owner Response", there was a single comment from the restaurant: "Thank you for your feedback. Our chef takes pride in innovation and is currently on extended leave."

I put the phone down and made a silent promise never to eat anywhere with a neon sign again.

The next morning, salvation arrived in the form of breakfast.

We stumbled down to the hotel dining room still carrying the emotional bruises of the previous night's culinary trauma, hollow-eyed, cautious, and quietly suspicious of anything that called itself "chef's choice". But then we saw it: a buffet that looked like heaven had decided to cater.

There were warm croissants so flaky they practically sighed when you touched them, baskets of bread that smelled of butter and forgiveness, and little glass jars of honey that caught the morning light like amber treasures. Platters of cheese and ham were laid out in soldierly precision, next to bowls of fruit so glossy they looked waxed. Even the coffee came in silver pots, dark and fragrant, with that reassuring hiss that says *everything's going to be alright now.*

Alex stopped in her tracks and whispered, "This… is real food; we're saved."

I nodded, misty-eyed. "And I shall never speak ill of France again."

We loaded our plates with cautious enthusiasm: eggs, pastries, a little jam, just in case it turned out to be a mirage. The first bite of croissant was pure redemption. After the horrors of last night's Franco–German Peace Accord in vinegar, this was divine intervention.

Alex leaned back in her chair, eyes half closed. "Now *this* is food," she said.

"Yes," I agreed solemnly. "And it doesn't smell like the river."

A waiter glided past with a basket of fresh baguettes. We took one, tore it open, and steam drifted out like a prayer being answered. I spread far too much butter, knowing I'd earned it.

By the time we reached the second pot of coffee, the nightmare of the previous evening had begun to fade. We could even joke about it now.

"Do you think last night's chef is still alive?" Alex asked.

"If he is," I said, "he's probably been reassigned to plumbing."

She laughed, that deep, genuine laugh that wipes the slate clean, and I felt human again.

We lingered over breakfast far too long, basking in caffeine, carbohydrates, and the quiet joy of survival. The city outside shimmered in the morning sun, the bells of Strasbourg cathedral chiming across the river.

We were glowing, from the coffee, the croissants, and the smug satisfaction of being once again culturally improved and nutritionally repaired.

As I poured the last of the coffee, I thought to myself: maybe, just maybe, life had finally calmed down. Of course, with us, it never does, but for one golden morning in Strasbourg, I could almost believe it.

CHAPTER TWENTY-FOUR

NEWS FROM HOME

The village never sleeps.

It pauses, yes. It slows. It sits down for long periods with coffee. But it does not sleep.

Even several countries away, we remained thoroughly informed. This was largely due to Maria, who regarded the telephone not as a device, but as a responsibility.

Her calls had changed tone now. The urgency had gone. No disasters. No accusations. Just updates. The kind that arrive wearing the clothes of concern but are really there for entertainment.

"Nothing important has happened," she said one afternoon, which is how you know something already had.

"That's good," I said carefully. "What kind of nothing?"

The village tavernas, it turned out, were beginning to think about summer.

This did not involve planning in the modern sense. Nobody was redesigning menus, consulting trends, or photographing plates from above. It was more a period of quiet reflection, conducted over coffee, cigarettes, and the occasional frown directed at the middle distance.

Last year, Adonia had been asked for hamburgers.

This request arrived via a tourist, translated twice, and treated with the seriousness usually reserved for medical news. Apparently, the visitor explained, there was a place called McDonald's where people ate meat inside bread and were somehow happy afterwards.

Adonia listened very carefully.

Clients were clients. If tourists wanted meat in bread, then meat in bread they would have.

She began sensibly, using her meatball recipe. Good meat. Onion. Herbs. Love. She placed it carefully inside a bread roll – the sort of roll only used when something foreign is being attempted.

She tasted it.

It was… fine.

This worried her.

She threw the roll away, made another meatball, and this time wrapped it in a rolled pita. She added tomato, onion, a little salad, and stood back.

This, she liked.

She called her son over.

"Nico," she said. "Try this."

He took a bite, chewed thoughtfully, and looked up.

"Mother," he said gently, "this is souvlaki."

She frowned. "No, it's a hamburger."

"No," he said patiently. "It's souvlaki."

She considered this.

"Tourists like hamburgers," she said. "They understand hamburgers."

"Yes," Nico replied, "but this is still souvlaki."

She waved a hand. "Fine. Then we call it Mc-Souvlaki. They will love it."

And that, as far as Adonia was concerned, was innovation concluded.

Not everyone was experimenting.

"Well," Maria said later, lowering her voice slightly, "Theodora had decided to change one dish on her menu."

This is not something done lightly.

For twenty years, her stuffed peppers had been exactly the same. Green peppers. Rice. Herbs. A flavour profile requiring no explanation. People ordered them without looking.

Last week, she used red peppers. This caused unease.

"Too sweet," Spiros said.

"Too modern," someone else muttered.

One man asked, very carefully, if it was temporary.

Theodora said nothing. She simply stood behind the counter, arms folded, daring anyone to complain again.

By the following day, the peppers were green again. Balance had been restored.

Elsewhere, Dimitri briefly considered adding quinoa to a salad.

"What is quinoa?" someone asked.

"Bird food," another replied.

The idea did not survive the morning.

Across the village, menus quietly returned to their proper state. Moussaka remained moussaka. Souvlaki stayed where it belonged. Anything wrapped in pita was called exactly that, regardless of what tourists thought it was supposed to be.

Summer, it was agreed, could come.

The village was ready.

As long as nobody asked for pizza with pineapple.

"This," Maria said, "is how democracy works."

There was also news of Yiannis, who had purchased a drone. No one knew why.

The drone had been flown once, briefly, over the olive groves, before disappearing into a tree belonging to someone Yannis did not speak to. Negotiations were ongoing. The drone remained in the tree.

"We think it is happier there," Maria said.

And then, of course, there was gossip. Not malicious. Not cruel. Just informational.

Someone was thinking of repainting their shutters.

Someone else had bought a new coffee machine, which made a noise "like an angry goat".

There was a rumour that a woman from the next village had been seen wearing trousers on a Sunday. This was reported with concern, but no follow-up.

Through it all, the village continued exactly as it should. Coffee. Arguments. Sun. Shade. The slow rhythm of nothing much happening, which is the whole point.

At the end of one call, Maria paused.

"When are you coming back?" she asked.

"We don't know yet," Alex said.

"That's fine," Maria replied. "Nothing is changing."

She meant it as reassurance. She was right. We hung up and sat quietly for a moment.

Back home, Theodora was watching her kitchen like a hawk. A drone rustled gently in an olive tree. Life was proceeding at exactly the right pace.

Somewhere along the way, the village had slipped out of my thoughts.

It was managing perfectly well without us. Adapting, improvising, reorganising itself in ways that didn't require our supervision or opinion.

Which, strangely enough, was the most reassuring news of all.

CHAPTER TWENTY-FIVE

Bubbles and Blood in Champagne

We checked out of our Strasbourg hotel with no plan whatsoever, which by now felt less like indecision and more like policy.

The car was packed, the satnav remained suspiciously quiet, and the map lay folded on the dashboard, pretending it had nothing to do with what was about to happen. Strasbourg, unhelpfully, sat right on the border, offering us a choice it had no business presenting.

One bridge led east into Germany. Sausages. Efficiency. Things happening when they were meant to. Another road drifted north-west towards the Champagne region. Lunch with bubbles. Possibly followed by another lunch.

"I think Germany," Alex said. "Sausages. Structure. Dignity."

"I think France," I replied. "Champagne. Leisure. Day drinking."

She narrowed her eyes. "We are not day drinking."

"Not intentionally," I said.

"Coin toss," Alex said, with the air of someone who already suspected the outcome but was willing to test fate anyway.

I flipped it.

Champagne.

She looked at the coin, then at me. "Again."

I flipped it a second time.

Champagne.

Alex exhaled slowly. "All right," she said. "That's enough."

"That's two out of two," I said.

"Exactly," she replied. "I don't need a third insult."

She took the coin from me and turned it over in her fingers, inspecting it closely, as if flaws might reveal themselves under pressure.

"This feels suspicious," she said.

"It's a coin," I said. "It's done its job."

She flipped it herself.

Champagne.

We both looked at it.

"Well," she said at last, with dignity, "the sausages aren't going anywhere."

"Neither," I said gently, "is Germany."

She folded her arms. "Next country, I choose."

"Agreed," I said, already adjusting the route.

And just like that, Germany was postponed, sausages were deferred, and the Champagne region of France was promoted from vague idea to immediate priority.

The road stretched ahead of us, obliging and open, and the coin went back into my pocket, no longer needed, its work complete.

Reims was everything the French do well: elegant, confident, and slightly disapproving of your shoes. The streets were wide and tree-lined, the buildings perfectly symmetrical, and even the pigeons seemed to have studied ballet. It's a city that sparkles, quite literally, built on the champagne that flows beneath it, miles of limestone caves holding the world's happiest secret.

The main square in Reims felt like a celebration that had forgotten why it started and decided not to ask.

Pavement cafés spilled out in every direction, tables pressed close together, chairs angled just enough to suggest intimacy without promising it. Every menu, without exception, featured champagne. Not tucked away in a corner. Not offered shyly. Champagne was the point. Glasses clinked constantly, the sound floating up and mixing with conversation, traffic, and the low hum drone of a city that knows exactly what it's good at.

We sat and watched.

In front of us rose Reims Cathedral, vast and calm, its stone pale and serious, as if it had seen every celebration before and was quietly unimpressed. Kings had been crowned there. History had happened there. And now, opposite it, people were drinking champagne and arguing about diner.

It felt right.

Alex ordered a Coca-Cola.

The waiter paused, just briefly, the way French waiters do when recalibrating their understanding of you.

"Coca-Cola," she confirmed.

He nodded, recovered instantly, and brought it as if it were a perfectly reasonable choice, which it was.

I ordered a glass of champagne.

It arrived cold and unapologetic, all bubbles and confidence. I raised it slightly, not in a toast, just in acknowledgement of the moment. Alex sipped her Coke contentedly, legs crossed, sunglasses on, entirely unbothered by the fact that she was possibly the only person in the square not drinking champagne.

"This is nice," she said.

I looked at the cathedral, the cafés, the fermented bubbles rising everywhere except her glass.

"It really is," I said.

And we sat there for a long time, doing very little at all. Watching the light move across the stone. Listening to the city talk around us. Feeling that quiet satisfaction that comes when you realise you're exactly where you didn't plan to be and wouldn't change it for anything.

We wandered through the market, surrounded by wheels of cheese the size of tractor tyres and sausages that looked home-made. There were flowers, lace, and pastries so perfect they deserved fanfare. Alex admired everything but bought nothing – she was already thinking ahead.

"Enough city," she said. "I want to see the vineyards."

It was spring, and the vines were waking up.

The buds were just opening, giving the vineyards a soft green haze, as if someone had breathed colour gently across the hills. Nothing shouted yet. There were no heavy leaves, no fruit. Just promise. The kind of promise that makes you slow down without realising you have.

We left Reims behind us and drove through rolling countryside where the vines stood in neat, disciplined lines, each one perfectly spaced, each one behaving exactly as expected. They climbed the slopes with quiet determination, rows curving with the land, catching the light differently as the road rose and fell.

It felt organised. Purposeful. Very French.

Every now and then a tractor moved slowly between the rows, as if careful not to wake anything too quickly. Small signs appeared, names we recognised and names we didn't, each one quietly suggesting celebration rather than promising it outright.

Somewhere between Épernay and a village that looked like it had been painted by Monet's tidier cousin, we found our hotel.

It wasn't announced. It simply appeared, tucked neatly among the vines, stone walls warmed by the afternoon sun, shutters half closed in a way that suggested confidence rather than secrecy.

We pulled in, turned the engine off, and sat for a moment.

Another stop. Another region making sense of itself. Another evening waiting patiently to unfold.

It had a moat. An actual moat, complete with ducks and the faint smell of history.

The Château stood in smug, aristocratic silence, all pale stone and perfect symmetry – the kind of building that looked as if it had never once been caught in the rain. A sign out front announced it as a *Monument Historique*, which immediately made me feel underdressed and unqualified to breathe near it.

Inside, everything gleamed and whispered. The staff glided, never walked. Even their shoes made no sound, which is always unsettling, like being served by polite ghosts.

Our room was enormous: four-poster bed, draped curtains. From the window, beyond the moat, the vineyards rolled endlessly across the hills.

"It's very beautiful," Alex admitted. "But I'm hungry; where do normal people eat?"

"Here," I said. "Apparently in absolute silence."

The dining room was a shrine to champagne, bottles everywhere, in glass cabinets, on gilded stands, in decorative pyramids. The air smelled of yeast and pride. In the centre, a huge oak barrel full of ice overflowed with bottles like an offering to Bacchus.

A waiter appeared. He was tall, solemn, and so precisely dressed that I felt like a hobo in my best T-shirt. He handed us the menu – a single piece of parchment.

There were two choices. That was all.

- **Option one**: Pigeon in its own blood.

- **Option two**: Fish with foam.

Alex frowned. "Blood or bubbles," she said. "Lovely."

"Maybe it's just a bad translation," I whispered.

She squinted at the paper. "I don't think so. They seem very proud of it."

We waved the waiter over.

"Excuse me," I asked. "Could you tell us what exactly *pigeon in its own blood means*?"

His eyes lit up. Finally, an audience.

"*Ah, monsieur!*" he said in a thick French accent, performing a small bow. "The chef takes a perfect pigeon, a beautiful, fresh bird, and he…" He paused dramatically and mimed strangulation. "He cuts the throat, saves the blood, cooks the bird very gently, and when it is almost ready…" He leaned in, lowering his voice reverently, "… he pours the blood back over the top."

Alex's mouth fell open. "He does *what*?"

"Ah *oui*," the waiter nodded proudly. "It gives *flavour*!"

There was a silence long enough for my appetite to pack up and leave the building.

"I'll have the fish," I said quickly.

"Me too," Alex muttered darkly. "Unless it's drowned in something's kidneys."

"Excellent choice," said the waiter. "It comes with foam."

He glided away before we could ask what sort of foam.

Alex turned to me, voice rising. "Foam? Foam! What is this, dinner or dry cleaning?"

"Calm down," I said quietly. "It's French. They do this."

Her eyebrows shot up. "*Do what*? Ruin food on purpose? Greece gave them civilisation and they repay us with pigeons in homicide?"

I tried not to laugh. "Just relax. We'll order wine. Wine fixes everything."

That was my second mistake.

There is something you should understand about Alex before this makes sense.

She hates snobbery. Not loudly or theatrically. She simply refuses to participate in it. Pretension, hierarchy, the idea that taste improves in direct proportion to price – all of it leaves her entirely unmoved. She is not impressed by labels, rituals, or men who hover while you make decisions.

I learned this early.

When we were first dating, I once decided to impress her. This was a mistake, but I did not yet know that.

I booked a five-star hotel; the sort of place where the carpets muffle your footsteps and the staff speak in voices designed not to disturb the furniture. At dinner, feeling pleased with myself, I ordered the most expensive champagne on the list.

The wine waiter arrived, immaculate, solemn, and opened the bottle with a practiced pop that suggested he had done this many times for people who wanted to feel important.

He moved to pour some into Alex's glass.

She placed her hand over it.

"Have you got any Seven Up?" she asked politely.

The waiter froze.

"I always mix my champagne with Seven Up," she added helpfully.

The silence that followed was educational.

The waiter looked at me as if I had brought a live animal into the dining room. I realised, in that moment, two important things. First, never try to impress Alex. Second, she had just saved us both from a lifetime of unnecessary performance.

Which is why, years later, when the wine waiter appeared, I knew exactly what was coming.

He was thin, elegant, and carried a silver tasting cup around his neck like a medal awarded for services to refinement. He presented the wine list with ceremony. It was heavy, leather bound, and roughly the size of a small suitcase.

Alex took it, flipped through the pages, sighed quietly, and looked up.

"Do you have any champagne?"

The waiter froze.

His lips parted slightly, as if she had just asked whether they served petrol or accepted payment in goats. Then, with infinite patience and a gesture that was clearly practised, he extended one arm in a grand sweeping arc that took in the entire room.

Every bottle. Every label. Every region.

It was, unmistakably, the Champagne region in liquid form.

Alex watched the gesture, unimpressed.

"Alright," she said. "How about retsina?"

The waiter's composure wavered.

"Non, Madame," he said, visibly trembling.

She nodded, as if this confirmed something she had already suspected.

"Then I'll have a Coke," she said, folding the wine list closed and handing it back to him.

The man blinked, swallowed, and retreated towards the kitchen, carrying the wine list like a wounded animal.

I watched him go.

"You realise," I said quietly, "you've just undone years of training."

Alex smiled. "Good," she said. "He can relax now."

And there it was. Not confusion. Not contradiction. Just Alex, refusing to pretend that enjoyment needs permission, or that pleasure improves when it is explained too loudly.

She didn't order champagne because she didn't want champagne.

She wanted to enjoy herself.

Which, as I had learned the hard way, is something Alex will always do on her own terms.

"Alex," I whispered, "you've just insulted two centuries of French culture."

"I don't care," she said, her voice sharp as vinegar. "If I wanted pretentious drinks, I'd order soda water. If I wanted blood on my plate, I'd go to war."

When the food arrived, it didn't help. My "fish with foam" looked like someone had dropped a sardine into a bath. Alex's plate was mostly empty, save for a single fillet surrounded by something frothy and suspiciously alive-looking.

She prodded it with her fork. The foam sighed and vanished.

"It's gone," she said flatly. "My dinner has evaporated."

"It's molecular gastronomy," I murmured.

"Molecular what? Peter, I don't want chemistry. I want food. Something with bones. Or sauce. Or dignity."

At that moment, a couple at the next table gasped over their plates, whispering about *texture* and *balance*. Alex watched them with growing irritation.

"They're pretending," she muttered. "That man's chewing air."

"Maybe he's just being polite."

"No," she said firmly, stabbing her fork into her disappearing fish. "He's lost the will to live and doesn't want to admit it."

The waiter reappeared, gliding silently towards us. "Is everything to Madame's liking?"

Alex smiled sweetly. "It's wonderful. I've always wanted to experience hunger in a castle."

He blinked. "Pardon?"

"She means delicious," I said quickly.

"I mean *tiny*," she corrected.

Dessert arrived: "deconstructed apple essence". It looked like the ghost of a crumble.

Alex put down her spoon, exasperated. "You know what I'd give for a proper Greek dessert right now?" she said. "Just one square of galaktoboureko. Sticky. Hot. Real."

"You're going to start a revolution," I whispered.

"Good," she said. "Let's start with the chef. I'll rebuild him with olive oil and logic."

We smelled the cheese trolley before we saw it.

Alex sat bolt upright. "Peter," she whispered. "It's here."

And there it was: a vast, wheeled altar to fermentation, gliding towards us in reverent silence. It was approaching from the far end of the dining room, slowly, ominously, like a fog bank rolling in from the Channel. At first, it was just a faint whiff, a polite introduction: a hint of dairy, a whisper of something rustic. Then came the second wave: deeper, darker, unmistakably French. By the time it reached our table, the air was thick enough to slice.

The waiter beamed proudly, as though unveiling a newborn. "*Le plateau de fromages, monsieur, madame.*"

I leaned back slightly, instinctively creating distance. Alex leaned forward, eyes wide with devotion.

Now, Alex loves cheese. Truly loves it.

She eats feta daily, sometimes twice if she's stressed. She'll happily nibble graviera with honey, melt kefalotyri over baked aubergines, or crumble manouri into her salad just to "give it attitude".

She even has time for foreign imports – cheddar on toast, stilton with grapes, brie if it's pretending to be polite.

But nothing, absolutely nothing, could have prepared her for this selection. The trolley was a battlefield.

There were soft cheeses that slumped against each other for support. Hard cheeses stacked in crumbling towers like dairy ruins. And in the centre, the real danger zone, a collection of unidentifiable specimens that looked like they'd been exhumed rather than aged.

Each one emitted its own distinct message. One smelled of feet. Another, of old socks left on a radiator. A third had a presence so commanding that the nearby candles seemed to flicker in terror.

Alex's eyes shone. "This," she breathed, "is heaven."

I held my napkin over my face. "It's something."

The waiter began the tour, gesturing with the solemnity of a museum curator.

"This one," he said, "is *Époisses*. Very strong. Was once banned on the Paris Metro."

"Because of the smell?" I asked.

He nodded proudly. "*Oui*."

Alex clapped her hands in delight.

"And here, the *Roquefort*, aged in caves. Made from the milk of very nervous sheep."

Next came a goat's cheese that appeared to be trying to

escape its rind, a Camembert that had given up, and something called Munster which, in my opinion, was a public health warning pretending to be a dairy product.

Alex was in rapture, nodding enthusiastically at each description.

Meanwhile, I had tears in my eyes, not from emotion, but fumes.

"Would you like to taste?" asked the waiter, already preparing a small plate.

"Absolutely," said Alex.

"Not for me," I began, but it was too late. A wedge of *Époisses* landed in front of me with the sound of wet fabric hitting tile.

The smell hit next. It was… complex. Like a compost heap that had been in the sun too long.

Alex took a bite, closed her eyes, and sighed with bliss. "Oh, Peter… this is divine."

I braced myself, took a cautious nibble, and immediately questioned my life choices.

It tasted exactly how it smelled: damp, determined, and oddly emotional.

"This cheese," I croaked, "is alive."

"Of course," said Alex happily. "That's the point."

The waiter hovered expectantly. "You like?"

I smiled weakly. "It's… unforgettable."

He seemed pleased, unaware that I meant that literally. The flavour had permanently attached itself to the inside of my skull.

Alex, meanwhile, was already moving on, sampling, commenting, ranking them as if judging an international pageant.

"This one's bold but misunderstood," she said.

"This one's shy but lingers nicely."

"This one's… oh my God, Peter, smell this one!"

I refused.

She shrugged and devoured it anyway, humming like someone being reunited with a lost love.

When the trolley finally rolled away, leaving a blue haze of aroma behind it, Alex leaned back in her chair, blissfully content.

"That," she declared, "was art."

I took a sip of wine to flush out the memory. "That was warfare."

She smiled dreamily. "You just don't appreciate good cheese."

"Good cheese," I said, "shouldn't require a fire alarm."

She laughed, reached across the table, and squeezed my hand. "You're such an Englishman."

"Yes," I said. "And I plan to stay that way: unscented."

As we left, the maître d' bowed low. "Did Madame enjoy the foam?"

Alex smiled, voice dripping with sweetness and threat. "It was… unforgettable. Next time, maybe the pigeon. But only if it comes with chips."

He nodded uncertainly.

Outside, under the moonlit vineyards, Alex let out a long sigh. "Pretentious food makes me tired," she said. "Tomorrow,

I'm choosing the restaurant," she said.

"Fine by me," I replied. "What are you thinking?"

She slipped her arm through mine. "Somewhere where you can smell the grill from the car park," she said, "and nobody feels the need to explain the food."

I nodded. "So Greece, then?"

She smiled. "Eventually."

She paused, then added, generously, "The French do breakfast properly. I'll give them that."

"And the cheese," I said.

"Yes," she agreed. "The cheese definitely saved the day." She squeezed my arm. "But for dinner, I like my civilisation louder."

We took a walk through the château grounds, the moon reflecting in the moat and frogs singing like drunks in perfect harmony. Somewhere a cork popped, perhaps in celebration of our survival.

"Beautiful place," she said softly.

"Yes," I agreed. "Full of history, elegance, and people who think foam counts as food."

And with that, the world felt perfectly balanced again: bubbles, love, and just a hint of mischief floating gently through the French night.

CHAPTER TWENTY-SIX

MEANWHILE, BACK IN THE VILLAGE

We were still in the château, which meant we had reached the planning stage.

This required breakfast.

We woke early and went downstairs to the restaurant, both of us in that cautious morning mood reserved for hotels where history has opinions. What we needed, urgently, was coffee. Proper coffee. The kind that restores balance and doesn't arrive with foam, blood, or an explanation.

I was relieved to find a buffet laid out with quiet French confidence. Croissants. Bread. Butter that knew exactly what it was for. Jams arranged as if colour mattered. No surprises. No performance. Just breakfast, doing its job.

I poured coffee and felt myself relax almost at once. Alex took a slow circuit of the room, taking in the tables, the food, and the general level of organisation with quiet approval.

She nodded. "That'll do nicely."

She sat beside me, set down her cup, and spread the map out beside the coffee pot, smoothing it flat with the careful attention of someone who likes things to behave themselves. The paper stayed put, the coffee stayed hot, and for once nothing appeared to require immediate intervention.

It felt like a good place to begin the day.

"Right," she said, wrapping her hands around her cup. "Where next?"

I took a sip, looked at the map, and felt that familiar flutter of freedom.

Breakfast, it turned out, was about to decide everything.

It hadn't felt like a journey in the usual sense. No grand departure, no sense of ticking destinations off a list. More a gentle drift through Europe, one road leading naturally to the next, as if the continent itself were quietly rearranging us.

Back home, things were still loosely hanging together. The village was functioning. The house remained upright. Maria was vigilant. We didn't feel urgently required, which in Pefki terms is as close to permission as you ever get.

And we were having a wonderful time.

Different countries slipped past almost unnoticed. Borders arrived politely, then vanished again. New languages floated through petrol stations and cafés. Road signs changed colour. Coffee tasted slightly different. That was often the only warning.

"How many countries have we actually been to now?" I asked.

Alex frowned and began counting on her fingers.

"Well," she said, "we started in Greece. That's one."

"We should definitely count Greece," I said. "It feels important."

"Then Italy," she continued.

"And San Marino," I added. "That counts. They're very proud of that."

She nodded. "Yes. San Marino. Then Switzerland."

"And now France," I said.

She paused, looked at her hand, then smiled. "That makes five."

I leaned over and checked. "Greece, Italy, San Marino, Switzerland, France."

She looked again, satisfied. "Five."

"Do you want to make it six?" I asked.

She didn't hesitate. "Of course."

"Any preference?"

She shrugged. "Somewhere nice."

I thought for a moment. "I've always heard Bruges is beautiful."

She looked up. "Belgium?"

"Yes."

She considered this, then nodded. "Alright. Belgium."

And just like that, the adventure stretched itself a little further. Just another gentle decision made somewhere between coffee and a croissant, adding one more country to a journey that had stopped behaving like a holiday and started feeling like a story.

It was morning in France, the road ahead lined with poplars and the promise of somewhere new, when Alex's phone began to buzz. She glanced at the screen, sighed in recognition, and put it straight onto speaker.

"Where are you now?" Maria's voice came through immediately, loud and unmistakable, filling the car.

"Still in France," Alex said.

"France," Maria repeated, sharply. Then, after a brief pause, her tone shifted. "Good. Thank God for that. At least you're not driving back."

She exhaled audibly, the sound of someone momentarily reassured but still deeply invested.

There was another pause. Then the unmistakable click of a lighter.

"Anyway," Maria continued, warming back up, "it's stopped raining here, but the river is still running straight down the road.

You should see it. Like a waterfall. Very dramatic."

"That sounds… energetic," Alex said carefully.

"Yes," Maria agreed. "But good news. The police came. They say it's probably caused by your drains."

I lifted my foot slightly off the accelerator.

"Maria," I said, leaning closer to the phone, "we don't have drains in the village. Nobody does. We all have tanks."

"Yes, yes," Maria said impatiently. "The tank is there. Everyone knows about the tank. But they say it's the way the water goes to the tank. The pipes. The angles. Something English."

I closed my eyes briefly.

"So," I said, "just to be clear. The rain has stopped. The road is still a river. And somehow this is because of our plumbing."

"Exactly," Maria said, sounding relieved to be understood. "But don't worry. They are only talking. For now."

Alex and I exchanged a look.

In Greece, this counts as reassurance.

There was a long silence on the line. Either Maria's throat had been cut mid-conversation, or she was digesting the radical concept of our innocence.

Finally, she spoke. "Well, yes, I told them that. But they said to tell you they still need to talk to you. Your jackal. It ate another chicken yesterday." Maria continued as if announcing the weather. "Yes. The man from Athens Zoo came. He says it's definitely a jackal, not a fox. He looked very excited about it. Apparently, we've never had one in Evia before. You should be proud."

Alex rubbed her forehead. "Maria, *it's not our jackal.* It just lives near the end of our garden."

"Well," Maria replied matter-of-factly, "the police said if it's been living in your garden, it must be yours. So they'd like you to do something about it."

"Like what?" I asked. "Take it for a walk? Fill in ownership papers?"

Maria ignored me. "Anyway, I told them you're away, but they said when you come back, you must report to the station."

Alex looked at me, half amused, half exasperated. "We leave the village for a few days and suddenly we own a wild animal."

"Yes," I said. "And apparently it's a repeat offender."

Maria sighed down the line. "Just come home soon, before it eats anything important. Oh, and Dimitri says if it kills a sheep, he'll shoot it. But don't worry, he usually misses."

The call ended with the usual Maria farewell – abrupt, affectionate, and faintly threatening.

Alex stared out the window at the French countryside, dotted with calm cows and obedient sheep. "You see," she said. "Even the animals here behave."

I nodded. "That's because none of them live near our house."

She smiled. "We really should get back."

"Why?" I asked. "Because we miss home?"

"No," she said. "Because apparently we're harbouring a fugitive."

And with that, we drove on, past vineyards and villages, the soft light of France glowing across the fields, wondering whether our garden was still intact, and whether the jackal was waiting to welcome us home.

CHAPTER TWENTY-SEVEN

BRUGES – CHOCOLATE, HORSES, AND BEER

We crossed into Belgium under a sky the colour of old pewter. Not dramatic rain, nothing that would justify a complaint; just that polite northern drizzle that never quite commits. The sort that dampens your coat, fogs your glasses, and leaves you smelling faintly of coffee, wool, and decisions you didn't fully think through.

By the time we reached the outskirts of Bruges, even the weather seemed to have softened, as if it too had decided to be on its best behaviour.

And then there it was.

Bruges.

It shimmered. Not with flashing lights or grand gestures, but with the quiet confidence of a place that knows exactly what it is and sees no reason to explain. Cobbled streets were arranged like carefully placed punctuation. Lace-curtained windows glowed softly. Gabled roofs inclined towards still canals, their reflections so perfect they felt rehearsed. Even the ducks moved slowly, deliberately, as if aware they were part of a protected cultural asset.

Alex stopped in the street.

"Peter," she said, eyes wide, "it's like being inside a Christmas card."

She was right. The entire town looked as though it had been designed by sentimental elves. Even the chimneys leaned artistically, as if posing for a calendar shoot.

Our hotel described itself as *charmingly historic*, which in brochure language means it had stairs that defied physics and corridors that required faith. The receptionist handed me a key the size of a frying pan and gestured vaguely towards a staircase clearly designed for monks with narrow hips.

The room itself was perfect. Low beams. A canal view. A bathroom so compact you could brush your teeth while sitting on the toilet and still reach the shower.

Alex flung open the window and inhaled.

"Listen," she said happily. "You can hear the bells."

They rang somewhere above the rooftops, softly and regularly, as if reminding the town to behave itself.

We went out to explore.

Bruges isn't a city you walk through. It's a city that gently ambles through you. Nothing rushes. Nothing shouts. Streets curve just enough to slow you down. Towers rise at a slight angle, thoughtful rather than precise, as if still considering questions they asked themselves centuries ago. It's built for wandering, not arriving.

We had taken perhaps ten steps when Alex stopped again.

"Look."

Lined along the square were horse-drawn carriages, glossy black, wheels shining, each pulled by a horse roughly the size of a small hatchback. Their harnesses jingled softly. Their breath misted in the cold air. Each animal stood with the serene authority of a creature that knows it is absolutely the main attraction.

"I want to go on one," Alex said.

This was not a request. This was destiny, clearing its throat.

I glanced at the price list. Then at the horse.

"Couldn't we just follow one," I suggested gently, "and imagine?"

She gave me *the look*, the one that ends negotiations and begins logistics.

Alex has always loved horses.

On our wedding day she arrived in a snow-white carriage pulled by white horses; the sort of entrance that makes you realise you are not marrying someone who plans to fade quietly into the background.

Her affection for horses has never been casual. It's instinctive, unquestioned, and, as I discovered, occasionally dangerous.

Years earlier, in England, we'd been walking through open pasture where horses wandered freely, unburdened by fences or expectations. They moved in loose groups, manes flying, hooves thudding softly against the earth. Alex slowed, watching them with that familiar expression: reverent, delighted, already emotionally invested.

Knowing her weakness, I had come prepared. From my pocket I produced several rolls of mint sweets. Horses love mints. I knew this because I'd read it somewhere, and because confidence often substitutes for knowledge.

"Come on," I said. "Let's feed them."

I demonstrated first, naturally. I placed a mint carefully in the flat of my palm and held my hand out, steady and calm, like a man who absolutely knew what he was doing. A small pony approached, sniffed cautiously, then took the mint with a warm, velvety muzzle. He lingered, hopeful, breathing gently into my hand, searching for more.

"See?" I said. "Easy."

Alex watched, impressed.

"Put the mint flat in your palm," I told her. "They'll come to you."

She nodded seriously, as though receiving classified instructions.

Satisfied with my mentoring, I wandered off towards the river to see if there were any fish, confident I had passed on all necessary wisdom and that nothing could possibly go wrong.

From the other side of the field, Alex called cheerfully.

"Look! I don't need to feed them from my palm, they eat mints this way too!"

I turned just in time to see her holding a mint delicately between finger and thumb, extending it towards a very large, very enthusiastic horse.

There was no time for advice.

No time for regret.

The horse took the mint, and then, quite reasonably from its point of view, continued forward. Alex's fingers disappeared into its mouth, followed shortly by most of her hand.

She screamed.

The horse, startled by the noise, panicked and bolted, still chewing.

For a brief, surreal moment, Alex was being carried across a field, her hand inside a galloping horse, both of them equally alarmed.

When the horse finally released her, she staggered back, white as chalk, her hand bleeding and torn, and very much not part of the feeding plan.

I ran towards her, my role as experienced horse consultant officially over.

She looked at me, shaking, furious, and said, "WHY DIDN'T YOU WARN ME?"

"I did," I said weakly. "About… palms."

This experience did nothing to diminish her love of horses.

If anything, it seemed to deepen it, as though being partially eaten was simply part of the relationship.

So now, years later, as we found ourselves in Bruges, standing in front of a line of immaculate horses waiting patiently for their next assignment, I understood immediately that this was happening.

The horses were magnificent. Glossy, calm, and entirely unbothered by tourists, cameras, or the fact that they were about to transport people who had not earned the right. Harnesses gleamed. Leather creaked softly. Tails were brushed with care. These were working horses, but proud ones, standing as if they knew they were part of the city's theatre.

Alex's eyes lit up. "This," she said, "is how you see a place properly."

I glanced at the horses, then at the carriages, then briefly considered suggesting a nice walk instead. Past experience told me this would only delay the inevitable.

Moments later, we were seated behind a horse named Napoleon, which felt like an ambitious name for an animal expected to remain calm in the presence of tourists with selfie sticks. Napoleon rose to the occasion. He set off at a steady, dignified pace, his hooves striking the cobbles with a rhythmic clop that echoed through the streets like polite applause.

From the carriage, Bruges revealed itself slowly, generously.

We rolled through market squares where cafés spilled outwards, tables crowded with people drinking beer that arrived in glasses shaped like experiments. Flower stalls brightened corners of ancient stone. Canals slipped quietly past, catching reflections of stepped gables and arched bridges. The buildings leaned in on one another like old friends sharing secrets.

Time softened.

Our driver wore a velvet jacket and spoke in a flowing commentary that moved effortlessly between languages. I recognised dates, the occasional name, and the word "medieval", which seemed to apply to almost everything. I nodded, respectfully, as though I understood all of it.

Alex waved to passers-by as if this were a civic duty. Some waved back. A child pointed. A couple smiled indulgently. Napoleon accepted the attention without comment, ears flicking occasionally as if taking note of the city himself.

We passed through quiet courtyards and broader squares, the carriage slowing naturally where the city seemed to want us to look longer. Bruges, I realised, is not a place that rewards speed. It prefers to be taken in at a pace slightly slower than modern life allows.

After about an hour, Napoleon came to a gentle halt.

The driver turned to us with a small smile. "Now," he said, "it is lunch time."

"For us?" Alex asked, hopefully.

"For him," he replied, nodding towards Napoleon. "He must eat. He must drink. He must rest."

This felt entirely reasonable.

"We ask you to take a walk," he added. "Enjoy the square. Come back in one hour, and we will continue."

Napoleon was unhitched with quiet efficiency and led away towards his meal, clearly pleased with the arrangement.

We climbed down, legs slightly unaccustomed to dignity, and found ourselves standing in the square we had just passed through without really seeing. Now, on foot, it revealed itself differently. The cafés. The details. The way the light moved across the stone.

"Good idea," Alex said. "He deserves lunch."

"So do we," I replied.

We wandered, unhurried, knowing we'd be back. Knowing the city would still be waiting. Knowing Napoleon would return, fed and refreshed, ready to carry us once more through a place that understood the value of slowing down.

And for once, so did we.

When we returned, Napoleon was waiting for us, refreshed, watered, and looking faintly superior, as if lunch had confirmed his belief that life was generally well organised.

The driver greeted us as though no time had passed at all. The harness was checked, the reins gathered, and we climbed back into our seats, resuming our positions in the small theatre of Bruges.

The afternoon light had shifted. The city felt softer now, shadows longer, colours warmer. Napoleon set off again, unhurried, his hooves tapping out a rhythm that seemed to belong to the place. The return journey took us through streets we hadn't seen before, past quieter canals and smaller squares where locals sat talking on steps, bicycles leaning patiently nearby.

From the carriage, Bruges felt timeless, suspended somewhere between postcard and reality, a city that had decided long ago not to rush for anyone.

Alex leaned back, content.

"This," she said, "is exactly right."

I nodded. There was nothing to add.

When the carriage finally stopped and we climbed down for the last time, I patted Napoleon's neck again. He accepted it with professional tolerance, already scanning the square for his next passengers.

We walked away slowly, neither of us keen to break the spell too quickly.

Bruges had done something rare. It had asked us to slow down, and then rewarded us for listening.

By the time we reached the edge of the square, the sound of hooves had faded, replaced by footsteps and voices and the gentle business of a city continuing exactly as it always had.

And for once, we were happy to keep pace with it.

Then came the chocolate.

Bruges does not *sell* chocolate. It presents it.

There are chocolate shops everywhere, glowing, beckoning, unapologetic. Inside, pyramids of pralines shimmered under soft lights. Truffles lined up like obedient soldiers. The air was thick with cocoa, caramel, vanilla, and temptation.

Alex vanished into the first shop like a pilgrim entering a shrine.

Ten minutes later she emerged radiant, carrying a bag full

of truffles, ganache, and "just a few essentials".

Ten minutes after that, she had another bag.

By evening, we were edging towards a sugar-fuelled financial incident.

We were standing on one of Bruges' many bridges. Alex leaned over the railing and looked down at a boat full of tourists drifting silently beneath us.

"They look cold," she said thoughtfully. "And sad."

Before I could intervene, she began dropping chocolates, gently, carefully, into waiting hands.

A woman caught a truffle mid-air and gasped. Applause broke out. Alex smiled, satisfied.

"See?" she said. "Good deeds are sweet."

While Alex shopped for more chocolate, and then redistributed it, I stationed myself strategically on a beer terrace overlooking the canal. The bar claimed to offer *over a million beers*. This was probably untrue, but standing before shelves of blondes, ambers, triples, monk-brewed legends and things that looked faintly radioactive, I decided Belgium had its priorities in order.

I ordered one.

Then another.

Then one that arrived in a tulip-shaped glass.

Another in something resembling a vase.

One in what looked suspiciously like a fishbowl.

By the third beer, I was convinced I could understand Flemish.

By the fourth, I was fairly sure I could speak it.

By the fifth, I was planning a life above the bar.

Alex eventually found me, glowing with a chocolate-based sugar rush.

"We're buying more chocolate, aren't we?" she said.

I nodded. "And possibly the bar."

That night, Bruges glowed. Canals mirrored gold and amber light. Swans slept on the water like decorative punctuation. Bells rang softly, as if approving the day's choices.

Alex stopped on a bridge and looked around.

"I think this might be my favourite place," she said.

I looked at her, at the city, at the moon floating perfectly in the canal.

"It's hard to argue," I said. "They have horses, chocolate, and beer. Civilisation has covered the essentials."

She smiled. "All it needs now is a little Greek spirit."

And as her laughter drifted across the water, warm, bright, and entirely at home, I realised something quietly comforting.

Some places impress you.

Some entertain you.

And some simply hand you a beer, offer you chocolate, and let life make sense for a while.

CHAPTER TWENTY-EIGHT

Sisyphus Moves to Pefki

We did not come to Pefki for drama.

This is important, because everything that followed suggests otherwise.

We came for peace. For quiet. For a simpler life. For mornings that began with light rather than paperwork, and evenings that ended without explanation. We came because we believed, naively as it turned out, that if you chose a small place and lived gently in it, the world might return the favour.

It seemed reasonable at the time.

You would think that after everything that followed, the

matter might eventually be considered closed. The flood. The engineers. The reports. The diagrams. The men with clipboards and expressions usually reserved for unpaid priests.

At some point, logic suggests there should be a pause. A collective intake of breath. A moment where everyone agrees that enough has been explained, documented, photographed, stamped, signed, and placed in a plastic folder.

That moment never comes.

Because Nemesis is always angry.

She does not arrive gently, or tentatively, or with questions. She arrives fully formed, already furious, already convinced, already pointing. Her anger is not spontaneous. It is sustained, rehearsed, and deployed with purpose.

When Nemesis speaks, it is with the certainty of someone who has no intention of being corrected.

"Your drains caused this," she will say, arms folded, jaw set.

Not might have.

Not possibly contributed.

Caused.

Evidence does not interest her. Explanations irritate her. Engineers are tolerated only until they contradict her. Anger, for Nemesis, is not an emotion. It is a method.

At some point during all of this – the flood, the accusations, the committees, the wildlife, the paperwork – I found myself thinking about Sisyphus.

In Greek mythology, Sisyphus was punished for being cleverer than the gods liked. His sentence was repetition.

Eternal, joyless repetition. He was forced to push a massive boulder up a hill, only to watch it roll back down again. He would then walk down after it, sigh the sigh of a man who has made some unfortunate life choices, and start again.

The myth is usually explained as a metaphor for the absurdity of human existence. Personally, I think it was written about village life.

Because every time we think we have pushed our boulder to the top of the hill, Nemesis appears and gives it a tap. Not a shove. Not a dramatic push. Just a small, angry nudge.

Down it goes again.

Sisyphus, poor man, had gravity to contend with.

We have Nemesis. And commentary.

"She says the river never behaved like this before you," Maria reported one morning down the phone, her voice carrying the familiar mixture of accusation and certainty. "Nemesis was standing there in the mud, shouting it while the rain was still falling."

I could picture it easily. Boots planted. Arms folded. The scene already fixed in her mind as evidence.

When someone suggested the water might simply have come down from the mountain, Nemesis dismissed it immediately.

"The mountain didn't change," she had said. "You did."

This is how it always works.

We repair the house.

Nemesis decides we changed the weather.

We hire engineers.

Nemesis proclaims that engineers can be bribed.

We show diagrams.

Nemesis explains diagrams lie.

We leave the village for a few days.

Nemesis concludes we fled to escape justice.

And then, inevitably: "Your jackal ate my cousin's chicken."

It is not our jackal. But in village logic, anything that passes your property becomes yours. Water. Blame. Responsibility. Wildlife.

Explaining this only makes Nemesis angrier.

She does not want clarification. She wants confirmation of what she already knows.

Village anger has a peculiar quality. It is loud, energetic, and absolute. But it is also exhausting. Nemesis burns brightly and completely, until eventually the outrage runs out of fuel.

Committees form. Coffee is served. People nod. Nothing is resolved. Not because anyone has been convinced, but because shouting is hard work.

And then, a few days later, something else happens. And Nemesis returns.

This was not what we came for.

We did not move to Pefki to argue about water, or jackals, or hypothetical plumbing crimes. We came because we believed that a small village might offer a smaller life. One with fewer voices, fewer demands, fewer explanations.

Instead, we learned something else.

Sisyphus knew something important. He knew the boulder would roll back down. He knew there would be no applause, no reward, no biscuit at the top of the hill.

And still, he pushed.

That is the lesson.

We push again.

We explain calmly. We deny politely. We accept coffee. We listen. We nod. We promise to "look into it".

We demonstrate how water behaves on a slope. We swear we did not summon anything. We deny responsibility for the jackal.

And when the boulder inevitably rolls back down, we take a breath, look at each other, and say something Sisyphus never got to say. "At least this time, we know we're right." Then, because this is Pefki, we add, "And at least the jackal didn't eat anything important."

Some battles are not worth winning.

In a Greek village, you do not survive by being right. You survive by understanding how gravity works here.

And just as we were beginning to think we had learned that lesson, the village found something new to discuss.

We now exist in a Greek version of *Groundhog Day*, except nobody warns you in advance and there is no soundtrack. Same village. Same problems. New day. Every morning begins with the same good intentions. Today, we tell ourselves, we will reset. Today we will move on. Today will be normal.

Then the village wakes up.

Floods come and go. People come and go. Opinions arrive early and stay late. Problems are declared urgent, then forgotten, then rediscovered with fresh enthusiasm as if they have never been discussed before. Yesterday's crisis becomes today's background noise, and tomorrow promises a brand-new variation on something we thought we had already dealt with.

Nothing ever quite ends. It simply pauses for coffee.

Each day begins like the last, but with new details added. A different rumour. A revised accusation. A familiar issue returning in a slightly different hat. The cast remains largely the same, but the script is improvised daily and nobody agrees on the plot.

We wake up. We assess the situation. We nod gravely. We say, "Let's see what today brings," as if it might bring silence.

It never does.

And yet, somehow, life carries on. Lunch is cooked. Cats are fed. The sun still sets. Tomorrow arrives, looking suspiciously like yesterday, only slightly louder.

This, we have learned, is how time works here. Not in straight lines, but in circles. Not forward, but around. Progress is measured not by resolution, but by how calmly you can repeat yourself.

This is why we went away for "a day or two".

Not to escape. Not to make a point. Certainly not to change anything. We knew better than that. Changing a Greek village is not a realistic objective. It has survived wars, occupations, earthquakes, and several mayors. It was not going to be undone by two tired people and a logical argument.

The village would remain exactly as it was. Opinionated. Talkative. Perfectly confident in its own conclusions.

So the only thing left to change was us.

We left to reset our ears, to give our nervous systems a rest from being permanently alert, to remember what it felt like to wake up without immediately wondering who might be cross and why. We went away so that tomorrow could arrive without carrying yesterday's arguments in its pockets.

A day or two, we told everyone. Long enough to miss it. Short enough not to worry anyone. Just enough distance to soften the edges.

The problems would still be there when we returned. The water would still know where it wanted to go. Nemesis would still have opinions. Someone would still be explaining something to someone else in great detail.

But we might come back slightly less reactive. Slightly more patient. Possibly even smiling.

And if nothing else, we would have proved one important thing: you may not be able to change a village, but you can, occasionally, change the channel.

What we did not know, as we continued our trip congratulating ourselves on a brief spell of sanity, was that the village had not paused in our absence. It had shifted. Quietly. Purposefully.

Without us there to observe it, comment on it, or drink coffee through it, things had rearranged themselves. Conversations had continued. Conclusions had been reached. Connections had been made that did not require our presence to be convincing.

We were not there to witness any of it.

We would simply return in time to be told what had happened, why it mattered, and exactly how it was, somehow, our fault.

CHAPTER TWENTY-NINE

Amsterdam – Mirrors, Canals and Questionable Hospitality

Bruges had been beautiful, welcoming, and dangerously good at making you forget responsibility.

Northern Europe, it turned out, suited us rather well. The cities were calm. The roads behaved. The coffee arrived on time. It was all very civilised, which only added to the sense that we were overdue for a mild crisis back home.

We were beginning to think about the village again.

Not in a panicked way. More in the way you think about a kettle you've left on when you're not entirely sure you *have* left it on, but you also wouldn't bet your house on it being fine.

We sat at a pavement café in Bruges, having breakfast. Croissants, coffee, the usual European reassurance. Alex spread the map across the table, flattening it with a sugar bowl as if it might try to escape.

We didn't say it out loud, but we were both thinking the same thing.

This might be the moment to start heading home.

Not rushing. Just… orienting ourselves in that general direction.

Alex traced a slow line with her finger, moving with the care of someone defusing a device.

"Amsterdam," she said.

I looked at the map. Then at the distance. Then back at her.

"It's not very far," she added quickly.

"That's how it starts," I said. "Every bad decision begins with 'not very far.'"

She ignored me. "We could spend a couple of days there. Then start heading back properly."

"Properly," I repeated.

"Yes," she said. "Homeward. But gently. So each day we're technically closer, in case something serious explodes."

I nodded. This felt like a sensible compromise. Adventure, but with an exit strategy.

"No rush," I said. "But within shouting distance of Greece."

She smiled. "Exactly."

We folded the map, finished our coffee, and sat there a moment longer, neither of us in a hurry to stand up. Home was calling softly, but not urgently. So we listened, nodded politely, and ordered another coffee.

Amsterdam, it seemed, could wait just long enough for us to finish breakfast.

We'd booked a lovely hotel on the River Amstel. Our ground-floor room was famous as the one where Empress Sisi stayed during her visit – a detail Alex adored, especially because of Sisi's Greek connection as the visionary behind Corfu's Achilleion Palace. The room featured four grand windows, two overlooking the river and two facing the street, all fitted with privacy glass. From the inside, we enjoyed clear views of the city and river, while passersby only saw their reflections. That night, we slept with the curtains open with a clear view of Amsterdam lit up before our eyes. It was spectacular.

Our first day in Amsterdam was one of those days that stay with you long after you've gone.

The city had a calmness about it, a sense of quiet confidence.

Tall, narrow houses stood close together, angled slightly as if in quiet conversation, their reflections breaking gently in the still canals below. It was daytime, technically, though Amsterdam on a grey morning has its own ideas about light. The sky was low and pale, and details stood out more sharply because of it.

Bridges arched between the houses, their strings of white lights still glowing against the gloom, not festive so much as practical, reflected clearly in the dark water beneath. Even in daylight, the city seemed to prefer a softer illumination, as if easing itself slowly into the day rather than announcing it.

Bicycles glided past like part of some silent ballet. Whole families rode together – parents, children, shopping bags, all balanced perfectly as if gravity worked differently here. I'm not sure how they do it. I can barely stay upright on two wheels without colliding with a lamppost.

We decided to explore on foot and walk until our feet protested.

The air carried that lovely northern mixture of coffee, damp brick, and cold spring air. We followed the canal paths at first, past houseboats decorated with fairy lights and small wooden decks that looked too fragile to stand on. Every turn seemed to reveal another postcard view, an old brick bridge, a row of trees perfectly aligned, a café with candles flickering in the window.

Alex walked ahead, taking it all in. "It feels peaceful here," she said quietly.

She was right. Even the city's sounds seemed softer somehow, the distant hum of trams, the ring of bicycle bells, the steady rhythm of footsteps on cobblestones.

We stopped for coffee at a tiny café that could only fit six people. The waiter brought two steaming cappuccinos and a slice of apple cake, which I pretended to resist and then didn't. The coffee was strong enough to keep us walking for hours.

Afterwards, we wandered through the floating flower market. Stalls overflowed with spring tulips in every imaginable colour, their scent rising through the cold air. Alex bought a small packet of bulbs to take home to Pefki. She said she wanted to plant them under the olive trees. I didn't have the heart to tell her they'd probably last about five minutes in Greek soil before giving up.

From there we made our way towards Dam Square. Trams rattled by, pigeons strutted around like they owned the place, and buskers played violins under the faint glow of fairy lights. We watched for a while, then followed the crowd down narrow streets lined with bakeries and souvenir shops.

By afternoon, the sun had faded into a silver mist. The canals caught the glow of streetlights, turning the water gold. Every bridge seemed to sparkle. It was beautiful in that understated way northern cities manage: quiet, unhurried, and deeply human.

We had planned to see as much as possible, maybe the Van Gogh Museum, maybe the Anne Frank House, but time slipped away, as it does when you're happy.

By the time we reached our hotel, my legs were protesting, and Alex's camera was full. We sat for a while by the canal outside, watching the boats glide through the dark water. A light drizzle began to fall; the soft kind that doesn't send you running for cover, just reminds you you're alive.

That night, as we looked out over the canals from our window, the whole city shimmered beneath the lights. It felt timeless.

For that first day at least, there were no deadlines, no floods, no taverna crises, no gossip from Pefki; just the two of us, a map full of possibilities, and a city that seemed to float.

We didn't know it yet, but Amsterdam had many surprises waiting for us, some involving interesting cakes, others red lights, and at least one unfortunate incident with a pair of underpants.

But for that first day, everything was perfect.

We woke the next day to see tour boats drifting past our hotel window. After a quick breakfast, we headed out again, map folded loosely, with no real plan beyond seeing what the city felt like at street level.

Outside, it was already busy. Camera-clutching tourists waved at anything that moved, whether it wanted to be photographed or not. Every few minutes a bell rang from somewhere – a tram, a church, a bicycle, or possibly all three at once.

The air smelled faintly of coffee, pastry, and damp pavements. For the first hour, as we wandered without urgency, I was completely entranced.

Then the smell changed.

At first it was easy to miss. Just a faint sweetness in the air, herbal and warm, the sort of smell that doesn't announce itself so much as linger, waiting to see if you'll notice.

The further we walked, the stronger it became.

Not floral. Not quite earthy either. More like passing a bakery that had abandoned bread altogether and decided to specialise in burning hay.

Alex slowed and took a careful sniff.

"It smells… nice," she said.

I breathed in again and frowned. "It smells confident. Possibly expensive. Possibly illegal."

She smiled. "You worry too much."

"Yes," I said. "But never without cause."

By the time we reached the end of the street, the haze had thickened into something you could almost lean on. Whatever was growing nearby was thriving, unapologetic, and entirely unconcerned with who approved of it.

Somewhere, someone was having a very relaxed day.

We turned a corner and found the culprit: a coffee shop. Only it wasn't selling coffee. Inside, the patrons looked far too relaxed to have consumed caffeine. Outside, a few lounged on benches, each holding what appeared to be a rolled-up bath towel on fire. Their eyes had that far-away look you only see in people remembering the answers to cosmic riddles.

Alex stopped to read the menu displayed in the window. It was less a drinks list and more a horticultural hallucination: *Purple Haze, Amnesia Haze, White Widow, Stardust Skunk, Trainwreck.*

"This is like the wine list from hell," I muttered.

"The space cake looks nice," Alex said, studying a man at a nearby table who was eating what looked like an innocent slice of sponge cake while staring lovingly at a paper napkin.

"I'll have that," she announced.

"No," I said. "That's how conversations with Greek gods begin, and paperwork follows."

Alex pouted. "But everyone's happy."

"They're not happy," I said. "They're orbiting."

I pointed at the man still gazing at his napkin. "You want to end up like him? He's halfway through a conversation with his fork."

"Fine," she sighed. "No space cake."

To cheer her up, I offered a compromise. "How about a safe dessert? Profiteroles. You like those. They don't make you see sound."

She wasn't convinced, but I managed to steer her away before curiosity could win.

We wandered on, crossing one of the city's countless little bridges, admiring the reflections of fairy-lit buildings in the dark water. It was all very romantic, until we drifted into a different kind of shopping district.

The shop windows began to glow red. The displays had changed too. Gone were the tulips, clogs, and cheese wheels. In their place stood women – confident, smiling, and wearing slightly less than the mannequins in Zara.

"Oh, look!" Alex exclaimed, delighted, as if she'd just discovered a new pâtisserie. Before I could stop her, she marched straight up to one of the windows and waved.

The woman inside, wearing what I can only describe as strategic optimism, waved back.

"Alex!" I hissed. "You can't just knock on the glass!"

"Why not? She's lovely!" said Alex. "She looks cold."

"She's *supposed* to look cold," I whispered. "It's part of the business model."

But Alex, being Alex, tapped again, smiled warmly, and asked through the glass, "Do you want a jacket?"

The woman laughed, genuinely laughed, and shook her head. Alex looked pleased, as though she'd just rescued a kitten.

"Come on," I urged. "Before you start offering to feed her."

"Oh, stop it," she said. "I'm just being friendly."

As the afternoon softened, the canals began to glow with reflections of light, and the city slipped quietly back into its own kind of magic. Couples wandered along the water's edge, unhurried, the air cool and alive with conversation and laughter. It was effortless, unshowy, and impossibly beautiful.

When we eventually reached our hotel, it was getting dark.

I froze. The lights were on in our room. The curtains were wide open. And through the enormous front window, I could see… everything.

"Hmm," I said slowly. "That's odd. I thought we had privacy glass."

We did. But, as I suddenly remembered, privacy glass only works in daylight. At night, with the lights on, it turns into an illuminated stage.

I felt my stomach drop.

Because the previous evening, I had stood in front of that very window, in my underpants. Not the sleek, Bond-on-holiday variety. The baggy, grey, post-laundry survivors. I'd been stretching, possibly humming, maybe scratching.

And I'd assumed, foolishly, that no one could see me.

The horrible truth dawned: I had spent an evening unwittingly performing near Amsterdam's red-light district.

I pictured it: tourists strolling past, whispering to each other.

"Ah, new act in Window 7. Not much costume, but a lot of enthusiasm."

The worst part? I'd had no customers. Not even a knock. Not one curious glance.

I had gone to bed under the comforting illusion of anonymity, convinced I was safely invisible to the street below. In reality, I had spent the night brightly illuminated, fully observable, and unknowingly performing for passers-by.

Note to self: in Amsterdam, draw the curtains. Always draw the curtains.

Alex, of course, found the whole thing hilarious.

"So, you were working the window last night?" she asked.

"Apparently," I sighed.

"And no one paid?"

"Not even an offer of hot chocolate."

She laughed so hard she nearly fell off the bed.

"Well," she said finally, wiping her eyes, "at least you now understand the business from the inside."

I groaned. "Next time, we're staying somewhere without windows."

I swear I heard the city chuckle.

Every hotel room promises possibility. Ours did this with a single, brightly coloured flyer on the desk, printed in cheerful type and untroubled by consequences: Hookah for your room – order now.

I stared at it for a long time.

The problem with hookah is not the object. It's the pronunciation. In my accent, *hookah* sounds dangerously close to *hooker*, and we were staying uncomfortably near the red-lit end of town.

I imagined phoning reception.

"Hello," I'd say, politely. "Could you send a hookah to my room?"

There would be a pause.

"Excuse me, sir?"

"A hookah," I'd repeat, louder, which never improves anything.

At this point Alex would look up from her book, take in the situation instantly, and begin planning my disposal. Canal. Night-time. No witnesses.

I tried rehearsing it in my head with added clarity.

"HOO-kah."

Still risky.

In the end, I did what experience has taught me to do in Europe. I left it alone.

The flyer remained on the desk, quietly offering temptation, misunderstanding, and possible marital harm. No phone call was made. No delivery arrived. No emergency apology was required.

And most importantly of all, I was not thrown into the canal – which, in Amsterdam, counts as a successful evening.

CHAPTER THIRTY

AMSTERDAM AND THE CALL FROM HOME

The morning light in Amsterdam was perfect.

Not dramatic. Not trying too hard. Just quietly flawless. A soft, golden wash slid through the hotel window, glinting off the canal water and bouncing politely off the rows of bicycles lining the railings below. Even the ducks looked organised, gliding past in neat formation, as if they'd attended a briefing and agreed on a route.

By breakfast we were laughing about the previous night: my accidental performance, Alex's coat donation, and the hookah flyer that never got its moment of glory. Amsterdam had been everything it promises: surprising, a little naughty, and full of good-hearted mischief.

It was the kind of morning that made you believe the world, on the whole, had things under control.

Today, we planned something modest and civilised. A long walk along the canals. Pancakes. Coffee. The glow of travellers who had mastered Europe.

We had just got back to the room after breakfast when Alex's phone rang.

She looked at the screen and her face changed instantly, from relaxed contentment to something darker, cloudier.

"Maria," she said.

Of course it was.

Alex put the call on speaker.

"Alex!" Maria's voice exploded into the room, loud enough to alarm a cyclist outside and possibly a duck. "Finally! Where *are* you?"

"In Amsterdam," Alex said carefully.

There was a pause. A sharp intake of breath.

"Still?" Maria demanded. "My God, what are you doing there? Smoking wacky baccy while Pefki crumbles? It's a disaster here!"

Behind her words came a familiar soundtrack: raised voices, meowing, something metallic being dragged across stone, and what sounded suspiciously like a goat being consulted.

I closed my eyes.

"What happened?" Alex asked.

"It rained again!" Maria announced triumphantly, as if rain were a personal betrayal. "A lot. The street became a river. Again."

I rubbed my temples. "Please tell me Nemesis isn't involved."

"It came out of the land next door and onto the road," Maria continued, ignoring me. "So the neighbours decided something had to be done."

My stomach tightened. Decisions in Pefki rarely involve paperwork and often involve tools.

"What sort of something?" I asked.

There was another pause. Then Maria spoke slowly, solemnly, like an oracle who had rehearsed this moment.

"There's good news and bad news."

Alex glanced at me. "Go on."

"The good news," Maria said, "is that Nemesis has stopped shouting at the water."

"And the bad?" Alex asked.

"They are building a dam."

I froze.

"A what?"

"A dam," Maria repeated, as if this were the obvious next step in any rainfall event. "Across the river where it comes out beside your house."

In my mind, a small alarm began ringing, the one that usually accompanies phrases like *beside your house.*

"They decided the river must be stopped before it reaches the road again," Maria continued. "So the men met outside

Costa's house, drank coffee, and agreed to take action. The mayor has not been told yet, because he will only ask for plans and permission."

I paused.

"Stopped how?" I asked cautiously.

There was a silence at the other end of the line; the sort that suggests thinking is happening, but not urgently.

"They will block it," Maria said finally. "So it cannot go onto the road."

This was presented as a complete solution.

I tried to picture it. If the water was prevented from leaving the land next to our house and spilling onto the road, there were only two other places it could go. Back up the mountain, which seemed unlikely, or sideways.

Sideways was us.

In purely logical terms, blocking the river before it reached the road didn't remove the water. It simply gave it a new ambition. And that ambition, I suspected, would involve our living room.

"So instead of running down the road," I said slowly, "it would run through our house."

Maria sounded unconcerned. "Well, it must go somewhere."

"Yes," I said. "And that somewhere appears to be our sofa."

She made a small dismissive noise. "Don't exaggerate."

I imagined our perfectly innocent house, the furniture unaware of its fate if the dam did what they said it would and held the water, and felt a familiar tightening in my chest.

In Pefki, problems are not solved. They are redirected.

And very often, they are redirected at us.

Through the speaker we could hear the unmistakable sounds of enthusiasm: laughter, shouting, metal striking stone.

"Who is building it?" Alex asked.

"Everyone," Maria said proudly. "Dimitri is in charge because he once worked on the ferry dock. Yiannis brought his tractor. Theodora made sandwiches. Father Andreas came to bless it, just in case. Nemesis is smiling."

I put my head in my hands. "What exactly is it made of?"

"Reinforced optimism," Alex muttered.

Maria ignored her. "Mostly rocks. And two old car doors. Someone found some bricks behind the kafenio. Also, Spiros brought his old washing machine because it has a very strong drum."

"A washing machine," I repeated.

"Yes," Maria said firmly. "It blocks the water perfectly. Theodora says Poseidon himself could not push through that drum."

We fell silent, the image forming slowly in our minds: a Greek river being restrained by faith, furniture, and domestic appliances.

Alex began to laugh. "Maria, you're telling me the village is building a dam out of car doors and a washing machine?"

"Yes," Maria said cheerfully. "And it's working! The water has stopped."

I knew better than to ask *where* it had stopped.

"And when it rains again?" I asked.

"They will fix it," Maria said confidently. "We are ready for anything now."

In village language, this means nothing is ready and everything is about to happen again.

Maria sent a photo.

Five men stood proudly in the riverbed beside our home, grinning like pioneers. At the centre was an upturned bathtub. Above it, a Greek flag fluttered from a broom handle.

The caption read simply: SUCCESS.

We were just digesting this information and worrying whether, if the dam actually worked and did stop the water, our home would flood again. Then Maria rang again. This time she was breathless.

"The dam has moved," she said.

"Moved?" I asked. "You mean collapsed?"

"No, no," she corrected. "It didn't collapse. It just… relocated."

Apparently, the water had risen behind the structure, considered it briefly, and then lifted the entire thing and carried it several metres down the road – bathtub, washing machine, flag and all.

"It's now in Costa's field," Maria said. "He says it's blocking the olives."

"And Nemesis?" Alex asked.

"She says it's still your fault," Maria replied. "Because the water is yours, and the water moved the dam. So the dam must also be yours."

"Of course," I said. "That makes perfect sense."

"They will try again," Maria added. "This time higher. Dimitri found metal poles from an old trampoline."

Alex was laughing so hard she had to sit down. "Maria," she said, trying to catch her breath, "please tell them to stop before they start charging admission."

"I already did," Maria replied. "But Theodora says if the water pools there again, even just a little, she will put fish in it and call it a lake. She says tourists like lakes."

It wasn't a lake, of course. What had actually happened was that the water, having nowhere sensible to go for a while, had spread out across a dip in the road and lingered there, shallow and temporary. But this was a Greek village, and facts are only the opening bid.

By the evening, the story had grown.

What had been a stretch of flooded road was now being discussed as a body of water. Not deep, not permanent, but promising. Something that might, with encouragement, become an attraction.

Maria said the whole village was talking.

Marily at the Island Hotel was calling it a miracle, on the grounds that nothing like it had ever happened before and it was definitely not her fault.

Eleni claimed she had seen dolphins, though Maria suspected this was a reflection, a plastic bag, or enthusiasm.

Nicho said it was the first time in living memory that the village had agreed on anything, which alone made it historic.

The final message from Maria came later. Wind in the background, laughter between words, her voice breaking as she tried to stay serious.

"They are talking about calling it," she said, pausing for effect, "Lake Peter."

I put the phone down slowly and looked at Alex.

"We've gone from owning a river," I said, "to owning a lake."

She smiled, entirely untroubled. "That's progress."

In Pefki, problems rarely disappear. They simply rebrand.

The dam – heroic but outmatched – was eventually swept away completely so the lake never materialised.

And that, in the end, is what I love most about our village.

Logic bends. Structures float away. Blame circles like seagulls after a storm.

But nobody gives up.

By next week they'll be planning a bigger dam. Or a bridge. Or, as Theodora suggested, a barbecue area beside the *new lake*.

Meanwhile, we'll keep travelling – one eye on the road, one ear on Maria, and the quiet certainty that somewhere in Pefki, the next great engineering project is already under construction.

Probably out of old bicycles.

Alex leaned back.

"We really should go back," she said.

"Because we miss home?" I asked.

"No," she said. "Because apparently we now own a lake, a dam, and a criminal animal."

We sat on the bed for a while after the call, staring at the serene canal outside. A man cycled past with a bouquet of tulips and a small child balanced in a wooden box at the front of his bike. The Dutch world carried on with impossible order. Meanwhile, in Pefki, the laws of gravity, property, and reason had clearly packed up and left.

"We've seen the canals, we've eaten the pancakes, and I nearly bought a coat for a prostitute. That's enough culture. Now we go home, before the jackal takes over the house."

I tried reason. "It's two thousand kilometres, Alex. Through snow. And tolls. And—"

She was already on her feet, suitcase in hand. "Let's go."

And that was that. The decision had been made, not by logic, but by instinct. Greek instinct. The kind that ignores maps and weather forecasts and simply knows when it's time to go home.

I dragged the suitcase onto the bed and began the usual routine, folding my clothes with the precision of someone who knows there's going to be a "Why doesn't this zipper close?" argument later. Then I moved on to Alex's pile, which, of course, was less about clothes and more about her relentless souvenir shopping spree.

I opened the carrier bags she'd stuffed into the corner of the room and started transferring her loot into the suitcase. Dutch cheese, fine. Pretty postcards, lovely. A pair of those tacky but endearing clogs, adorable. But then, I pulled out… a rather suggestive, oversized penis-shaped lollipop. I stopped mid-pack and gave Alex a raised eyebrow.

"What?" she said, utterly unapologetic. "It's for Maria. She'll love it."

Before I could respond, my hand brushed against something else at the bottom of the bag. I pulled it out slowly, like it might explode. It was a suspiciously dense, foil-wrapped lump. On the front of the pack was a picture of a green cannabis plant and big letters spelling: "SPACE CAKE EXTRA STRONG". My eyes widened. She bought space cake?!

"Alex!" I exclaimed, holding the incriminating lump of baked goods in the air like a piece of radioactive material. "You bought space cake while I wasn't looking?!"

She gave me her most innocent, wide-eyed look. "It's just cake. Relax."

"Relax?!" I sputtered. "We're about to drive through half of Europe, past customs, with sniffer dogs. You know, the ones trained to find stuff like this!" I could already picture it – port police pulling us over, dogs barking like maniacs, me being handcuffed while trying to explain that my wife wanted a snack for the road.

"Oh, stop being dramatic," Alex said, swiping the cake out of my hand and tossing it back into the bag. "It's perfectly legal here."

"Here! Yes! But the minute we hit the border, this goes from being a fun souvenir to me starring in an episode of *Locked Up Abroad*! You're turning me into an international drug smuggler!"

Alex shrugged. "If they ask, just tell them it's your lunch."

I stared at her, dumbfounded. "Lunch?! It's a brick of drugs disguised as dessert! You think the sniffer dogs are just going to be like, 'Oh, monsieur, enjoy your gâteau?'"

She rolled her eyes and went back to packing her postcards like she hadn't just potentially ruined my clean criminal record. "Honestly, Peter, you're such a worrier."

By the time we zipped up the suitcase, I was mentally preparing for how I'd explain this to the Italian border agents. "Good morning, officer. Yes, I know my wife bought a large piece of space cake. No, I didn't eat it. No, I don't want to share. Please, no cavity search."

As we finished packing, I muttered, "I can't believe I might end up in prison because of your snack choices."

Alex just grinned and patted my arm. "Relax. If they stop us, I'll smile at them. It always works."

Somehow, that didn't make me feel any better.

When Alex wasn't looking, I stealthily fished the incriminating space cake out of the suitcase and left it on the bedside table with a 20 euro note. The maid was going to get the tip of her life, and possibly the most "relaxing" cleaning shift ever.

The receptionist wished us a pleasant onward journey in flawless English. Alex smiled sweetly and replied in Greek, "If the gods are kind."

He looked mildly alarmed, which felt appropriate.

Outside, the air was crisp, the sky a perfect northern blue as we climbed into the car. "Ready?" she asked.

I nodded. "If we leave now, we can be in Munich by night-fall."

She took a sip of her coffee, smiled, and looked south in the direction of home and brewing trouble.

For a moment we sat together, watching the neat Dutch world go about its business. Somewhere far to the south, Maria was no doubt narrating our absence live to the entire village. Dimitri was servicing his dam with optimism and no real materials. The priest was running low on holy water. And Nemesis… Nemesis was probably already writing her next speech.

So we started the car.

Because in Greece, as Alex always says, when the gods start laughing, you may as well join in.

CHAPTER THIRTY-ONE

MUNICH – LEDERHOSEN, LAGERS
AND LESSONS IN SPEED

We'd gone far enough north.

Belgium had been beautiful, Amsterdam enlightening, and the situation back home – involving a jackal, a river, and several men with tools increasingly troubling.

But now we accepted that we were heading back.

Not rushing. Not fleeing. Just… orienting ourselves vaguely in the direction of responsibility.

We were having far too lovely a time to do anything dramatic. We felt refreshed, lighter, and only mildly haunted by the knowledge that we did, in fact, still belong to a Greek village that notices absence. We didn't want to go home yet, but it was time to begin behaving as if we might, eventually.

So we did what sensible people do.

We planned.

Maps came out. Distances were calculated. Fingers traced optimistic lines across Europe.

The route emerged slowly. A long drive from here to Munich, a quick overnight stop, then on to Salzburg for two days. After that, a longer haul to Venice, where we'd stay another two days to wander, get lost, and pretend we understood the place. Then the ferry. Thirty-five hours across the Adriatic to Patra. Then home.

It was measured. Balanced. Mature.

I agreed with it completely.

Which is why I immediately attempted to renegotiate.

"What about a full day and night in Munich?" I suggested casually. "Then only one day in Salzburg. Venice stays the same."

Alex looked at me.

"Why Munich?"

"Well," I said, choosing my tone carefully, "beer halls."

"No."

"I haven't finished."

"You don't need to."

To me, Germany has always meant beer served in quantities normally associated with buckets.

A German beer hall, in my imagination, is not a place so

much as a system. Vast wooden rooms built for serious purposes. Long tables designed to remove personal space and encourage conversation whether you want it or not. Benches polished smooth by generations of elbows.

You don't order beer in a beer hall. It arrives. A litre appears in front of you without discussion, negotiation, or judgement. It lands with a solid thud that says this is not your first and will not be your last.

People laugh properly in beer halls. Loudly. From the chest. Strangers talk to each other as if they've known each other for years, or at least since the previous beer. Food arrives in similarly ambitious proportions. Sausages the size of plumbing. Pretzels that could double as flotation devices. Mustard applied with conviction.

There is music somewhere in the background: usually brass, always confident, sometimes live, sometimes played by men who look like they were born holding a tuba. It doesn't ask for attention. It simply exists, steady and reassuring, like the building itself.

Time behaves differently inside a beer hall. A morning can drift into afternoon without anyone noticing. Nobody checks their watch because nobody needs to.

It is civilised chaos. Structured joy. Happiness served in glassware designed to build arm strength.

At least, that's how I've always understood it.

Which is why Munich without beer felt like turning up to the Parthenon and finding it closed for lunch.

Alex, meanwhile, imagined something else entirely. Driving.

"Peter," she said, folding the map with finality, "we are driving. That means no beer."

"I could have one," I offered. "A ceremonial beer. For cultural reasons."

"No."

"A half?"

"No."

"A sip?"

"Absolutely not."

This clearly required further discussion.

I pointed out, reasonably I felt, that she was already getting Salzburg.

Salzburg came with mountains. Salzburg came with fresh air. Salzburg came with history, culture, and Julie Andrews twirling energetically on hillsides she did not personally own but had made famous.

All I was asking for was Munich.

One modest day. A gentle pause. Beer. Pretzels. Wooden benches that had supported generations of thoughtful drinking. History you could sit on.

She listened without interrupting, which is never a good sign.

"I'm not asking for much," I added. "Just one day devoted to hops and contemplation."

She folded her arms. "You've already had Champagne."

"That was decided fairly," I said. "By coin toss."

Her eyes narrowed. "You cheated."

"I did not."

"You changed the rules."

"After you lost."

"I still lost," she said. "Which proves cheating."

I felt this was drifting away from evidence.

She shook her head slowly. "Fine. We toss a coin."

Relief washed over me.

"But," she added, "I choose the coin."

This seemed unfair. Deeply unfair. But I was buoyed by recent success and the quiet optimism that comes from selective memory.

We flipped.

Alex won.

She smiled with the calm satisfaction of someone who had never doubted the outcome.

"Well," she said, picking up her bag, "Salzburg awaits."

I nodded, already adjusting my expectations.

Munich, it turned out, would have to wait.

She smiled. "See?"

I sighed, folded myself into the passenger seat, and watched Munich slip past in my imagination, full of beer I would never drink.

We joined the Autobahn.

Some negotiations, it turns out, are symbolic rather than successful.

The Autobahn is not so much a road as a national philosophy. It begins politely enough – smooth surface, clear signs, a sense of calm – and then suddenly reveals itself as a place where German cars travel at speeds normally reserved for aviation.

In my mirror, a small black dot appeared. Two seconds later it was a Mercedes, overtaking us at what I can only describe as disrespectful velocity. The driver glanced at me as he passed, not angrily, but with pity.

I pressed the accelerator. The Citroën responded with encouragement rather than urgency and managed a dignified 130 kilometres an hour.

Then a Porsche arrived, overtook us, and disappeared into the future.

"Peter," Alex said calmly, "we are stationary."

"We are moving," I replied. "Just… symbolically."

An Audi shot past, followed by another, then something low and expensive that looked like it had escaped from a racetrack.

Alex started timing them on her phone.

"That one took three seconds from horizon to horizon," she said. "That's faster than a priest in confession."

We survived the Autobahn through concentration, mutual support, and the fact that the Citroën eventually refused to go any faster on ethical grounds.

It was late when we finally arrived; the sort of late where your body has given up pretending it's enjoying itself. We were due to stay one night in a hotel and leave early. This, I assumed, meant a brief pause. A recovery. Possibly a beer.

Alex was already talking about our next destination, Salzburg, with the kind of brightness usually reserved for childhood heroes and saints. Munich, in her mind, was not a city. It was a corridor.

I would have loved to stay a little longer, but I lost the toss, and a deal is a deal. The deal, to be clear, was that we moved on.

This was unfortunate, because Munich beer is not really beer. It is a commitment. A litre arrives whether you asked for it or not, and once it's in front of you, you feel a moral responsibility to see it through, even if it alters your posture and your afternoon.

Alex, however, already had her sights set firmly on Salzburg. Julie Andrews. Mountains. Singing. Purpose.

Which meant Munich would be reduced to a brief stop.

With admiration.

And no beer.

Alex loved Munich instantly.

"It's so clean," she said, turning slowly, taking it all in. "Even the pigeons look organised."

She was right. Munich pigeons don't flap or argue. They queue politely, take turns, and appear to have a shared understanding about personal space.

"Because you love it, let's stay an extra day," I tried.

"No."

We parked near Marienplatz just as the Glockenspiel began. Above us, the clock tower came alive. Little wooden doors opened. Painted figures stepped out with solemn purpose. Knights emerged and began to joust, circling each other with mechanical dignity, lances raised, honour intact. Bells chimed. Figures turned. History replayed itself on schedule.

A small crowd gathered, watching in respectful silence, as if this happened only once a year rather than twice a day. Children stared. Adults filmed. Nobody questioned why medieval tournaments were happening above a shopping square.

"It's impressive," Alex said.

The knights clashed again. A drummer spun. A rooster crowed with what I assume was enthusiasm.

"Do they ever get tired?" Alex asked.

"Probably," I said. "But they're German."

The performance ended. The doors closed. Normal life resumed immediately.

The next morning we were up early. Alex was keen. Focused. Determined to get me out of Munich before the beer halls opened and ruined her schedule.

I glanced wistfully at a passing sign pointing towards something involving hops.

"Quick breakfast," she said. "Then we go." Julie Andrews awaited.

My Munich dreams faded from my mind. No beer had been consumed.

And somehow, that felt like a loss worth documenting.

Munich without beer, I knew, would haunt me. Some regrets fade. This would not.

As we checked out of the hotel and dragged our suitcase towards the car, the city was already awake.

The Hard Rock Café across the street was serving breakfast, its doors wide, guitars polished, eggs presumably on standby. Alex didn't even glance at it.

My eyes, however, were fixed on the building opposite.

A beer hall.

Open.

At breakfast time.

I stopped walking.

Inside, visible through tall windows, a brass band was at work, jackets neatly pressed, sheet music clipped in place, cheeks puffed with effort. They were playing something that sounded suspiciously like ABBA, only slower, louder, and with the sort of dignity that comes from having played the same instruments for decades.

Men in traditional jackets sat at long wooden tables, drinking beer the size of small aquariums with the calm confidence of people who had made excellent life choices.

I watched, transfixed, mourning not just the absence of beer this morning, but yesterday's failure to drink any at all.

"This," I said carefully, choosing my words like a man negotiating his release, "would be the ideal moment."

Alex kept walking.

"Breakfast," I continued, louder now, "in a beer hall."

She stopped, turned, and looked at me the way you look at someone who has suggested sleeping in an airport for fun.

"No."

"They're playing music," I said, gesturing wildly. "It's cultural."

"It's eight in the morning."

"Exactly," I said. "Peak beer-hall hour."

She shook her head. "You are not starting the day like this."

I looked back through the window one last time. The band hit a triumphant note. A man raised his stein. Somewhere, a sausage was being honoured.

"One look," I tried. "We don't have to go in."

"No."

"A photograph?"

"No."

I sighed. "History will record this as a missed opportunity."

"It will record you as the designated driver," she replied.

As we walked along the Isar, sunlight glinting on the water, cyclists gliding past with serene efficiency, I looked south, towards the Alps and Italy beyond. Venice awaited. Sunshine. A ferry. Greece.

And behind us, Munich carried on efficiently: bells chiming, brass bands playing, sausages being haggled over, and beer halls quietly waiting for people who weren't driving.

"Munich will remember this," I muttered.

Alex smiled sweetly. "You can regret it forever."

And so we left Munich behind, sober, disciplined, and emotionally bruised.

Some cities give you memories.

Munich gave me unfinished business.
Next time, I promised myself.
Next time, I'm taking the train.

CHAPTER THIRTY-TWO:

SALZBURG – THE HILLS ARE ALIVE (BUT ALEX HAS QUESTIONS)

I left Munich in a sulk.

This wasn't because Munich had disappointed me. Quite the opposite. Munich had been warm, elegant, welcoming, and filled with beer halls, not a single one of which I had entered.

Who goes to Munich and doesn't visit a beer hall?

It's not normal.

It's not civilised.

It's not something a man recovers from easily.

Alex, meanwhile, was radiant.

As we drove south, the air itself seemed to change. It felt thinner somehow, cleaner, as though it had been filtered through mountains and discipline. The road softened into gentle curves. Meadows opened out. Wooden chalets appeared, balconies lined with tidy wooden boxes of flowers, cows grazing with the serene confidence of creatures who had never seen a Greek village.

Alex rolled down the window and inhaled deeply.

"Ah," she said. "Austria."

"It smells organised," I muttered.

She ignored me.

By mid-morning we were drawing closer to Salzburg, the scenery growing more theatrical with every kilometre. Peaks rose calmly, forests thickened, rivers slid beside us like silver ribbons.

"This," Alex announced, "is how Greece would look if everyone stopped arguing for ten years."

"That would require a miracle," I said.

She nodded. "Or a dictatorship. But a nice one."

Salzburg appeared gently, like it didn't want to show off. Spires and domes caught the light. Mountains framed the city like theatre curtains. Church bells drifted through the air, sounding approving rather than alarmed.

Alex pressed her nose to the window.

"Oh, Peter," she breathed. "It's *The Sound of Music*."

I groaned.

"We are not singing."

She smiled sweetly. "We'll see."

Our hotel sat quietly in the centre of Salzburg, tucked into an old building that looked as though it had been minding its own business for several centuries. Nothing announced itself. There were no grand gestures, no dramatic flourishes. The place whispered rather than spoke.

Inside, everything was hushed. The carpets looked faintly offended by shoes, as if they had expected slippers and better behaviour. Doors closed softly. Voices lowered themselves without being asked. Even the lift seemed reluctant to make a sound.

From the window, the city laid itself out with quiet confidence. Red-tiled rooftops stepped neatly towards the river. Church spires rose at careful intervals, each one claiming its share of the skyline without competing too hard. Beyond them, the hills held their position, green and immovable, as if keeping Salzburg contained by mutual agreement.

It was a view designed to reassure. Everything in its place. Everything accounted for. A city that had decided long ago what it was and saw no reason to revisit the matter.

Alex stood beside me for a moment, taking it in.

"Well," she said, approvingly, "this feels organised."

In Salzburg, even the silence seemed to have a plan.

I was still thinking about beer when we left the hotel to explore the city.

Then we reached the bus station. A sign stood there, bold and unavoidable: THE SOUND OF MUSIC TOURS – SEE WHERE MARIA SANG!

Alex stopped dead.

I did not.

"We're going," she said.

"We're absolutely not."

She turned to me slowly, eyebrows raised.

"Why not?"

"Because," I said, "it involves singing, buses, and forced joy."

"And?"

"And I am British."

She considered this. Then nodded. "Yes. That explains a lot."

Ten minutes later, I was on a coach painted with dancing nuns, surrounded by fifty people vibrating with excitement. The driver wore a feathered hat. The guide wore lederhosen so tight they raised ethical questions.

He bounced to the front.

"*Guten Morgen*, my musical family!"

Alex clapped.

I looked for the exit.

The singing began almost immediately. Half the bus joined in without hesitation. Alex sang softly, happily, eyes shining. She nudged me.

"Sing."

"I'm observing."

The guide clapped enthusiastically. "Feel the freedom!"

Alex leaned forward. "Excuse me," she said brightly. "Before we feel the freedom, can I ask a question?"

The guide beamed. "Of course!"

"Are we seeing the real places," she asked, "or just the places that look nice in the film?"

A pause.

"Well," he said carefully, "these are the filming locations."

Alex nodded. "Yes. But the real family. Where did they actually live?"

Another pause.

"They lived… nearby."

"Nearby like next door," Alex pressed, "or nearby like somewhere completely different but less cinematic?"

The Americans leaned in. I sank lower in my seat.

"Well," the guide said, adjusting his enthusiasm slightly, "the film used locations that captured the spirit—"

"The spirit," Alex repeated. "So not the reality."

The guide smiled bravely. "The hills are alive."

"They're also real hills," Alex said. "I just want to know which ones."

Stop one: the gazebo.

People twirled. Alex did not. She stood with her arms crossed, examining it like a crime scene.

"So," she said to the guide, "this is not where the family lived."

"No."

"And not where they sang."

"No."

"But it looks romantic."

"Yes."

She nodded. "Good. As long as we're clear."

I tried not to laugh.

On the bus, lyric sheets were handed out. The singing resumed.

Alex sang. I did not.

Between verses, she leaned across the aisle to interrogate another tourist.

"You really believe they sang all the time?" she asked kindly.

"Well," the woman replied, uncertainly.

"In Greece," Alex said, "if someone sings this much, it means something is wrong."

At the meadow – *the* meadow – people spun joyfully.

Alex stepped out, looked around, then turned back to the guide.

"And Julie Andrews didn't actually sing here, did she?"

"No, this was filmed later."

"And the real family didn't spin here."

"No."

"And they didn't escape over these mountains."

"No."

Alex smiled. "So this is like Instagram."

The guide laughed nervously. "Yes! Very much Instagram."

"Good," Alex said. "I hate Instagram."

Despite herself, she eventually spun – once – arms wide, laughing. I took a photo.

"You look happy," I said.

"I am," she replied. "But I'm still right."

At the abbey stop, the guide explained that the real von Trapps took a train.

Alex lit up. "Ah! Practical. Sensible. I like them already."

On the final sing-along, even I hummed, quietly, defensively.

Alex leaned over. "See? You're enjoying it."

"I'm tolerating it musically."

When it ended, the guide shook my hand.

"Did you enjoy it?"

"I learned," Alex said before I could answer. "Which is better."

Outside, bells rang softly. Alex slipped her arm through mine.

"See?" she said. "You need to question things."

"Yes," I replied. "But next time, I'm questioning the itinerary before I get on the bus."

That evening, Salzburg redeemed itself quietly.

Not with choreography. Not with spinning nuns. But with schnitzel the size of a small roof tile, beer served without ceremony, and locals who sang only when the mood genuinely took them. This felt more reassuring.

Alex hummed contentedly as we walked back through the streets.

"I still don't believe they escaped singing," she said.

"I don't believe anyone sings that much without wine," I replied.

We decided to stay another day. Salzburg, it turned out, deserved it.

The following morning we crossed the river early, the water moving steadily beneath us, pale green and purposeful, carrying reflections of the Alps downstream one careful ripple at a time. The mountains rose around the town like quiet guardians, close enough to feel protective rather than dramatic, as if Salzburg had been placed there deliberately and told not to move.

We wandered through the old town market, past stalls selling cheeses with confidence, sausages with opinions, and bread that looked as though it had been baked by people who took history personally. Nothing here felt rushed. Even the tourists behaved.

Alex stopped frequently.

"This smells honest," she said at one stall.

"This smells dangerous," I said at another.

We crossed the bridge heavy with padlocks, thousands of them clinging to the railings, each one marking a declaration of love, hope, or optimism. Names were etched everywhere. Dates. Promises. Entire relationships reduced to metal and belief.

"It's romantic," Alex said.

"It's also structural," I replied. "At some point the bridge will file a complaint."

She laughed and squeezed my hand. "Ours would hold."

I wasn't entirely sure whether she meant the bridge or us.

Salzburg carries its history lightly, but it never lets you forget it. Everywhere we walked, there were gentle reminders that this was the birthplace of someone very important. His face appeared on chocolates, postcards, shop windows, and mugs. His hair was immaculate. His expression suggested mild irritation, possibly at tourists.

Wolfgang Amadeus Mozart was born here, composed here, and then sensibly left. Salzburg is very proud of him for all three.

There is a quiet confidence to the way the city handles Mozart. It doesn't shout. It assumes you know. Churches hum faintly with echoes of his music. Courtyards feel acoustically superior for reasons no one fully explains. Even the silence seems organised, as if waiting for the correct note.

"This is where genius came from," Alex said, pausing outside one of the many Mozart-related buildings that Salzburg scatters about with admirable confidence.

"Yes," I said. "And possibly why it needed fresh air."

Like most visitors, we had assumed Salzburg's name had something to do with music. It feels plausible. A place this neat, this composed, this full of violins in shop windows surely must be named for sound.

It isn't.

Salzburg, we learned, has nothing to do with music at all.

It's named for salt.

Saltzburg.

Which, once you know it, explains rather a lot.

Long before symphonies, the fortress above the town guarded the trade routes that made the city wealthy. White gold, they called it. Salt paid for churches, palaces, fortifications, and the quiet certainty that still hangs in the air. The river once carried barges heavy with it through the valley.

Music came later. Salt came first.

We climbed slowly towards the fortress, stopping often, partly for the view and partly because Salzburg insists you look at it properly. Red roofs spread out below us. Church domes rose with calm authority. The river looped through the town like it had important places to be.

By the afternoon, we were walking without purpose, which is usually how you know you're enjoying a place. No checklist. No urgency. Just streets, river, mountains, and time behaving itself.

When we finally packed the car the next morning, it felt earned.

Salzburg had been kind. Thoughtful. Balanced.

A city built on salt, refined by music, and perfectly content to let you wander through it at your own pace, quietly humming, whether you realised it or not.

As we drove south again, Italy waiting ahead, I leaned back and sighed.

"Alright," I said. "I forgive them."

"For what?" Alex asked, still faintly humming.

"For all the singing."

She laughed. "You were singing."

"I was participating defensively."

Behind us, the hills were still alive. But now, at least, they had been properly explored.

CHAPTER THIRTY-THREE

The Underground River

We were having breakfast at the hotel when Maria sent the message.

It was early morning. The Alps were glowing softly, sunlight catching on their white tips like a blessing applied with care. The breakfast room smelled of coffee and warm croissants, and for once, everything felt calm. Balanced. Solved.

Which, in hindsight, should have worried us.

Alex was buttering bread with the quiet concentration of someone at peace. I was pouring coffee and thinking that

Salzburg, all things considered, had been remarkably free of complications.

My phone buzzed.

A message from Maria.

I stared at it for a moment.

"Well," I said, "here we go."

Alex looked up. "What?"

"I don't know yet," I said. "But judging by the timing, we're about to discover that the hills are alive with something."

Alex smiled faintly. "How do you solve a problem like Maria?" she said.

"You don't," I replied. "You manage it. Briefly. Then it evolves."

Outside, the mountains sat quietly, perfect and unconcerned. Inside, coffee cooled, croissants flaked, and somewhere far away, Maria was warming up.

Salzburg, it seemed, had given us music.

But home was already clearing its throat.

Alex groaned. "What now? Has Lake Peter expanded?"

My eyes widened as I read. "No. Something better. They're building the new river."

Alex blinked. "At last."

Readers who remember *The Parthenon Paradox* will know that when the water came, we weren't standing heroically in it, pointing at the sky. We were woken by the storm, realised something was very wrong, and then did what sensible people do in Greece when faced with biblical weather.

We left.

By the time we could get back to Pefki, the roads were impassable and our house unreachable. We stayed at Marily's hotel, damp, stunned, and waiting for news like people whose lives had been temporarily handed over to gravity.

What we know about what happened next, we know second-hand.

The mayor told us later. Proudly. As if he'd personally diverted the weather.

According to him, while we were away, the situation had escalated. There were inspections. Visits. Raised voices. At some point, a minister had toured flood-damaged areas of Evia, and the mayor, thinking quickly, had arranged for our house to be included.

This was done without telling us.

The minister never met us. He didn't drink coffee in our kitchen. He didn't wade through our living room while Alex offered biscuits. Those details belong to Nemesis's version of events, which is always more theatrical.

What actually happened was simpler, and more Greek.

The minister saw the damage. He was shown the path of the water. He was told, with great conviction, that something must be done. He nodded in the way ministers do when they want to look concerned but also to catch a ferry.

And a promise was made.

The river, the not-quite-a-river behind the houses, the one that behaved itself for years and then lost interest in subtlety, would be dealt with properly. Engineered. Redirected. A new channel would be built to take the water safely away, once and for all.

Athens had agreed. Funding had been approved. Plans would follow. A solution was on its way.

When we heard this, we laughed. The tired laugh. The one that arrives when relief and disbelief turn up together and neither quite knows what to do.

The danger, we were assured, would be removed. The village could move on. Our house could finally recover.

We rebuilt. Slowly. Carefully. We replanted. Alex resurrected the garden with determination and threats. Life resumed its normal rhythm.

And for a long time, nothing happened.

No new river. No machinery. No men with notebooks. Just time passing, and the unspoken assumption that, like many things in Greece, the promise was resting somewhere between intention and memory.

Until now.

Because when water appears again, attention sharpens. Old promises resurface. Conversations restart. And suddenly, everyone remembers that a new river was supposed to exist.

It hasn't arrived yet. But now, at least, it's being started. Which, in Pefki, is how all major projects begin their second life.

"A new river," Alex said slowly, scrolling through the messages from Maria on my phone. "From Athens."

"From Athens?" I said. "That's ambitious. Does it start at the Acropolis?"

She didn't look up. "Funding from Athens. The money. Apparently it's official."

That word again.

Official.

In Greece, *official* is not reassuring. It's a warning.

Maria's message was a breathless cascade of optimism, rumour, and prophecy, written in the unmistakable tone of someone leaning into the future while still standing firmly in chaos:

Good morning my dear friends.

Big news. Huge machines at the beach. They are building the new river.

Engineers say no more floods. Everything underground. Concrete river. Very modern. The mayor says this is progress.

Also Nemesis is furious because they will dig the road in front of her house and she cannot enter. She says this is targeted. But this is democracy.

I read it twice.

"An underground concrete river," I said. "So… plumbing."

Alex smiled. "They've finally decided to domesticate water."

For a moment, just a moment, it felt like the end of a long story.

No more floods.

No more accusations.

No more police officers looking at us as if we'd personally offended the clouds.

No more Nemesis standing in her wellington boots, pointing at rain.

The village, predictably, exploded with enthusiasm.

"They started from the beach," Maria explained later, "because the sea looks important. The road near your house looks like a mistake."

The plan, in theory, was elegant.

They would dig backwards, from the sea, through olive groves, under the road, past our garden, following the old river's unruly path.

Only this time, the river would be obedient.

Contained.

Civilised.

Invisible.

In theory.

The first problem appeared immediately: Nemesis.

Her house, it turned out, sat directly above the planned route of what the engineers were now calling the New Aquatic Management System.

Maria was delighted.

"They told her they must dig the road in front of her house," she said. "All of it."

"And?" I asked.

"She said, 'Then how will I enter my house?' They said, 'You will wait.' She said, 'Wait where?' They said, 'Wherever you can.'"

According to eyewitnesses, meaning everyone, Nemesis stood in the street for nearly an hour.

The foreman pointed at blueprints. Nemesis pointed at the sky.

He explained hydraulic flow. She explained moral responsibility.

He mentioned drainage capacity. She mentioned destiny.

Eventually, she called her lawyer, who, upon hearing the phrase *funding from Athens*, made a thoughtful noise and disconnected.

By lunchtime, the photos arrived.

A trench the size of an Olympic swimming pool cut straight down the road outside Nemesis's house. Concrete walls rose on either side. A digger crouched nearby, idling patiently.

And at the centre of it all stood Nemesis, arms crossed, immovable, flanked by villagers who had brought chairs.

Maria's caption read simply: *Nemesis says this is personal.*

By the following day, the village had taken sides.

Most believed the new river was a miracle; proof that Athens still remembered Pefki existed. Others insisted it was an ecological disaster; a concrete insult that would confuse the mountain and anger the water.

Theodora announced plans to sell souvlaki to the construction crew.

Dimitri claimed the tunnel would be lit "so the fish don't panic".

Spiros muttered that it should have been built ten years ago, before the Englishman made his lake.

And Nemesis said nothing at all. This, we knew, was not a good sign. She didn't come to the café. She didn't raise her voice in the street. She didn't explain herself to anyone. She stayed at home.

Instead, letters began to appear.

Formal ones. Typed. Carefully worded. Delivered by hand. Objections. Clarifications. Requests for review.

She discovered regulations. She cited protections. She referenced clauses nobody else remembered existed. Roads were described as "historic". Olive trees were referred to as "established". Boundaries were mentioned with a precision that suggested recent measurement.

The project, she wrote, benefited only certain properties.

Ours.

Maria relayed this information calmly, as if describing the weather.

"The machines are working," she said one evening. "The mayor came again. He wore a helmet. It was too big."

Work continued for a while. Slowly. Carefully. Until it didn't.

The excavators reached a section where the planned channel passed close to an olive tree Nemesis claimed as protected. Discussion followed. Then a pause.

That night, Maria called again.

"They moved the channel slightly," she said. "The engineer says it still works."

After that, everything stopped. No machines. No noise. No progress.

Alex stared at the phone. "She's doing it properly now."

"Yes," I said. "She's gone legal."

The next call came without preamble.

"She says it's encroachment," Maria said. "That the works crossed onto her land."

According to Nemesis, the revised channel followed a contour that ran too close to her boundary. A boundary she had, over the years, adjusted with quiet persistence. The measurement, Maria explained, had been done personally.

"With what?" Alex asked.

"A broom," Maria said. "She trusts it."

More letters followed. Requests for inspection. Claims of damage. Appeals for compensation.

And so the machines stopped completely.

The site was left as it was. Half-finished concrete. Exposed steel. An excavator parked slightly askew, as if uncertain whether it should still be there.

In Greece, once paperwork begins, movement ends.

The unfinished river settled into village life. Cats slept on the concrete. Children cycled through it. Officials arrived occasionally, nodded, and left again.

Nemesis remained at home.

She did not argue. She did not shout. She simply waited.

The village was with us, quietly. Athens had approved the funds. The plans still existed.

But Nemesis had found the one thing stronger than water. Paper.

And paper, in Greece, is patient.

The real problem was not the river construction. She must have secretly agreed that it was in everyone's interest, including hers. No, the real problem was that the people gaining the most from the river were the ones most seriously affected, and that happened to be us.

Somewhere beneath Pefki, the future waited.

And above it, Nemesis stood firm, daring the river to pass.

CHAPTER THIRTY-FOUR

THE FOR-SALE SIGN
(or: How Nemesis Finally Won)

The village did not defeat Nemesis with facts.

That had already been tried.

It did not defeat her with law.

That had merely encouraged her.

Instead, the village did what it does best when cornered by stubbornness, paperwork, and one very determined woman.

It lied.

Gently. Collectively. With style.

The idea was born, as most great Greek ideas are, over

coffee that had gone cold and biscuits that had been eaten by someone who had claimed not to want any.

"We cannot fight her," Maria said finally. "She enjoys fighting."

"She doesn't want the river," Dimitri added. "She wants to win."

This was important.

Nemesis had no deep emotional bond with floodwater. She did not commune with it. She did not sit beside it at dusk and reflect. What she loved, what sustained her, was *victory*.

And victory, the village realised, did not require us to lose.

It only required her to *believe* she had won.

Maria leaned back in her chair, eyes narrowing slightly. This was the look she gets when a solution has just arrived fully formed.

"We sell their house," she said.

There was a pause.

"Won't Peter and Alex have something to say about that?" asked Theodora.

"We don't actually sell it," she clarified. "We perform a sale."

Within an hour, the plan was in motion.

A local estate agent, one who owed Maria a favour dating back to a disputed inheritance and a goat, was summoned. He arrived with a measuring tape, a clipboard, and a complete understanding that he was not to ask questions.

By lunchtime, a FOR SALE sign appeared outside our gate. Large. Tasteful. Impossible to miss.

The effect was immediate.

Nemesis noticed it before the concrete set on the road.

Maria reported live.

"She is standing very still," Maria whispered down the phone. "Like a heron. She is reading it."

"Does she look happy?" Alex asked.

Maria went very quiet.

"She's gone back to the sign," she said slowly. "She's standing right in front of it now. Reading every word. Carefully."

A pause. Longer this time.

"Oh no," Maria added. "She's smiling."

Another pause, as if Maria were bracing herself.

"It's not a normal smile," she said. "It's the smile she does when something terrible has finally behaved properly. No teeth. Just satisfaction. Like she always knew this would happen and has been waiting for the world to catch up."

I could picture it perfectly. The slight tilt of the head. The arms folded. The stillness of someone absorbing victory rather than celebrating it.

"She just nodded," Maria continued. "Just once. Very small. Like a judge confirming a sentence."

Then, quietly, almost respectfully, she said, "She thinks she's won."

That afternoon, the second phase began: information. Carefully leaked. Never announced.

"Oh yes," Theodora said loudly in the bakery, "they loved Austria. Very clean. No flooding."

"I heard it's on a mountain," Spiros added. "High. Dry. Very foreign."

"Peter never liked damp," Dimitri agreed. "He prefers snow."

Maria, who understands narrative, refined it further. "They've bought already," she told anyone who would listen. "Near Salzburg. Or maybe Innsbruck. Somewhere musical."

By evening, the story had reached Nemesis.

She did not ask directly. That would have shown interest.

Instead, she mentioned casually to Maria that *foreigners never stay*.

Maria nodded sympathetically. "It's true. They always leave when they are defeated."

Nemesis smiled for the first time in weeks.

The next morning, something extraordinary happened.

Nemesis crossed the road, stood beside the trench and looked at the digger.

"Well?" she demanded of no one in particular. "Why is this river still not finished?"

The foreman blinked.

Maria nearly dropped her coffee.

"You want it finished?" the foreman asked carefully.

Nemesis folded her arms. "Of course. I don't want to live next to a hole. Now that they are leaving, there is no problem."

The village did not smile. That would have ruined everything. Instead, everyone nodded gravely.

"Yes," Dimitri said. "Now it makes sense."

"The timing was important," added Theodora.

Nemesis sniffed. "I knew this was the right outcome."

That afternoon, she phoned the municipality. The next day, she phoned Athens. By the end of the week, Nemesis had become the river's fiercest advocate.

"It must be finished properly," she told the engineer. "Not cheaply."

She complained about delays.

She criticised the concrete.

She demanded progress reports.

At one point, Maria reported that Nemesis had shouted at the digger for taking a cigarette break.

More men appeared. More machines. Better biscuits.

The river advanced.

The FOR SALE sign remained.

No one mentioned it. Not once. Nemesis walked past it daily, chin high, victorious.

She had driven us out. She had protected the village. She had won.

Alex read the updates, shaking her head.

"They're evil geniuses," she said.

"No," I replied. "They're Greek."

The river was completed: the concrete smooth, the water obedient. Floods were redirected elsewhere, preferably into history.

On the morning the final section was sealed, Nemesis stood at her gate, watching.

"It's good," she said. "This is how it should have been from the beginning."

Maria smiled. "You were right."

Nemesis nodded. "I usually am."

That afternoon, the FOR SALE sign quietly disappeared. The estate agent collected it, tipped his hat, and went back to selling apartments to Athenians who would never move in.

Nemesis noticed nothing.

Why would she? She had already won.

And somewhere beneath the village, the river flowed silently, efficiently, and with the faintest hint of laughter.

Because in Pefki, justice doesn't arrive with a verdict.

It arrives with a story everyone agrees not to correct.

CHAPTER THIRTY-FIVE

VENICE, VICTORY, AND THE ART
OF GOING HOME

We were happy.

Nemesis was happy too, mainly because, in her mind, we'd finally left the country and would never return.

Pefki was happy.

And the fact that everyone was happy at the same time should probably have made me check my pulse.

The new river was apparently doing what rivers rarely do in Greece: behaving. Maria said it was gliding through its concrete jacket like a well-trained dog on a lead, not barking, not biting, not flooding anyone's oregano.

Nemesis had already been spotted inspecting the ground outside her house, hands on hips, chin slightly raised, nodding at the soil as if she'd personally given the water a firm talking-to.

"The river knows its boundaries now," Alex said, when Maria reported this with the gravity of a weather bulletin.

"So do I," I told her.

Which was optimistic. But after weeks of being followed across Europe by phone calls about floods, committees, cats and wildlife politics, I felt entitled to one small lie.

Because that's the thing about travelling when you live in Pefki: you don't really leave. You just change scenery while the village continues to sit on your shoulder, whispering updates into your ear like a dramatic parrot.

We'd crossed borders, climbed mountains, eaten our way through half a continent, and still, every time Alex's phone lit up, it wasn't Italy calling. It wasn't Switzerland. It certainly wasn't the Netherlands.

It was always Pefki.

And now, at last, we were in Venice, the final stop, the calm at the end, the reward. Not because Venice is quiet (it isn't; it's full of people confidently walking in the wrong direction), but because for the first time on the whole trip, it felt like nothing back home needed fixing. No repairs. No explanations. No "just a few questions". Just water... behaving like water is supposed to behave.

We had left Salzburg with a boot that still smelled faintly of schnitzel, and a GPS that had taken on the tone of a tired marriage counsellor. It continued to give directions, but without any real belief in us as people.

The road south had drawn us into the Austrian Alps, through tunnels and over bridges, around sharp turns that opened suddenly into valleys so perfect you felt you should apologise for being there without a ticket. Snow still clung to the peaks like unfinished laundry. Water ran everywhere, neat and orderly and utterly uninterested in destroying anyone's property.

Alex had pressed her nose to the window.

"Look," she had said quietly. "The mountains touch the sky."

I had nodded, trying to look like the sort of man who routinely drives through landscapes like that, rather than someone who normally gets emotional about a well-organised supermarket.

We had stopped for coffee at a mountain café where the espresso arrived with apple strudel the size of a paving slab. I had eaten it with the gratitude of a man who had survived both Dutch cycling lanes and Greek flood gossip.

"This," Alex had said, stirring her coffee as if it required her personal approval, "is freedom."

"Yes," I had replied. "The kind that comes with small print."

She laughed, and I loved her for it, because that is our relationship in miniature. She finds the beauty. I quietly check what it's going to cost us.

By afternoon, the mountains had eased away, the light had softened, and Italy had arrived like an old friend who immediately puts food in front of you. Vineyards appeared. Rivers slowed. Even the air felt gentler, as if it had decided to stop shouting.

Alex had put on music, something Italian, full of strings and sunshine, and pointed theatrically.

"South," she said. "Towards the sea. Towards Venice."

And when the sign finally appeared – VENEZIA – something had loosened in my chest. Not excitement exactly. Relief. The quiet satisfaction of realising we had reached the end of one journey without dropping the plates.

Venice doesn't announce itself with a skyline. It announces itself with a change in the air: salt, diesel, and water that's always moving, as if it has somewhere important to be.

We did what every guidebook tells you to do: parked the car on the mainland, and then attempted to carry our suitcases as if we were still young and athletic. Within three minutes, I was reminded that I am neither.

We got on a vaporetto – a floating bus that behaves like it's running late – and as it roared across the lagoon, Alex stood at the rail laughing, hair flying, looking like she'd been born for this sort of arrival.

"This is wonderful!" she shouted.

I held onto a pole and tried to look brave. "It's like public transport," I shouted back, "but it wants to drown you."

And then the city rose ahead of us, domes and spires

and leaning buildings reflected in the water like a painting that somehow still functions as a place where people live and hang laundry.

For a moment, I just went quiet.

Venice had done what it always does. It made me stop narrating. It made me simply look.

We wandered the alleys and bridges, getting lost in that cheerful Venice way where you don't mind being lost because every wrong turn gives you something beautiful. Even I couldn't complain, and if you know me, you'll understand the significance of that.

At St Mark's Square, the bells rang, the pigeons behaved like they owned the place, and tourists posed as if they'd discovered Venice personally.

And then Alex danced.

At first it was nothing. Just a pause. A breath. The kind of stillness that comes right before a Greek woman decides that standing still is no longer appropriate.

She reached into her bag, the small one she carries everywhere, capable of producing passports, receipts from 2009, and emotional surprises, and pulled out a little Greek flag. The proper one. Blue and white, neatly folded, clearly brought along for reasons that had nothing to do with Venice and everything to do with being Greek.

She held it up, smiling to herself, and gave it a gentle wave, as if testing the air.

That's when I noticed the pavement café.

It sat right on the edge of St Mark's Square, tables crowded close together, chairs scraping stone, waiters weaving through with trays held aloft like offerings. White tablecloths fluttered slightly in the breeze. Coffee cups clinked. Spoons tapped. Conversations hummed in half a dozen languages, all competing with the bells, the pigeons, and the general sense that something important might happen at any moment.

Just outside the café, slightly elevated on a small wooden platform, sat a modest orchestra. A violin, a clarinet, an accordion, a double bass. Nothing flashy. The sort of group you assume will play pleasant background music while tourists drink overpriced cappuccinos and pretend not to notice the bill.

The conductor stood in front of them, jacket slightly shiny at the elbows, hair carefully arranged, baton resting casually against a small rostrum. He had the relaxed authority of a man who has seen everything Venice can throw at him and is still prepared to be surprised.

He saw Alex.

He saw the flag.

He paused.

Then, very deliberately, he tapped his stick once against the wood. The musicians looked up. Another tap. They exchanged glances – the kind musicians exchange when something unscripted is about to happen.

And then, softly, unmistakably, the first notes began.

Zorba the Greek.

Slow. Careful. Almost tentative. The melody unfurled gently into the square, like someone telling a secret.

Alex froze for half a second, that tiny moment when joy catches you off guard, and then she stepped forward.

It wasn't a performance; it was just movement. A few small steps. A turn. Arms lifting slightly, elbows loose, wrists soft. The flag moved with her, not waved so much as *included*, as if it too had been waiting for this moment.

I stood there, rooted to the spot.

"Peter," she called, smiling at me, eyes bright, "why are you standing like a lamppost?"

"I'm British," I said. "This is my dancing."

She laughed, that deep, easy laugh that says she already knows exactly who she married, and kept moving.

As the music continued, the beat began to change. Still slow, but fuller now. The clarinet leaned in. The violin found confidence. The rhythm started to gather itself.

That's when another woman approached.

About Alex's age. Dark hair pulled back. Sensible shoes. The sort of woman who looks like she's spent her life holding families together and finally decided she deserved five minutes for herself.

She didn't ask. She simply stepped up, smiled, and linked arms with Alex. They exchanged a look, instant, wordless, unmistakably Greek, and began to move together.

The music picked up again. The rhythm deepened. People started to notice.

A couple abandoned their table, forks still resting in half-eaten pasta. A group of teenagers stopped filming each other and turned their cameras outward. An elderly man in a hat began clapping softly, experimentally, as if checking whether this was allowed.

It was.

The beat quickened. More people joined. Not choreographed. Not rehearsed. Just instinct. A man with his jacket slung over his shoulder. A woman still holding a shopping bag. Someone's aunt. Someone else's grandmother.

They formed a loose line, then a curve, then something that looked suspiciously like a circle.

Those who didn't dance stepped back, naturally, creating space. A semi-circle formed around them, widening as more people stopped, drawn in by the music, by the joy, by the fact that something genuine was happening in a square usually reserved for postcards and pigeons.

Clapping spread through the crowd, first unevenly, then in time.

The orchestra leaned into it now. The conductor smiled – actually smiled – his baton cutting the air with more confidence. The bass thumped. The tempo rose.

Alex's steps grew bolder. The turns sharper. Her arms lifted higher now, flag trailing, her face alight with pride.

I watched her, my Greek wife, dancing Zorba in the middle of St Mark's Square, and felt that familiar, ridiculous mix of pride, love, and the quiet awareness that I would never, ever be the most interesting person in the room when she was around.

The square pulsed. People clapped. People laughed. Someone shouted "Bravo!" A waiter paused mid-step, tray balanced impossibly on one hand, and joined in with his free palm.

And I stood there thinking: *This is it.*

This is the end of the trip.

This is the moment we'll talk about when we're back in Pefki, when the river misbehaves again, when Nemesis has a new theory, when Maria phones with urgency in her voice.

This – Alex dancing, strangers joining, music filling the square – this is the memory that will carry us through the noise.

Eventually, as all good Greek things do, it ended not with a neat finish but with laughter, applause, and people who had not known each other ten minutes earlier hugging.

Alex came back to me, slightly breathless, cheeks flushed, flag folded again and tucked away.

She took my hand.

"Well?" she said.

I smiled.

"Yes," I said. "That. That was worth the whole journey."

And for once, Pefki didn't interrupt.

Because the truth is, we'd been carrying Pefki with us the whole way, like a noisy bag we couldn't put down. Floods, jackals, Nemesis, committees, rumours… always hovering, always waiting to jump back into the front of our minds.

But Venice, for one day, pushed it all to the side.

We were happy. Properly happy. The uncomplicated kind.

Nemesis was in Pefki nodding at the soil like a victorious general, and everyone believed, for a brief, suspiciously peaceful moment, that the worst of it might be over.

Which, of course, is never how it works in Greece.

But in Venice, under those bells, with Alex dancing and me pretending not to be moved by it, I allowed myself to think: *Maybe. Just maybe. We've earned a calm ending to this trip.*

And if nothing else, we'd made it to Venice without being arrested, flooded, or asked to register a jackal.

That felt like progress.

CHAPTER THIRTY-SIX

Homeward Bound

It was dark when we finally arrived.

That felt right somehow, returning under cover of night, when nothing is required of you except to unlock the door and breathe. We were tired in that deep, accumulated way that comes from too many borders, too many languages, and too much living out of a boot. Happy, yes. Relieved. But carrying that faint, unsettled feeling that comes when you've been away long enough for home to start feeling slightly theoretical.

From our regular calls with Maria, the village had sounded calm. Almost suspiciously so. Her updates had become shorter.

Fewer exclamation marks. Less urgency. According to her, things had "settled".

That alone should have concerned me.

We left Venice late in the afternoon, heart-light but suitcase-heavy, driving towards the ferry terminal with the focused optimism of people who just want to get on the boat without incident. The car felt swollen with our lives, bags stuffed with clothes that smelled of different countries, coats that hadn't been needed when we packed them, half-eaten snacks that had seen too much, and that odd emotional weight you carry when you suspect you might have escaped somewhere a little too easily.

Boarding the ferry was its usual exercise in humility.

We squeezed the Citroën into a slot clearly designed for something slimmer and more obedient. On one side, an iron girder. On the other, a gigantic air-conditioning unit blasting hot air directly into my ear like a creature with digestive issues. I folded mirrors, twisted sideways, and negotiated with the steering wheel in low whispers.

Alex watched, amused. "Just like old times," she said.

I gave her a look that suggested I might remember this later. She smiled sweetly and offered no assistance whatsoever.

The ferry from Venice to Patra takes long enough to make you reflective. Long enough for your thoughts to wander back to everything you thought you'd left behind. Long enough to realise that journeys don't erase problems, they just put them on hold.

We ate dinner in the ship's restaurant as the sky faded completely. The windows flickered with reflected waves. The ship lurched now and then, just enough to remind us we weren't done yet. We didn't talk much, just shared looks, small smiles, the unspoken agreement that we were suspended between worlds.

Outside, there was only night. The sea didn't reflect much, just absorbed light and thought. Through the porthole, moonlight traced a silver line across the waves. For a moment, everything stilled – the ship, the sea, our thoughts. I reached for her hand. Some moments don't need commentary.

Morning arrived pale and reluctant. We disembarked in Patra after thirty-odd hours, blinking into Greek light with the enthusiasm of people who had had quite enough Europe for now. The air felt different immediately. Warmer. Looser. It carried dust, coffee, hot metal, and the faint promise of something unplanned.

We were back in Greece.

Alex stretched and smiled at the hazy hills beyond the port. "Home."

"Almost," I said.

We crossed the Rio–Antirrio bridge – that long sweep of steel and cables stitching one part of Greece to another – one more time, and drove east into mountains that felt immediately familiar. Roadside shrines flickered past. The air smelled of pine. A bouzouki drifted from the radio.

The road north unwound through dusk. Olive groves flickered under the headlights. Every bend felt loaded with memory. Every stretch of tarmac carried echoes of previous arrivals – hopeful, anxious, exhausted.

And then, finally, Pefki.

The village lay quiet. Not asleep exactly, just holding its breath. No barking dogs. No late-night voices. No music drifting from a taverna. The silence of home is different from the silence of nowhere. It knows you.

We pulled into the drive. The gate creaked familiarly. The keys felt oddly cold in my hand. The house stood there, lights off, patient.

Alex stepped out first. "We're back," she said softly.

Inside, the house smelled of stillness. Dust had settled. The air hadn't moved much while we were gone. The walls looked exactly as we had left them, though we both knew what they carried with them. The memory of the flood. The repairs. The weeks of worry that linger long after the water has gone. Waiting.

We stood in the hallway for a moment, slightly disoriented, noticing how some rooms felt smaller than we remembered, how shadows gathered in corners we hadn't noticed before. But also, grateful. We had crossed borders and seas, trusted ferries and instincts, and arrived.

Alex slipped her arm through mine. "We did it," she said. "All the way."

I nodded. Part of me still felt out at sea, humming with engines. But here, in the quiet, something began to settle.

Tomorrow we would open windows. Walk the garden. See what had changed. See what hadn't. Maria would appear, full of updates. The village would resume its commentary.

But tonight, we were home.

Journeys don't always end with celebration. Sometimes they end with keys in the door, shoes kicked off, and the quiet understanding that whatever comes next can wait until morning.

And that was enough.

CHAPTER THIRTY-SEVEN

We went to Theodora's taverna for lunch because we were hungry, jet-lagged, and foolish enough to believe that one quiet meal might ease us back into village life gently.

This was optimistic.

Theodora's taverna is not just somewhere you eat. It is where information goes to stretch its legs. News doesn't arrive there, it waits. If you want to disappear in Pefki, you do not sit down anywhere that serves wine by the jug.

We chose a corner table, backs to the wall, the posture of people who have learned that survival here is largely about angles. Theodora greeted Alex with kisses, pinched my cheek hard enough to confirm I was solid, and poured wine without asking.

"Welcome back," she said.

We raised our glasses.

One sip.

That was all it took.

The grapevine whirred into life like a well-oiled generator. Chairs scraped softly. Phones appeared. Someone leaned out of a doorway "for air" and did not return. I felt it in my bones, that subtle shift when a village recalibrates.

By the time we reached the bottom of the first glass, the village knew we were back.

By the time the second arrived, the village had decided to join us for lunch.

Spiros wandered over "just for a minute". Eleni pulled up a chair. Dimitri appeared, followed by Kostas, then two men I vaguely recognised and one woman who clearly knew me far better than I knew her. Tables were dragged together. Plates arrived without explanation. Bread multiplied. Meat followed. Someone shouted for more wine.

Theodora watched it all with satisfaction.

"You see?" she said. "You leave, and nothing works properly."

News poured out.

The goats.

The electrician who rewired the church so the bells rang during funerals but not weddings.

The cats, now organised enough to require a rota.

Then, inevitably, we arrived at the river.

"Oh," Eleni said casually, as if mentioning a new haircut. "See, the river is finished."

"Completely," Dimitri nodded. "Underground. Concrete. Very modern."

"And quiet," Spiros added. "Like it was never angry."

I looked at Alex. She smiled slowly.

"And Nemesis?" Alex asked.

A pause. Smiles exchanged. Wine poured.

"She tried," Theodora said carefully. "Of course she tried."

Apparently, once construction resumed, thanks to the village's masterstroke involving a For-Sale sign and a collective refusal to tell the truth, Nemesis had reinvented herself yet again. No longer opponent, no longer victim.

Visionary.

"She told everyone she had pushed Athens," Eleni said.

"She said the Minister listens to her," Dimitri added.

"She says without her," Spiros concluded, "the river would still be a hole."

Alex raised an eyebrow. "And nobody corrected her?"

The table laughed.

"Why would we?" Theodora said. "It worked."

"And today," Eleni said, leaning in, "there is an opening ceremony."

"A ceremony?" I asked weakly.

"Yes," she nodded proudly. "This afternoon. Speeches. Blessings. Photos. Nemesis will be there."

"Of course she will," Alex said.

"She says she should be guest of honour," Dimitri added. "Because she suffered the most."

"And does she know," I asked carefully, "that we are back?"

A silence fell.

Then Theodora smiled.

"No," she said. "Nobody has told her."

I felt something settle into place. A perfect, terrible symmetry.

Nemesis would arrive believing she had driven us out, forced the river into obedience, saved the village single-handedly. The mayor in his good jacket. The priest with his water. The village nodding solemnly.

And then—

Us.

Alive. Present. Sitting politely near the back.

Alex leaned into her glass, eyes bright.

"Well," she said, "it would be rude not to attend."

Theodora clapped her hands. "Exactly."

Lunch continued. Laughter rose. Plates emptied. Wine flowed. Outside, beneath the road, the new river moved silently where it had been told to go, obedient at last.

The ceremony was waiting.

And Nemesis, blissfully unaware, was about to enjoy the surprise she had so carefully earned.

CHAPTER THIRTY-EIGHT

THE DEDICATION

Nemesis arrived early.

She always does. Victory, in her experience, improves with punctuality. She took her position beside the newly finished river, or rather, above it, since the whole point of the thing was that you couldn't see it any more, and stood with the posture of someone expecting applause to break out at any moment.

She wore her best coat. The wellington boots, naturally, were the same. Some things are non-negotiable.

The mayor arrived next, stepping from his car with the careful dignity of a man wearing his *important jacket*. It was navy, pressed, and worn only on occasions involving microphones or funerals. Today, it was doing civic duty. He shook hands, nodded gravely, adjusted his lapels, and positioned himself so the sunlight caught him at his most responsible angle.

The priest followed, swinging incense with enthusiasm and little regard for wind direction. A small cloud of holiness drifted towards the sea and was immediately absorbed by cigarettes and gossip.

By the time Alex and I arrived, the village had gathered. Not dramatically – Pefki never does drama openly – but fully. People leaned on walls. Sat on plastic chairs. Hovered near the coffee machine pretending not to watch. Children were positioned strategically in front. Cats occupied the warmest concrete slabs, unimpressed by infrastructure.

Nemesis was radiant.

She spoke quietly to anyone within range, explaining how difficult it had been. How much resistance she'd faced. How persistence and courage had prevailed. She gestured towards the invisible river with the proprietary air of someone who'd personally laid the concrete using moral strength alone.

Then she turned.

And saw us.

It wasn't a gasp. Nemesis doesn't gasp. It was more of a recalculation, a visible, internal reorganisation of reality. Her smile froze. Her eyes narrowed. For a second, she looked genuinely uncertain, like someone who's just spotted a ghost doing the shopping.

We smiled.

Politely.

Alex waved.

I nodded, the way one does at people who once had you arrested. Twice.

Nemesis blinked.

Then she did the only thing left to her: she turned away and stared very hard at the river, as if refusing to acknowledge us might erase us entirely.

The mayor cleared his throat. He stepped forward, clasped his hands, and began.

"Friends," he said, beaming. "Today is a great day for our village."

Murmurs of agreement rippled through the crowd.

"This river," he continued, gesturing vaguely at the road, the air, the general concept of water, "represents progress. Safety. Cooperation."

Nemesis nodded solemnly.

"It represents," the mayor went on, warming to his theme, "the end of suffering."

Nemesis nodded again.

"And above all," he said, pausing for effect, "it represents perseverance."

He turned. Towards us.

"I would like," he said loudly, clearly, and without hesitation, "to dedicate this new river to Peter and Alex."

There it was.

Clean. Simple. Irrevocable.

You could hear the moment land.

Nemesis's head snapped round.

"What?" she said. Loudly.

The mayor smiled. "Peter and Alex. Our friends. Without whom—" he gestured expansively "—none of this would have happened."

The priest nodded. The village nodded. Even the cats appeared to nod, though that may have been the heat.

Nemesis stepped forward. "Excuse me," she said sharply. "I believe there is a mistake."

The mayor glanced at her kindly, the way one does at someone who has misunderstood the rules of a game that has already ended.

"No mistake," he said. "They suffered most. They showed patience. And they brought attention."

Alex leaned towards me. "Attention," she whispered. "That's Greek for disaster."

Nemesis tried again. "But I—"

"Yes, yes," the mayor interrupted gently. "You were very… involved."

That was the most Greek insult possible. Vague. Absolute. Inarguable.

The priest stepped forward and raised his hand.

"Let us bless the river," he said. "And those who gave us reason to build it."

He sprinkled holy water.

Some of it landed on the road. Some on the mayor. A surprising amount on Nemesis's boots.

She looked down. Then up. Her mouth opened. Closed. For once, Nemesis had nothing to say.

Applause broke out. Not wild, but real. Sustained. Village applause – the kind that means consensus has been reached and will not be revisited.

The mayor shook our hands. Photos were taken. Someone clapped too early. Someone filmed, portrait-style, without shame.

Nemesis stood very still.

Later, as people drifted away and the ceremony dissolved into coffee and commentary, she passed us.

"Well," she said tightly. "Enjoy it."

"We will," Alex replied warmly.

Nemesis hesitated, then nodded once, sharply, and walked off.

That evening, the village returned to normal.

Water flowed obediently beneath our feet. The river said nothing. The house stood dry. The past stayed where it belonged.

And somewhere in Pefki, Nemesis began quietly planning her next victory.

Because rivers may be redirected.

But Nemesis never is.

CHAPTER THIRTY-NINE

Zorba Joins the Family

Something unexpected happened after we came back.

The jackal stopped being mysterious.

Up until then, Zorba had existed largely as a rumour with teeth. A blur at dusk. A shadow slipping between olive trees. A half-chewed sandal with opinions. He was discussed far more than he was seen, which is always dangerous in a Greek village.

But once we were home, he made a decision.

He adopted us.

The first time it happened, I was in the garden pretending to tidy something that no longer recognised order. I heard movement by the fence and turned, bracing myself for the usual stand-off. Instead, there he was.

Sitting.

Not lurking. Not slinking. Sitting.

His head tilted slightly, ears alert, tail moving gently from side to side like a cautious handshake.

"Oh," I said, intelligently. "Hello."

He wagged.

A jackal wagging his tail is unsettling the first time you see it. It challenges assumptions. It suggests betrayal of the species handbook. I looked around, half-expecting a camera crew.

Alex came out behind me.

"He's smiling," she said.

Zorba stood, stretched, and walked a little closer. Close enough to make a point. He sniffed the air, assessed us, then lay down by the fence as if this had always been the arrangement.

From that moment on, he was ours.

Or rather, we were his.

He greeted us every morning. A small wag when I appeared. A fuller one for Alex, who he clearly regarded as the senior authority. He accepted the cats with the weary tolerance of someone who understands bureaucracy – they existed, they had rights, and fighting them would involve paperwork.

The cats, for their part, were unimpressed. They sat on

the wall above him like a committee, watching his every move. He ignored them completely, which annoyed them more than aggression ever could.

Zorba became a fixture.

He sat near the fence, watching the road. Guarding the garden with quiet dignity. When friends passed, he wagged. When children pointed, he blinked. When scraps appeared, he accepted them with the careful politeness of someone who didn't want expectations.

Sometimes people stopped.

"That's your jackal?" they'd ask.

"Yes," I'd say, as if this were the most normal sentence in the world.

Theodora started bringing him bones.

She'd appear at the gate with a small bag, glance around conspiratorially, and lower her voice.

"For Zorba," she'd say, as if delivering classified material.

He adored her.

Maria took photos. Eleni told people he was good luck. Dimitri claimed he'd seen Zorba chase away a bad dream once, though this may have been wine-related.

The village, inevitably, chose sides.

Most were on Zorba's.

Nemesis was not.

She filed complaints. So many complaints.

Dangerous animal. Wild predator. Threat to public safety. Threat to moral order. Possible foreign agent.

The police stopped answering her calls.

Zorba, meanwhile, made his own assessment.

The first time Nemesis walked past the fence while he was there, he stiffened. The wag stopped. His ears flattened. Slowly, deliberately, his lips lifted to reveal teeth that had very clear opinions about the situation.

A low growl rolled out of him, deep and unmistakable.

Nemesis froze.

I watched, fascinated.

She pointed at him. "You see?" she shouted. "This is what I mean!"

Zorba held her gaze. Calm. Still. Professional.

I reached into my pocket and produced a biscuit.

"Well done," I said quietly, handing it to him.

He took it gently, eyes never leaving her.

This became routine.

Nemesis would pass. Zorba would rise. The hair along his back would lift like a warning flag. The growl would come, controlled and deliberate. I would give him a biscuit.

Positive reinforcement.

Alex raised an eyebrow the first time.

"You're training him," she said.

"No," I replied. "I'm encouraging discernment."

The village noticed.

"He only growls at her," Spiros observed one afternoon.

"He has instincts," Eleni nodded.

"He knows," said Theodora, with finality.

Soon, people began joking that Zorba should be made official guardian of the village. Someone suggested honorary citizenship. Someone else suggested a small ceremony.

"He contributes more than some people," Dimitri pointed out.

Even the mayor, passing one morning, stopped to admire him.

"Good dog," he said.

Jackal, technically.

Zorba wagged anyway.

Nemesis stopped using the road. She took the long way round. That, perhaps, was Zorba's greatest service.

He never barked. Never chased. Never crossed his line. He simply was. Present. Watching. Choosing sides quietly.

Nature, it turned out, didn't need paperwork.

Zorba belonged because he decided to.

And in a village built on stories, accusations, and carefully misplaced blame, the jackal – unregistered, unofficial, and faintly amused – became the most popular resident of all.

We'd gained another family member.

One with better instincts than most of us.

And sharper teeth.

CHAPTER FORTY

We came home quietly.

Not because we had learned anything, but because Greece teaches you that confidence is best exercised slowly, like testing water with a toe. The village was exactly as we had left it, which is to say, completely different.

The road was dry.

The house was standing.

The cats were fatter.

A new river flowed obediently, silent as a secret everyone had agreed to keep.

It felt wrong at first. Too calm. Too settled. After weeks of movement, of borders and breakfasts and borrowed languages, of Maria's voice crackling down the phone with daily bulletins of catastrophe, peace in this village felt unfamiliar. Almost suspicious.

Odysseus would have understood.

He left Ithaca thinking he'd be gone a few weeks. Ten years later, he arrived home disguised, scarred, and mildly traumatised, only to find his house full of people who had misunderstood his absence as an invitation. He had Cyclopes. Sirens. Gods with personal grudges.

We had Nemesis.

Every day of our journey had been accompanied by messages from the village – floods, goats, machinery, lawyers, cats, paperwork, rumours, and the occasional jackal update. We crossed borders, climbed mountains, drank wine in foreign squares, and still Pefki followed us, neatly folded into our phones.

Odysseus was lashed to a mast to resist temptation.

And like him, we thought the danger was out there, in storms, in roads, in the unknown. But the truth, as it always does, waited patiently at home.

When we returned, the village did not applaud. Instead it absorbed us, quietly, efficiently, as if we had merely popped out for bread.

Nemesis still lived along the road.

Theodora still poured wine without asking.

Maria still knew everything before it happened.

But something had shifted.

The river, once a rumour, then a threat, then a weapon, was now gone from sight. Domesticated. Buried. Obedient at last. Water no longer burst through doors or accused us of wrongdoing. It flowed where it was told, beneath concrete and collective amnesia.

The jackal still guarded the garden. Zorba sat by the fence each evening, tail swaying gently, watching the road with the quiet authority of someone who understood territory better than any planning office ever could. He accepted the cats. He accepted offerings. He did not accept Nemesis.

Neither, it turned out, did the village.

Odysseus had to fight to reclaim his home.

We just had to leave it long enough for everyone else to solve the problem creatively.

That was the lesson Greece kept trying to teach us: sometimes you don't win by standing your ground. Sometimes you win by stepping aside and letting the story finish itself.

We had gone looking for peace.

We thought it lived elsewhere – in ordered countries, tidy systems, roads without potholes, places where water stayed politely inside its designated channels and neighbours minded their own business.

But peace, it turns out, doesn't live in silence.

It lives in familiarity.

It lives in knowing which chaos belongs to you.

Our peace was not the absence of trouble. It was the presence of understanding. The shared glance across a taverna table. The way the village closed ranks when it mattered. The way Nemesis, even now, continued scheming, because that, too, was part of the balance.

Odysseus returned to Ithaca to find his kingdom waiting.

We returned to Pefki to find something better.

A place that had argued with us, accused us, flooded us, arrested us, and then quietly, collectively, decided we were theirs.

The house stood dry.

The garden grew wild but loyal.

The river behaved.

The jackal kept watch.

And the village – flawed, loud, contradictory, and endlessly inventive – settled back into its rhythm.

We hadn't escaped it after all.

We'd just gone away long enough to understand that this – mud, madness, neighbours, and all – was home.

Odysseus reached Ithaca and laid down his oar.

We reached Pefki and poured a glass of wine.

Which, in the end, felt like the more sensible ending.

The End

… for now.

Credits

First, to the friendliest corner of the internet I know. *We Love Memoirs.* A group that reads, encourages, laughs, and reminds writers that words are meant to be shared, not hidden in drawers. You are generous, curious, and endlessly patient. This book exists more happily because of you.

To Chris Moore, my one and only beta reader. Every writer needs someone brave enough to read the early pages, the uncertain chapters, the bits that wobble before they stand upright. Chris does far more than read. She lifts, encourages, questions gently, and reminds us why we began writing in the first place. She sees the heart of a story before it quite knows itself. Her support of writers is generous, constant, and deeply felt. Chris is not just a reader. She is our champion.

To the world's best editor, **Debbie Chapman**, who has once again performed a small miracle. She took my jam-stained notes, rescued them from a bin bag, shook them into some kind of order, questioned everything that needed questioning, and gently moved the words until they sat where they were supposed to. She has an eye for clarity, a feel for rhythm, and the rare ability to make a book better without changing its soul. I am deeply grateful.

To **Alex.**

My wife. My best friend. My muse. My everything.

Without her, not a single word of this book would exist. She is the reason the stories happen, the reason they get noticed, and the reason they get told at all. She walks beside me through every place, every argument, every absurd situation, and somehow manages to see both the comedy and the truth at the same time.

For the walking, the arguing, the laughing, the grounding, the eye-rolling, and the unwavering ability to cut through nonsense without ever losing warmth. For the courage to say what she thinks, and the generosity to let me write about it.

Every page carries her voice.

Every book carries her heart.

To the people of **Pefki.** For the coffee, the opinions, the interruptions, the theories, the arguments, the warmth, the generosity, and the certainty that nothing is ever simple and everything is worth discussing. You are the village that keeps on giving, whether asked or not.

This book is yours too.

And finally, to **Nemesis.**

She had no idea, of course, that having us reported, investigated, blamed, arrested and briefly treated like international criminals would turn out to be the most helpful thing anyone in the village ever did for us. Possibly not to herself. In the end, it benefited us more than anyone.

This must be very irritating.

Without her, our river would never have been redirected, our home would still be at risk, and the village would still be flooding with admirable regularity. Her tireless dedication to accusing us of everything from rainfall to wildlife eventually proved that even government departments have a heart, and that justice, while slow and deeply in love with paperwork, does sometimes prevail.

Her persistence was impressive. Her confidence unwavering. Her theories… ambitious.

We will, inevitably, see her again.

In the next book.

Whether she likes it or not.

Love Peter xxx

Scan the QR Code for more
information about
Peter Barber and his books.